Up the Bumpy Lane

Up the Bumpy Lane

by

Harridave Dutton

DIADEM BOOKS

Up the Bumpy Lane

Published by Diadem Books
An imprint of Spiderwize

For information, please contact:

Diadem Books
Mews Cottage
The Causeway
KENNOWAY
Kingdom of Fife
KY8 5JU
Scotland UK

www.diadembooks.com

ISBN: 978-1-907294-64-8

*This is the story
of the first twenty years
of my life...*

For Jane, Allan, David and Amy

Acknowledgements

Grateful thanks are due to my wife Gill for her support in so many ways in the writing of this book. Also for putting up with me! Also, to my sister Jill who has frequently refreshed my memory and helped practically, especially with the photographs. Thanks, too, to my cousin John Neller who inspired and encouraged me.

My gratitude to my brother-in-law Derek Pike for his editing is immeasurable. Without his skills and patience there would be no book at all.

"Some bumpy lanes are short, others just a little longer..."

Table of Contents

Chapter One

The Start

I T ALL STARTED for me in the upstairs' back bedroom above my mother's hairdressing shop at 121 Stoke Lane, Westbury-On-Trym, Bristol on July 30th 1940. This was not a good time to be born, really. For all the world it seemed that Britain was about to lose the Second World War and that the future of the country was to be that of a German conquest ruled by Nazi tyranny.

I have often wondered at the wisdom of my parents planning to have an additional child at such a ridiculous time (they already had my older brother Allan and sister Jill). The answer of course is there was absolutely no 'planning' involved at all. My father William, as he showed throughout his life amongst his marriages and numerous affairs, was quite incapable of keeping it inside his trousers whatever the outcome may be. Don't get me wrong—I loved my father and he had good qualities.... generous (on the occasions he had money in his pockets), charming, humorous (he had a distinctive and an infectious laugh), affectionate and sociable (everyone 'loved' Billy).

Young Billy Dutton aged 18.

Unfortunately, he was feckless, obsessively jealous-natured, irresponsible, had a foul temper and, above all, treated his three wives (and probably numerous girlfriends over the years) very poorly. He married three fine women|: Kitty (my Mum), Eve (Johnny's and Faith's Mum) and Olwen (Peter's Mum). He was to make all of them unhappy to some degree and leave them all with children and years of struggles to get their lives together

1

again (which they all seemed to do eventually but no thanks to father, although he couldn't help dying at the young age of 53 (from multiple myeloma) and leaving Olwen with a baby less than a year old). In spite of the ducking and diving sort of life he led as he skipped around his ever increasing responsibilities, he did achieve success in his job as a 'sports' promoter' and manager, being, at different times, manager of Exeter, Swindon, Cardiff, Weymouth and, indeed, the England Speedway Teams. Speedway racing was in its heyday just after World War 2, attracting for a few years crowds even bigger than football. Father was fortunate to catch the crest of this wave and he became, at that time, something of a minor celebrity doing several broadcasts on the B.B.C. as the expert summariser from the great speedway occasions such as the annual World Championships from Wembley Stadium. So that was my Dad. He was a shadowy figure to me in my first years as he was always away, although I remember he would occasionally be home on a Sunday and fall asleep in the afternoon with all the Sunday Papers spread out around him and covering his face (he was a voracious newspaper reader, something I may have inherited from him).

With Father it was always 'balls over brains'

In those days it was amazing how many more Sunday Newspapers there were. In addition to the ones we have today there was *Empire News*, *Reynolds News*, *Sunday Graphic*, *Sunday Despatch* and probably others, titles long forgotten now. My father would buy them all though. He was an informed and an intelligent man but as my old Nanny remarked once to me, 'Billy Dutton was a lovely man but he shouldn't have had a "dicky"!' Put another way, with Father it was always 'balls over brains'.

I have several clear memories of those first years... being whisked, wrapped in a blanket, into the air raid shelter we had in our tiny garden at the back of the shop. Bristol was badly bombed up until 1943 with the Docks at Avonmouth and the aircraft factories at Filton being prime targets for the Luftwaffe and our home was situated equidistant and only a couple of miles from both. Consequently, when the siren sounded we headed quickly for the shelter. I really only have an impression of these events but it was a fug of humanity inside as we shared the shelter with a few neighbours and, as well as all 'us', I'm sure my Nanny (Mum's Mum, Clara) was there too with Mum's father, my grandfather 'Pom Pom' Webb. I DO remember my mother whispering into my infant ear when we heard the slow engine drones of a bomber—'that's theirs' and then the more continuous buzzing engine sound of a fighter aircraft—'that's ours'.

My brother Allan was much older than me (14 years) and I don't remember him much at that time except on the occasion when he jumped off the balcony roof with a homemade parachute... daft bugger nearly killed himself as it was about a 30-foot drop into the 'back lane' which ran at the side of our home. On another occasion, one winter, he made us (me and Jill) a homemade sledge, which he hauled with us to the steep slope on Westbury Golf links (always 'flinks' to us). It was great having a big brother to drag the sledge to the top and then give us a push to start us hurtling downwards. It was such fun and was the only thing I can ever remember we three children doing together (Allan must have been in his late teens then). He was very occupied with his sport (he was an excellent rugby player, eventually good enough to play regularly for Bristol Rugby Club, a promising rugby future brought abruptly to an end by a severe injury to his knee a year or so later). Although I didn't appreciate it at the time, my brother was something of a star: captain of his Grammar School (Cotham), clever enough to obtain a place at Medical School, a girlfriend (!) and generally moving so fast in life I hardly ever saw him.

My sister Jill and I spent quite a lot of time hating each other. She was always bossing me about and I was being the obnoxious (and favoured) younger brother, always telling tales and getting her into trouble. Our only joint enterprise was often on a Sunday when we would have this game with our parents (Jill would have known it was only a game but I thought it was for real). Anyway, our Mother would shout from her bedroom 'Don't you children dare go down to that back kitchen!' which of course we did in order to make our parents a cup of tea. I can feel now the pleasure of basking in their approval as we entered the bedroom with the tea. Another time my sister announced a 'midnight feast' (I think one of her friends was staying the night and was also part of this great adventure). Anyway, the feast turned out to be brown sauce spread on pieces of cake!

Selman

We used to have a lady come in who helped look after us whilst Mother worked long hours in the hairdressing saloon which took up most of the ground floor of the premises. We called this lady 'Selman' (which was actually her surname). In fact she was a somewhat sad, Bristolian spinster lady who had been badly buffeted by life and somehow she had ended up with us. (My mother almost made a career out of attracting unfortunate and stray people to whom she always gave a helping hand. As my sister put it much later, 'Our Mum was always helping stray dogs over stiles.') Anyway, Selman loved me but had a permanent down on Jill... 'He's been perfect,' she would report to our mother after a day looking after us... 'But her... she's bin dretful!' Poor Jill, she always felt a bit rejected throughout her childhood and having Selman around can't have really helped her self-esteem. Jill felt the impact of our father's almost continual absence from the home more than anyone else (and a little while later our parents' divorce). She really did love her 'Daddy', as did I, but I was more insulated from the consequences of his conduct.

At some point during the first years I must have had one of the rooms at the front of the building as a bedroom. This room looked out on to the main road, Stoke Lane. I recall lying in bed in that room and following the car headlights as they swept up one wall, across the ceiling and down the opposite wall. This seemed to be something I did for hours but was probably only for a while. If I looked out onto Stoke Lane in the evening there was a gas lamp at the side of the road and a man on a bicycle would arrive at dusk each evening and reach up with a pole to switch the light on... it seems incredible now that there were still lamplighters in Westbury-on-Trym, Bristol up to the 1940's, so much so that I wonder if my memory is playing tricks on me... but I don't think so.

More certain is that my sister Jill was a regular bed-wetter. On many occasions I remember a warm jet of liquid bathing my back in the 'wee' small hours and as any other bed-wetters' victims will testify, that initial moment of warm pleasure turns rapidly into cold, miserable discomfort! It never seemed to occur to the adults in control that it wasn't really such a good idea that my sister slept with anyone. Most of the clean sheets in the home had large circular stains on them from previous contents of my sister's poor weak bladder. Poor Jill (again) carried on as a bed-wetter right up to her teen years and I know it caused her much embarrassment. (I probably used to tell other people about it, which, again, must have done a lot for her self-esteem. It's a wonder really that we have always genuinely loved each other so much!)

A nice thing that Jill and I would often do, again on a Sunday, would be that we were sent to the home of one of mother's 'posh' customers (mother always seemed to be recounting anecdotes about her customers and they were invariably described as 'posh'). Anyway, we were sent to collect some freshly grown mint as a gift from the posh lady's garden which we duly took home and gave to mother who would chop the mint, mix it with a little vinegar and sugar to make a lovely mint sauce for the Sunday roast. Mum was an extremely 'average' cook (extremely!) but the one meal at which she absolutely excelled was a Sunday 'roast'. To this day I have always loved the smell of mint and lamb, and it has always been, by streets, my favourite meat. I loved that wooden circular chopping board she used and I kept it and used it for many years... but one day, just like that, it split and broke in two and I threw it straight out without a sentimental flicker. I've always been able to 'tighten' up emotionally when the need arose... that chopping board meant a lot....

We used to stand outside on Stoke Lane when the American troop lorries rolled past in convoys from time to time. The soldiers were standing at the rear of the lorries smiling and waving. 'Got any gum chum?' we would shout and they would toss us sweeties... those little different coloured sweets called 'life savers' (a bit like 'Spangles' which came much later after the war). We really couldn't get sweets at all. (I don't think I actually knew what sweets *were* before those 'Yanks' were so kind.) Maybe funny, but I've always liked Americans (later in life I was to work in The States for a year) and I'm sure I am influenced by my first encounters with those soldiers who were 'over-paid, over-sexed and over here' as they threw us things from the backs of their lorries.

I loved going to Canford Park to play football with my pals. There were several playmates. I cannot recall all their names, but there was a John Cottrell and a Terry Hobbs. (I remember Terry Hobbs lived in one of the little cottages just down the road on the other side of Stoke Lane. He had a sister called Bridget and I remember we all went into the bushes at the side of the car park on one occasion for a game of 'you show me yours and I'll show you mine'... This little first innocent skirmish with Bridget was really the time that the notion that girls were 'different' lodged itself in my head.)

A game of 'You show me yours and I'll show you mine'

Anyway, back to football in the park. I can't say we were actually poor or I ever felt really deprived. After all, mum was taking money in the shop every day and although she was no businesswoman and Father often had his hot little hand in the till for some gambling money or 'meeting-a-previous-debt-money', Mum nevertheless always had tips. Those tips used to seem quite important in making the financial wheels of the home go round. Sometimes, though, the well must have dried up and 'make do and mend' became the order of the day. This must have been the case one time when I desperately wanted to get off down to the park to play football and I simply had no socks to wear inside my football boots. Ever the improviser and ever the kind of facilitating person she was, Mum produced a few pairs of her nylon stockings. All were placed one inside the other to form what was, in effect, an extremely bulky pair of nylon stockings... 'I can't wear those, Mum!'... 'Of course you can, they don't look anything like a pair of stockings now... tell your friends, if they say anything, that they are the latest style in football socks and your uncle sent them from Brazil...' I was only about six or seven, so if my mum told me something, I believed her. I rushed to join my pals who had already gone to the park. Never shall I forget the whoops of mirth into which they all descended as they ran around pointing at my ridiculous 'football socks'! I ran off back home with the shame of the whole thing burning my cheeks and, honestly, a few tears of humiliation too. From that day forward I always had my eye on my Mum when she told me things!

(ii)

I have often been told that I was by no means an easy child... being very strong willed and always very noisy. Most adults, apparently, gave me a wide birth lest they were sucked into my demanding, noisy and selfish orbit. My Mum, of course, bore the brunt of having to keep me pacified to prevent my temper tantrums which could embarrass everyone as they went about their daily business in the hairdressing saloon. There were two apprentices employed by Mum in the business. Dilys and Olwen—I remember their names... very Welsh sounding, but they were probably from Bristol. Anyway, they were warm and kind figures towards me and used to do their fair share of 'shooing' me out of the saloon part whenever I intruded and helping to keep the peace. It must have been really hard for mother having a holy terror like me always around to threaten the good order of things and undermine mother's whole position.

The worst incident was when (I only have the vaguest recollection of this) I had a terrible tantrum one day and threw myself down on the floor of the saloon bawling and shouting and refusing to let go of a chair and rejecting all efforts to calm me down and gain my co-operation. Apparently, one of Mum's customers tried to do her bit to assist in handling the little brat and I bit her on her leg for her trouble! Whether or not she ever booked any further appointments I never did discover... but I have my doubts! No wonder mother decided to get me away from there if possible. Jill had already been sent off to Boarding School (where, she told me many years later she was very unhappy and was sexually abused, don't want even to think about that).

It was decided that, young though I was, by my remaining in the home whilst mother tried to run her business posed a greater threat than the whole of The Luftwaffe. So, I was sent to join my sister at the Boarding School. I was very young, no more than three or four. It turned out that the good folks (!) at the Boarding School couldn't handle me either and I'm not sure how long they put up with me there, but it was a very short time.

There was one huge trauma (which I do remember), when I drank a cup of milk and came face to face with a large spider (presumably dead) at the bottom of the cup. Probably the proprietors of the school put it there deliberately as an act of revenge against this ghastly child who had descended on them. Anyway, according to Jill I screamed for about a day and a half... so if they had put the spider there on purpose, they must have eventually regretted it! Anyway, the upshot of it all was I found myself back in Bristol pretty promptly. (Jill must have returned with me; they probably concluded that the Dutton kids were trouble one way or another..)

Avalon, Touchstone Lane, Chard. This is Auntie Dorrie's house where Jill and I were evacuated.

Next, mother had the idea of sending Jill and I away to stay with her sister Dorrie Neller who lived in a little town in Somerset (Chard). This arrangement worked out well, I think, for there we were away from the threat of the bombing and in the care of our family (my grandparents Nanny and 'Pom Pom' were there too). Also Auntie Dorrie, who had three young children herself (our cousins John, Tony and Wendy... not sure if Wendy had been born then) was there with husband Leslie Neller. Mum's youngest sister Margie was there too with her new baby (our cousin Bobby Kent). Where and how all this lot were accommodated I have not the slightest idea... it must have been one heck of a business to feed, maintain and look after such a tribe. For sure, my Nanny and Aunts would have had pivotal roles (they were all lovely ladies) in the general maintenance and good order of things. My own memories are again vague, but even here, in the warm and kind bosom of my family, I apparently was virtually uncontrollable. I would scream in protest every night at bedtime and throw everything I could lay my hands on at anyone who entered the bedroom. I was told later that my grandfather, Pom Pom, would eventually approach my cot with an open umbrella for protection against the missiles. What a little bugger I must have been! Jill and I always say we were evacuated in the war and I suppose, in a way we were, but I suspect there was an awful lot of 'let's get them out of the way, especially him' about it—and, I suppose, it's easy to understand why, with my being such a difficult child.

(iii)

My mother, and just about everyone else, must have been greatly relieved when the day came for me to start officially at school. In those days, unlike today when young children seem to join the long educational journey well before they turn the age of five, it was only once the age of five was reached that parents were able to start loosening the tether. In my case it was not so much a case of 'loosening', I imagine, but unwinding as rapidly as possible. The upshot was that on a day at the beginning of September 1945 my brother Allan was given the job of taking and depositing me for my first day at school. I think I went willingly, even obediently, holding his hand as we walked along Stoke Lane in September sunshine, my brother pushing his bike as we walked, I seem to recall, to Stoke Bishop Primary School.

At that time, Stoke Bishop Primary was a large old House with a small tarmac playground, a temporary hut used as a classroom and a small garden area situated on the far side of the house (where we little folk were not allowed to venture). A lane led to the school, which was enclosed by a stone wall. We entered through a gate onto the playground and thence into the crumbly old house (or so it seemed to me) where the rooms of the house formed the classrooms. There was one other part I remember... the toilet block was outside and also 'open air'. The 'boys' was on one side and, over the roofless wall that divided them, was the 'girls'. I remember, to this day, not only my first encounter with the smell of stale urine but also what a freezing and uncomfortable experience was the whole toilet business. In winter, especially, we were in and out of there as rapidly as possible. Spring and summer allowed for an altogether more leisurely and enjoyable toilet experience. In the manner of boys the world over, I suppose, we played the game of 'how high can you make your pee shoot up the face of the urinal'. I remember our ambition was to try and get it high enough so it would actually go over the wall into the girls' part. We would do this giggling and laughing as we strained. No one succeeded of course but it didn't ever stop us trying!

Most of what I remember at that time was to do with 'playing'. We had a really great way of collecting volunteers for the games we wished to start. At the beginning of breaks, you would extend your arms like a plane and start perambulating around the playground shouting 'all in for robbers and cops' or 'all in for cowboys and indians' (these were the two most popular I recall). Anyway, another would join on to you, linking one arm around your shoulder and extending his 'free' arm, making now a 'wider aeroplane'. He would add his voice to the 'all in' call until another joined on and linked up and extended his free arm, then another and another and so on until enough had joined to actually begin the game. Usually, we would make two sides, one 'the cops', the other 'the robbers'; or one the 'cowboys' and the other 'the indians'. The object of the game was to kill as many people on the other side to you as quickly and efficiently as possible!

So you belted around at a thousand miles an hour shooting people with finger-guns, each shot accompanied by a noise that always sounded like… '*ku, ku*'.   Variations were throwing imaginary punches and chopping imaginary chops, accompanied by the sound of '*bam, bam*' and '*splat, splat*', or firing imaginary arrows to the sound of '*ss..huuw*', '*ss..huuw*'. All this frantic helter-skelter activity came to an abrupt halt after about ten minutes on the piercing blast of the teacher's whistle. Then we stood still, panting, waiting to return to lessons. Naturally, only boys played these sorts of games. I have but a minimal awareness of any girls present *at all* in that playground! They must have been there of course doing sissy stuff like skipping and hopscotch and generally keeping out of the way probably.

I remember four teachers at that time… Miss Kerswell, Miss Barkell and Miss Dudridge (she was the Headmistress I think). They seemed very old to me and in the tradition of grey haired spinster ladies who have always been the sort of glue of England's primary schools. All these ladies I remember as kindly. I must have turned some kind of corner in my behaviour over my time in their care, it seems, for by now I had calmed down quite a bit and the 'leg biting, venom spitting, temper-tantrumed, spoilt brat, little horror' of 121 Stoke Lane had begun his journey to normality.

The fourth teacher is altogether etched differently into my memory box—Miss Elliot. I was in her class at some point and our classroom was the temporary hut across the other side of the playground that I mentioned earlier. I had a 'thing' about Miss Elliot (I was only seven or eight I suppose, but Miss Elliot was (a) young and (b) had a 'shape' that interested me. Somewhere very, very, very deep down, something stirred). To get to the classroom she had to walk across that playground and I would look forward to seeing her and most days when I saw her coming I would rush across and offer to carry her bag and say 'good

The most polite child in the class

morning Miss Elliot' as nicely as I could. My never, never to be forgotten reward, was the day Miss Elliot told us all to 'put down your pens'. (We had those wooden pens with metal nibs you dunked into an inkwell that always got clogged and so, often, a 'blob' of ink would form at the tip and drop off onto your work and make a blue stain. You then proceeded to make it ten times worse by dabbing at it with one of those pieces of green blotting paper we all used. End result—a *very* messy page in your exercise book.... *most* of my books were like that, trust me!) Anyway, back to Miss Elliot. 'We have been talking about politeness,' she said, 'and I want to tell you the name of the most polite child in the class. Stand up... David Dutton!' Oh boy, what a joyous moment! Recognition! Praise! Pride! She went on to tell the others about my offering to carry her bags and saying good morning and the rest. Apart from those stirrings Miss Elliot caused in me I know that (except for my mum and my sister) I had bonded with her and not quite in the same way as with my mum or my sister either! It was a first step, sort of growing up thing for me. Incidentally, what Miss Elliot had put her finger on must be an integral part of my personality as, honestly, I've always been a generally polite and charming person!

A feature of life at school was the daily trek 'up the bumpy lane' to the huts on Stoke Lodge Playing Field where we had our dinner. A small army of us little ones would 'get into two's please' and advance, often in haste, up the hill, over the rugged stones (hence 'bumpy lane') along the small stretch of main road. 'Keep together, no running!' barked our teacher 'shepherds', and thence into one of the long huts just inside the wall of the playing field. There used to be several huts along there, and now, amazingly, after some 60 years there is one still remaining, just as it was when our hungry little tribe would arrive for our daily nourishment.

You have to hand it to those good folks who put hot meals in front of us each day... after all, this was austere post-war Britain, slowly recovering from its physical, emotional and economic battering of the previous six or seven years. So, I suppose, one has to be charitable... but the fact is that those meals I ate each day in that hut on Stoke Lodge Playing Field went a long way to destroying my liking for food permanently. In particular, the vegetables were totally 'massacred' into an evil tasting pulp... to this day I can't eat swede or parsnip and only recovered a liking for cabbage after many years of convalescence. I remember the meat always had a funny smell... was it just old or was it the way they cooked it? I guess we'll never know. The gravy too was highly suspect... a sort of thin brown water which actually seemed to float the other bits of mess on the plate. Anyway, the whole process of sitting at long trestle tables was overseen by grumpy ladies in green overalls who urged us (somewhat menacingly I used to think) to 'come on now, eat everything up, we don't want any fuss!' So, hardly an encouraging atmosphere then, and not a very good foundation upon which to begin one's education on the pleasures of the table. We survived, nevertheless.

Our school was a 'Church of England' Primary school... I'm not sure then, or even now, quite what this meant, but one thing for sure, it did mean we often had to climb up the hill on the main road (the other way than up to Stoke Lodge, towards The Downs) to the church (St. Mary Magdalene, Stoke Bishop I'm almost sure it was called). Anyway, we were always being marched up that hill to that church for one service or another. As a matter of fact, these occasions were the very first on which I came across the whole God business. It's fair to say that God and I never got on right from the start. I never really took to all that 'hands together, eyes closed' business at the start and end of each day.... 'What for?' I always used to ask myself and couldn't help noticing how silly the other children looked standing around me (I used to peep between my fingers) with their faces all screwed up tightly, their noses wrinkled and daft words coming out of their mouths. Sorry God, I really started with a clean sheet but you've never really made a lot of sense to me. Neither have I ever really found you very helpful in my life at times when it occurred to me that you just *might* step up to the plate. Anyway, that's neither here nor there... back at St. Mary Magdalene's the plot was getting ever thicker. You know, we'd sing away (enjoyed the singing, first time I knew I had a nice voice) and what puzzled me often was who is this 'Percy Vere' to whom we have to 'give grace' and I'd worry about those 'little brown children who lived over the sea with their Mummies and Daddies.' I kid you not, in the Church of England Hymn book there was a hymn that went like that, and the tune forever resonates in my head... 'Over The Sea There Are Little Brown Children, Mummies and Daddies and Babies Too, They Have Not Heard of The Dear Lord Jesus, They Do Not Know That He Is Near...' There were other verses that I don't remember, but *really*, I ask you, even then, in my tiny mind a little voice was saying 'something daft about all this lot'. Memorable though were the 'harvest festival' services and I used to love to see all the tins and jars (and veggies!) piled up at the end of the Nave of the church.

Back in the classroom, two things about me were becoming evident. First I couldn't draw for toffees. I used to sit by a boy called David Oliver and I would honestly marvel at his drawings... buses, houses, dogs, soldiers, just about anything it seemed... all symmetrical, perfect representations of the subjects. Did I envy and resent him! No matter what I did with my pencil there was absolutely nothing you could recognise ending up on the paper! I often wonder what became of David Oliver (I vaguely remember he had a sister, maybe even a twin). Being brilliant at one thing doesn't really guarantee anything in life, but it probably helps. Like being able to play a musical instrument, for example (I could never do that either and have always envied those who can).

The other truth that I was having to face was that I wasn't much good at 'sums', especially 'problems'. How did I know this? Well, Miss Elliot (!) had 'groups' for sums and, although I'm not quite sure which group I was in for ability, one thing was certain, it was one of the 'bottom' groups! Bugger me, 'adding' wasn't too bad, nor 'take-aways' but mention 'division' or 'multiplication' and the shutters in my brain started to descend. As for 'long division', this was moving onto a higher plane altogether inhabited by super brains... trouble was that there were kids in the class who could *do long division*, and needless to say I hated and envied them too. As for 'problems'—impossible, frustrating: couldn't understand them no matter what... 'If it takes two men half an hour to plough a field, how long would it take one man'... da, read it again and again, and still nothing; get angry (no help)... feel the tears welling up... Though I eventually acquired enough basic numeracy to be able to cope with the world, this inability to solve 'problems' as a child highlights that I have never really been much good at any kind of 'reasoning' or 'logical' thinking (of the kind that makes good barristers for example). I've never been any good at thinking quickly on my feet... otherwise my life would probably have worked out differently.

(iv)

My world shook a little when it was announced that we would be leaving the crumbly old house and moving to a new school on brand new premises. This was just before my last year of primary so I must have been ten, or thereabouts. That old house, that had been a school and had done so much to put the first bricks into my wall, is still very much 'there'. It has been done up somewhat and last time I strolled the lane alongside and paused, gazing and musing a few years ago, a top window of the house opened and a lady shouted down: 'Used to come to school here, did you? We get quite a few come around to have a look!' We chatted a while. She went over all the 'alterations' since 'your day' and cheerfully popped back inside as though her exchange with me was an established routine. I did hear, not so long ago, that there is in existence an 'Old Stoke Bishop

Primary School Association'... crikey! The average age of the members must be whopping as the school closed in around 1949! The new school on the new premises took a new name and assumed a new identity... Cedar Park Primary... so the old Stoke Bishop Primary really did cease to exist. Do I really want to join a worthy 'band of ancients' such as these and temporarily increase their ever-diminishing number? Not really, bless 'em; think I'll give it a miss now but thanks anyway for being my school chums all those years ago.

Anyway, that last year I spent at Cedar Park imprinted on me for two main memories. One, I had, for the first time a *man* teacher. A nice man, too, called Doug Silverthorne (not that we called him 'Doug', oh my God no, he was 'sir'). Apparently, all our schools had been bereft of 'sirs' during the war years and now they were starting to reappear... many teachers just after the war were 'emergency trained' which I think meant they were thrust into the classrooms after not much more than a few weeks of talking nicely about children and what was best to do with them between 9 in the morning and 4 in the afternoon! I got on well with my 'sir' because he promoted the one thing that really interested me at that time and at which I excelled—football! All those lovely lady teachers knew little about the great game and the fact that it was what most little boys really wanted to do with their time (*this* little boy for certain!). Anyway, Doug Silverthorne formed a school team and I was in it! Never was I happier at school than when playing 'proper' football matches against other schools. Sure, a persistent 'fog' hung across any actual learning I was supposed to be doing and alas, I think I may have been 'sidelined' academically already. The all important and dreaded 11+ exam was right on the horizon (this was the exam all eleven year olds took in England at that time. It is no exaggeration to say it more or less determined your whole future... 'Pass' and you moved on to 'a life'... 'Fail' and you were lumped into the vast pool of 'no hopers' who would spend their lives as little more than industrial serfs and economic peasants, forever struggling to get one's head above the pit of failure into which you had fallen...in short, an exam of hardly any consequence then for its takers!) What I am saying is that I think the teachers had decided that there were probably several kids who would have absolutely no chance of vaulting this 11+ fence (including David Dutton) so let them get on with doing 'easy peasy' things in class... 'That's *very good David*, now see if you can draw another cat'. So, we were left alone pretty well, blissfully unaware of the reality. So, lovely football it was as much and as often as possible!

(v)

It's the little scar I have always had on my forehead that links me permanently with Cedar Park Primary School. Our 'sir', Doug Silverthorne, was not only the man who gave my life some kind of shape at school, he was also the person who allowed us to go into the school Hall one day and listen to the commentary on the radio of the 3rd Round FA Cup Replay from St James' Park between Bristol Rovers and Newcastle United. This was an amazingly 'progressive' thing for a teacher to do with his pupils in those days when everything was done in such a formal way. Deviations from 'the norm' were rare and very little was done all day not involving pens, paper or crayons and 'sit still, get on with your work and be quiet!'. Allowing kids to listen to a live football commentary during school hours... wow! Good old Doug had set it up though for us. The game was something of a major event for Bristolians (Rovers' fans at any rate). Bristol's two soccer teams were united throughout the years by one common factor... neither really ever achieved any success! Both (Bristol City being the other club) had always limped along in the lower echelons of the football establishment. Not that the rivalry between the fans of the two clubs was any less partisan and passionate than that between the aristocrats of the game... the Arsenals and Spurs, the United and the City in Manchester and so on, indeed, wherever teams shared localities. So, Newcastle United in those days was one of the giants of the game... a leading First Division Club. This was the Newcastle of Jackie Milburn and Co, in all their pomp. The Newcastle who seemed to win the Cup almost every year around that time. Well, the previous Saturday this mighty team had come to Bristol and the Rovers had held them to a draw. Now, this being the following week, it was the replay. We were agog with the excitement of it all! I had a Bristol Rovers' scarf and I remember Mr. Silverthorne allowed me to drape it across the climbing bars along the side of the Hall. There we sat listening to the breathless commentator crackling through the airwaves. (Radios *always crackled* in those days, sometimes with a continuous sound when, if you concentrated very hard, you could *just* make out the voices or the music underneath the crackle or, more annoyingly, with the occasional burst of short, sharp crackling that would obliterate totally everything else... 'The Prime minister announced from Downing St today that *KKKKKRRRRRCCCCCCCC* and this will take immediate effect'.... 'the jury returned a verdict of *KKKKKRRRCCCCCCC* today in the trial of *KKCCRRR*, sentencing him to *KKKKKRRRCCCC*, the judge said *KKKKRRRRCCCC*'....you get the idea! Well, that's what it was like with what I think were called 'crystal sets'. They were certainly not 'crystal clear' though but we were so glad to have them.

Along with 'going to the pictures' radios were what we mostly had for entertainment.) So, back in the School Hall, there we kids sat listening with 'our sir' who was as keenly interested as the rest of us. Well, I can't honestly say that it was the moment the Rovers scored (as I don't remember if they actually did in that game; they were eventually beaten, I know that). What is certain is, at some point, possibly a 'near miss' for Rovers, we lads all started tumbling around and jumping about. During the course of this little mêlée I fell and cracked my head on the sharp edge of a chair and, blow me down, the next thing is I'm lying unconscious on the floor, blood gushing from my forehead! This must have kicked off a right panic (more amongst the adults I suspect, as my pals would have probably been more pissed off with me for spoiling the game!). Next thing I'm in an ambulance and then in The Bristol Royal Infirmary where I had, just prior to these events, more or less set up permanent home anyway, but more about *that* later.

What turned everything even more interesting was that my very own brother Allan (who was a just-qualified doctor) was on duty in the Casualty Department when they brought me in. Not only did he help to calm me down (I almost certainly would have been making a fuss and a lot of noise) but he actually helped to thread the stitches into my gashed forehead—wow! He might have done it all on his own but I can't quite be sure. I know that he did a good job as the scar on my forehead is very neat, barely discernible, in fact. When I returned to school I was the focus of a lot of concern and interest (which I almost certainly milked like mad). I was certainly proud of my scar and the fact that 'my brother's a doctor and he put my stitches in'. I used always to say that for several years after until the time when the testosterone and the vanity combined to make me think that scarring might spoil my looks and sex appeal! Then I would spend ages looking at that scar in the mirror and wondering if I was disfigured or not!

Now, though, is as good a time as any to sort out my side of 'are you a Rovers' fan or a City fan' which has always puzzled some people and about which I have endured much teasing. As I've insisted, I actually support Bristol City more than Bristol Rovers nowadays and, as it's an unprecedented (some may say even shocking!) position to be in, I'd like to put my case on the record, as it were...

(vi)

Here was the dilemma... my Dad and all my Mum's brothers—Allan, Sonny and Bertie (who was only actually ever a lukewarm follower of football) were really keen Bristol City supporters. Thus my first and natural inclinations, imbibed through my male relatives' beery talk among the tobacco clouds on a Saturday evening, were towards City. So far so good... but here's the rub. My Aunt Margie's (mum's sister's) husband, Uncle John, used to go to watch *both* teams. Unusual, but my Uncle John, who fought the Japs in Burma, was the only one in the family with a proper war record; all the other male folks in the family somehow managed to avoid direct military service. Although, to be fair, they did their bits, albeit at a somewhat lower level as Air Raid Wardens and such like. Even my Dad, Billy Dutton, was an Air Raid Warden, although he managed to combine *his* war service with plenty of wheeling and dealing on the black market (never short of pairs of nylons or extra ration coupons for all the lady folk in my family as the bombs rained down).

Anyway, Uncle John was a man of some substance and he, it was, who took me, as a boy of about six or seven, to watch my first professional football match. Now if only that first game I saw could have been a City match it would have avoided a lifetime of confusion. Sod's Law of course, Rovers were at home that week (Uncle John used to alternate Saturdays between City and Rovers). Anyway, the crowd and the crush inside The Eastville Stadium were enormous and I couldn't see a thing till Uncle John swung me in the air and fixed me, legs astride a single spike, onto the great green railings which ran around the back of the enclosure. Outside and behind rose the great gasometer from which Rovers fans derived their nickname... 'Gasheads'! I'll never forget that first view as the pitch stretched out way below the uncomfortable eyrie where I had been perched. Bristol Rovers, in their blue and white quartered shirts (with *red* numbers on the back!) against Swansea Town in their brilliant white shirts and black shorts. Don't remember the score, just the indelible impression and, for now, it was Rovers for me! Without labouring the point, it wasn't long before Uncle John was taking me regularly to see City and Rovers. When we went to see City we often went after the game to see Uncle John's mother and other family of his who lived very close to the City ground at Ashton Gate... I remember a house full of friendly people in a road along which streamed crowds of fans making their ways homeward from the match. We waited with a cup of tea or some sweets for it to 'die down' so we could more easily get a bus home. As the years went on I really always followed both Bristol teams, inclining to one or the other to annoy whoever I was with.

For instance, some years later, after school, I always used to walk from my Grammar School (Q.E.H.) in Berkeley Square, down Park Street to the Tramway Centre with a few pals from my class... 'Grumpher' Steeds,

'Susan' Stallard—he was slightly effeminate and we were always completely heartless in the attributing of nicknames. There were many others at the school cruelly named: 'Oola' Garnett, so called as he *didn't* have a Bristol accent, 'Oneball' Stewart.... self-explanatory, 'Slug' Jennings, and so on.

Also walking to The Centre with my little group was 'Feisal' Pratten (so called as we were reading a book in English about Lawrence of Arabia and it features a character named 'Feisal'... God knows how Richard Pratten, a lovely lad from Knowle, got *that* nickname, but he did!) To get to the point, All these mates I walked with were ardent City fans and I would pose to them as a Rovers' fan. They would be cracking on about Johnnie Atyeo, City's top player of that time, and I would counter with the greatness of Geoff Bradford, the then Rovers' great champion. I was just being contrary, see. I have to admit that being awkward at times and going against the tide, deliberately, might just be a characteristic of mine—one that has not always served me well.

(vii)

Saturdays were turning out the best days during this time (come to think of it they've always been best, one way and another). There were fairly regular trips with Uncle John to the football which was pretty good. Saturday mornings though were just magical.... off we went (some pals and me and my sister too sometimes I think) to 'The Orpheus Club'! This was 'the picture house' in Henleaze (one of Bristol's posh districts, next to mine, Westbury-On-Trym, which was also considered 'posh', to my mum's continuing pleasure as she, bless her, always considered herself (and her family) as 'middle class' and a clear cut above the 'oiks' who lived in such places as Bedminster... and, heaven forbid, a place even worse, inhabited by villains and cutthroats... *Knowle West*!). Such places as these were used to terrify us as to where we might end up if ever we were to topple from our elevated social position.... really! We lived in a flat above a hairdresser's shop... but to mum it was all-important, its location protecting us from 'Bristolians' who lived beyond the frontiers of Westbury and Henbury. The English class system, eh, I could write volumes...

When you entered 'The Orpheus' it was packed with kids making an awful din even before the lights were dimmed (to a universal cheer of excitement and anticipation!). The first film flickered onto the screen, usually a comedy. We loved the 'Three Stooges' and I especially liked 'Leo Gorcey and The Bowery Boys'. One thing throughout all the films which were ever shown, it was never possible actually to hear any words spoken at all, as the racket we kids made was unrelenting. Action was what we liked, slapstick or violent, as long as people were getting slapped, kicked, falling over things or off things, shot, stabbed, tied up, dragged, chopped, run over, chased or just about any other indignity capable of being suffered or inflicted. As long as the screen was 'jumping' with all this, the more we liked it. Louder and louder we yelled, the noise rising to a crescendo of derision, even 'booing' if the film reached a quiet section or worse, a 'soppy' section, where the hero and heroine were approaching that most embarrassing of moments, when they *kissed*! I remember I found these moments so excruciating that I would cover my eyes and (perhaps) just squint through my fingers...

So, first a comedy... I adored the bit in the 'Bowery Boys' when Huntz Hall (the stupid one) did something wrong and Leo Gorcey (the boss and the brains) would take off his hat and batter Huntz mercilessly on the head. Sometimes the comedy would be Laurel and Hardy or Charlie Chaplin (never used to find him very funny actually, never really liked 'mime' from that day to this). Then came the main feature... nearly always a 'cowboy'. My favourites were Johnnie Mack Brown, Gene Autry, Roy Rogers and his horse Trigger. Roy spoilt himself somewhat in my eyes for two reasons... first he used to *sing* (whistles and boos, quite right in my view) and second, he always had a girlfriend (Dale Evans if my memory serves)... I think I liked Trigger a little more than Roy, come to think of it! My absolute favourite though (and I still get a little buzz writing his name) was Hopalong Cassidy! 'Hoppy' had it all for me: immaculately attired and coiffeured, sort of large 'pearl' looking gun handles protruding over the tops of his black leather holsters. A 'shimmering' white horse ('Topper'), fast fists and a lightning 'draw' that didn't give a man time to take a breath before he was well and truly 'plugged'! 'Hoppy' always had a bandana type scarf around his neck and a hat which he rarely put on but hung on his back secured by a cord on his chest attached to a sort of broach (what we called in the boy scouts, a 'woggle') in the shape of cow's horns. God, that man was totally immaculate! He filled the screen and he filled all my boyhood yearnings to be tough, handsome and fearless!

The session always ended with 'the serial'... usually something like 'Robin Hood' or 'Black Arrow'. The serial would be fairly short and always ended with a cliff-hanger... 'Will Robin escape from the evil Sheriff's clutches?' boomed a voiceover from the screen… 'Will Marion succeed in smuggling a sword into Nottingham Castle?'... 'Find out in the next thrilling episode of Robin Hood'!

We would all excitedly tip out into the daylight glare, our imaginations fired up to a peak. We would enact our own adventures all the way home. Just fix the top button of your macintosh (my doting mother always made me take mine whatever the weather!). Anyway, fix that button and you had a cloak. Extend the arms and hands, voila, two-finger guns! Then, gallop! Yes, gallop, firing at all around you. Slap your arse with the flat of the palm of your hand as you raced through North View. Across the road by The White Tree ('Be very careful crossing that busy road, David!'), on to the Downs, across to the big wall around St Monica's School and down the path that led to Westbury... firing, tumbling, lassoing, feigning death, coming back to life, ambushing others from behind walls and trees, firing off shots and arrows, lobbing grenades, lashing whips and bunging 'Jim Bowie' knives... what wonderful *fun*! These Saturday mornings were the start for me of a lifelong love of films and the idolising of those we called 'Film Stars'. Cooper, Mitchum, Flynn, Bogarde, Niven, Holden, Brando, Clift, Peck—I loved them all. Watching their films was a large part of my young years.

(viii)

Our Sunday routine was often a long bus trip across Bristol to see Mum's Mum, my dear 'Nanny', who was living at that time with her son, my Uncle Bert in Staple Hill. Her husband, my grandfather 'Pom Pom' Webb had died just before the end of the war (of stomach cancer) and Nanny had been living since then with Uncle Bert.

At that time, Uncle Bert (and his wife Auntie Bonnie, the very sweetest and kindest of ladies), lived in a house that doubled as his business— 'Hamilton's Photographic Studios'. This business had originally been started by Nanny's father, Allan Hamilton, who had come down from Scotland towards the end of the nineteenth century. Photography, of course, was in its infancy then and it was probably a prosperous business for many years. However, by the time my Uncle Bert inherited it during the war years, it was in decline... I guess because photography was moving away from the fashion of people visiting studios to have portraits and group photographs taken and had rapidly been overtaken by the mass production of film and the usage of smaller cameras and easier means of getting photos developed. In short, the business was 'on the skids' and, not too long after, my Uncle sold it and moved directly across the main Staple Hill High Street to a shop which was a sort of general grocer's shop, specialising in cooked meats—'Table Delicacies' was its rather overblown name. So, when they moved, Nanny went with them (indeed she spent her remaining years there, dying in 1958). Nanny lived at a time when Nannies dressed like Nannies, usually in black. She always smelled of lavender and spent her days crocheting and reminiscing... Nanny's stories were legendary. She'd ramble on with a story for ages and we would 'take shifts' sitting by her and listening and she wouldn't even notice that her audience was changing! Thing was, she wasn't really, really very 'old' at all! Certainly she would not be considered old by the standards of today. When first we used to travel on those Sundays across to Staple Hill, she was probably only about 60! Yet she dressed 'old', acted 'old' and was certainly treated as old. I wonder why it used to be that way with older people? One up, here methinks, for the changing attitudes of society, as older people are certainly a lot younger these days!

The fortunes of Uncle Bert and Auntie Bonnie in their food business got worse. It turned out Uncle Bert was no businessman at all and, in spite of the fact that he and Auntie Bonnie seemed to toil for hours to bring it round, the business was sliding irreversibly onto the rocks. I can see them both now, in white coats, working most of Sunday out the back making 'faggots' to sell during the forthcoming week. God knows what they put in to those faggots but there were several pots bubbling along which, when you peeped in, seemed to contain masses of scummy fatty stuff floating in greyish water and not really smelling at all nice.

One thing though, Uncle Bert had a television! He was the only person we knew, the very first, to possess one of these magic little machines (which of course were to change the world, although such a notion would have seemed very far fetched if anyone had suggested it at that time). One of the reasons we travelled home so late on a Sunday evening was because Mum liked to watch a popular programme of the day called 'What's My Line?'. We would all gather around the flickering little black and white screen, squashed up on the settee to watch the panel try to ascertain someone's job. First they would be introduced by Eamonn Andrews (the host of the show), chalk their name on a blackboard, do a piece of mime of their job and then be questioned to see if that job could be guessed. The panel was, Gilbert Harding (who had a reputation for being rude to people), Barbara Kelly (a pleasant blonde lady with big teeth and a funny laugh), David Nixon (a bald magician, cracked some good jokes, always had a cigarette on the go) and 'Lady' Isobel Barnet (she was brainy and used to screw her face up somehow). It was always a very jolly programme and the adults seemed to really love it. One person's job which caused much merriment one time was 'a saddle maker's bottom knocker'... that sticks in my mind.

A saddle maker's bottom knocker

When this programme finished it was the signal for me, Mum and Jill to say our farewells to Nanny and the others and walk down to the bus stop which was just past the 'Portcullis' pub, to which my Uncles Bert and Sonny had scuttled after 'What's My Line' ended. Uncle Sonny was another of my Mum's brothers and he and his wife (Auntie Ada) with their daughter (Cousin Valerie) would also have joined this weekly pilgrimage to see Nanny at Staple Hill. Sonny's family would stay longer than we Duttons as, even though they lived 'our' side of Bristol (Sea Mills... not *quite* as nice as Westbury or Henleaze of course but OK!) they had a car, so whilst Sonny was down the pub with Bert, Auntie Ada could settle down to watch that other great Sunday evening television favourite of the day—'Armchair Theatre'.

I was always so sleepy on those long, late bus journeys, frequently just falling asleep nuzzled into Mum's coat. The problem was, we always had to change buses half way, usually at Old Market or The Tramways Centre. If it was at Old Market we waited for the Westbury Bus (a no.1. I think) outside a pub called 'The Pie Poudre Court', which had a sort of projecting Elizabethan façade. Across the wide expanse of Old Market Street was 'The Kings Cinema'. I recall standing, cold and tired, at that bus stop watching the to and fro of people passing the 'Kings' opposite and those going in and out of the 'Pie Poudre Court' behind us. The latter pub had a great deal of history, being the site of a real Court in medieval times, I believe. Glad I was to clamber on the bus for the second leg of the journey back to Westbury. We always went upstairs, perhaps because Mum would want to smoke a cigarette which was only permitted upstairs... then again, maybe not, as there was still then a considerable stigma attached to women smoking in public places.... 'One thing I really hate to see,' would say Uncle Allan, another of Mum's brothers, tapping his own cigarette on the side of his nickel-plated cigarette case which was what people customarily did before smoking in order to 'compact' the tobacco at the end of the cigarette which was going into your mouth. 'Yes, I really *do* hate to see,' he would continue, 'a woman smoking in public'! Usually, nods and murmurs of agreement from others, men probably, would follow!

We'd get off the bus in Westbury Village or, if the bus had gone down the steep Falcondale Rd., at the end of Stoke Lane. We still had to walk along to the rank of shops where we lived. I would be totally shattered at the end of such days and certainly didn't relish the prospect of 'school tomorrow'.

On one occasion, going for a visit to Nanny on a Sunday, we saw quite the most dreadful thing. At the top of Falcondale Road a tank (American I think, but not sure) had collided with an Austin Seven car and squashed (literally) all the people inside the car. We must have got there shortly after the accident. Being on the top deck of the bus as it slowly edged past, I beheld such a sight as I have (thankfully) never seen anything the like of since. I have often wished I had not seen what I saw that day as it really has flashed back to me many times throughout my life and sent a tiny shock wave through my mind at the thought.

(ix)

It was about this time that Steve came into our lives. He was a friend of my brother Allan. They had got friendly through playing rugby, I think. They had gone to different schools (Allan to Cotham Grammar, Steve to Queen Elizabeth's Hospital, both being Captains of their respective schools). Steve's father had been killed in a bombing raid on Southampton and he had ended up with his grandmother at Knowle (not Knowle *West*!). Being exceptionally bright, he had won a scholarship to be a Boarder at Q.E.H. This school, at the time, was famous for granting clever, bright boys the opportunity of a 'Grammar School' education. Steve therefore was what, you might say, the quintessential Q.E.H. pupil. On leaving school he had a place to do a Maths' Degree at

Michael Arthur Stephens, 'Steve', a big influence in my life.

Bristol University. I'm not quite sure why it was not convenient to carry on living with his grandmother (whom he dearly loved incidentally) but he ended up coming to live with us... I must have been six or seven or so when Steve came. He was to become a really big influence in my life.

Actually, 'Steve' was not his name at all. His correct full name was Michael Arthur Stephens (I think 'Arthur' was his father's name). It wasn't for a few years that I realised he was known as 'Mike' or 'Michael' to the rest of the world... he was always 'Steve' to us. I remember how much I liked it when he arrived upon our domestic scene. He was always funny and kind and had a lot of time for me and Jill. He seemed immediately to get on very well with my mother and, indeed, it was the start of a lifelong friendship between them. They were always teasing each other and he began to call her

'Mrs. D' which made me laugh (later he would alternate between calling her Mrs. D. and 'Dolly D'). They used to argue at times as Steve was a very untidy person but they were friendly arguments, somehow, always with an amusing sort of edge. I think Steve was possibly the first person who treated Mum as the intelligent woman she actually was and I think she responded to the fact that Steve wanted to really discuss things with her, perhaps in a way no one ever had before. After all, mother left school at an early age and she had never known anything but kids and work and a hopeless husband. What had been Mother's salvation was her own large and loving family with caring parents and five close brothers and sisters. I think Steve's arrival in the house gave Mother another perspective.

For Steve's part I think he found a sort of domestic stability with us which perhaps had been lacking hitherto. He clashed with Selman (our sort of home help) really badly and she was always complaining loudly about ''im'. Their little feud kept everyone amused. I think I remember Selman crying one day over something Steve had supposedly done or not done, said or not said. I remember giving her a cuddle and feeling sorry she was upset. I didn't really understand the things which grown ups seemed to think important. I was probably usually too busy ploughing my own selfish little furrow.

I soon got attached to Steve and he was always making us laugh. He used to sing a song he made up about me... 'Little Davy, blow on your horn, fal di, di, fal di di...'. There were more words—I think he made them up as he went along, but this was always the chorus. I don't think Steve had a very high opinion of my father at all. Over the period of my mother's divorce from father I think Steve gave her friendly support—something he was to do for the next forty years or so, as a matter of fact.

Divorce was a really major business back then and I knew something big was going on although I don't think anything was ever explained to me. What I do know is that, to her eternal credit, my mother never ran our father down to us. You would think she would have every reason to have been embittered but she really wasn't. I don't think she had any feelings left for him by the time he finally left, but, amazingly, she always spoke well of him (certainly in front of us). She remained on good terms with him thereafter, in spite of the fact he provided virtually no maintenance. She always encouraged us to see our father when the opportunity occurred and to keep in contact with him in other ways. I once heard someone ask her how it felt to be divorced (as though it were a disease or something) and I remember mother's answer: "I came out of that Court and I felt just like a bird out of a cage." Mother never remarried, although at the time of her divorce she was only a very attractive 43-year-old. Mum was vain, it has to be said.... 'Pretty

Kitty', she called herself, and she was forever looking in the mirror or appearing in a new hat or dress and asking, 'Now how do I look in this?' Yet she never had a really lasting relationship with another man. There were a few clearly unsuitable men she got a little mixed up with... John Reece and Bill Surtees were two. I think there were one or two others. I did discover many years later (since I was very jealous of my mother giving her affections to anyone but me) that she did enjoy one passionate and fulfilling affair with a man she met in South Africa, a ship's Captain, named Bill Snyder. He was already married. I like to think now that she had that sexually satisfying affair as, by all accounts, my father was 'wham, bam, thank you m'am' in the bedroom. Had I known about my mum's affair at the time of course, like all silly jealous little boys, I would have been upset and angry at the thought.

They stick a red hot poker down your throat

Well, with all this going on in my formative years you wouldn't really think I would have had time for nearly two years in Hospital, now would you? Wrong! It came on literally over one weekend. Suddenly, it seemed, my knees and ankles became swollen, the pain made me cry and I could barely walk. What the hell was *this*? I had had many of the 'usual' childhood ailments... the miseries of toothache and earache had been endured and survived with oil of cloves, hot water bottles under pillows and lots of mummy love. I'd even had my tonsils out—something my caring sister had helped me prepare for by telling me, as I set off for the Hospital, 'They stick a red hot poker down your throat!' All of these had been largely overcome. Nothing so far in my seven-year-old life had prepared me for the stunningly painful full stop to which I had come. I remember it went on for several days before my medical student brother Allan (who must have known a thing or two by then) insisted that we send for Dr. Coulter and observed, quite correctly to our mother, 'That boy ought to be in hospital.'

Our family doctor was a large-limbed, elderly and genial Irishman who seemed to have his nose blocked up all the time since he made a curious 'blowing' noise as he bent over me. He poked me around a little and pressed my painful swollen joints. (By now I was rather past caring and my pillow was wet with my tears.) There was some hushed talking outside on the landing and I heard the word 'Hospital'. Poor Mum, not only the worry of this sudden catastrophe to deal with, but the emotional strain of having to get me to accept this looming unknown, and just as important, the pain of separation.

(x)

Mother was a totally non-violent person, yet had to keep control of her errant brood. (My sister Jill was a self-willed and difficult child at times with a perfectly horrible temper... a temper 'just like her father's', it was always said.) On top of that she had 'yours truly', who most parents would have probably quite happily given away.

Poor mother, she had to put up with a lot... an absent and unfaithful husband, a business which was at best financially 'dodgy' and, at worst, downright worrying. On her feet, working all day and then, two difficult kids who, although loving her to bits, were always a strain on her patience and her limited resources... and, oh yes, almost forgot, a little matter of a war going on...

No wonder she smoked a lot. No wonder she had her 'phobias' (which got *much* worse in her later life and were to drive us all potty). Mum could 'put it on' though and in a different life she could quite easily have made a career in the theatre. She had a number of strategies to maintain some control. Eschewing any kind of literal force or violence (not even that popular method of the day, 'a good clip round the ear'), she adopted more subtle methods. First she would try to make you feel guilty by stressing her own 'pain'... as in 'you kids are giving me the 'ab-dabs'' (never really clear what they were). 'I might as well jump off the Clifton Suspension Bridge!' or, 'I mean it, if you don't stop, I'm going to run away!' This approach probably would work better with Jill who lived with chronic insecurities. What worked best with me was the threat to embarrass me, especially in public, as in (walking along the road): 'Pick your feet up and behave, David, or I'm going to *stop and talk* to the next man I see and tell him you've got something to say to him....' 'Oh no, Mum please don't show me up!' Or, same idea, but a variation (Jill used to join forces with Mother on this one): 'Pick your feet up and behave, David, or we're going to *sit down in the road*!' Oh, God, the shame... 'Please don't do it Mummy, please, say you won't!' The absolute ultimate was, usually on a bus: 'Sit still and stop fidgeting, David, or I'm going to start *singing*!' This would lead to a storm of begging for restraint and, sure as anything, I would behave for the rest of the time!

I think the tactic of threatening to embarrass your kids in public was a clever and effective one for Mum to use, especially in her circumstances. (I used it often on my own kids later.) The fact that it seriously impaired my social and psychological development I suppose is neither here nor there!

(xi)

To be frank, Mum and I were really tightly bonded. I suppose I filled a big need in her for affection and she was pretty much the centre of my emotional universe. So, leaving all the security of our daily warmth was at least as difficult as adjusting to the totally alien environment of Ward 20, The Children's' Ward at Bristol Royal Infirmary.

It was the winter of 1947, the worst winter weather for many years. It seems amazing now, but for reasons I don't know to this day, there was *no visiting* allowed. Consequently the ward was filled, not only with sick children, but desperately unhappy ones too. So, not surprisingly, what did we do for hours on end? We yelled and cried in a continuous cacophony of misery! There was a small porthole window in the door to the ward and faces would appear at that window to wave at us. I watched that window, waiting for my Mum's face to appear and, such, I suppose, was the unendurable heartbreak that seeing her face caused, I would turn away and not look at her! Poor little sod—me!—at that time for sure.

Now I don't know how she did it (perhaps because my brother was a medical student at the hospital) but Mum somehow got around the rules and she would appear at my bedside when no other visitors were around. There would be lots of cuddles and she usually had a small gift of some sort, probably sweets or a comic. (I loved my comics. I remember that, however deficient I was numerically, as it were, I made up for it in part by being a good reader—straws in the future wind perhaps. Back then it was 'Desperate Dan' and 'Korky The Kat' I loved, stalwarts from 'The Dandy'.)

This special treatment clearly helped me to calm down and accept my lot. There was a very kind ward sister, too, called Sister Eyrebrooke, who gave me some fuss and attention between my mother's appearances at my bedside.

What I had contracted was 'Rheumatic Fever' or 'Rheumatic Heart Disease' as it is known now. This blight (mainly of youngsters) has all but disappeared nowadays, but was very common back then. The first effects usually wore off quite quickly (fever and swollen painful joints) but it was the long term effects of the damage the virus did to the heart which made it so dangerous and such a threat to children back then.

There was little known treatment for the disease except bed rest. I didn't know it but I was extremely fortunate to have come under the care of Professor C. Bruce Perry. He had a special interest in the treatment of Rheumatic Fever and, indeed, was in the very forefront of understanding the disease and pioneering the first effective treatments. Large doses of aspirin were prescribed (to toxic levels I learned later). All I know is that, although my pain and swellings had gone, all those aspirins (only tablet form available in those days) were making me feel permanently nauseous. I had constant ringing in my ears and started truly dreading the next dose and fighting, literally, against it being forced down me every few hours by a team of nurses. All in all, my little world was really upside down and worse was to follow when almost daily blood tests were ordered. The dreaded, feared 'needle' was to add to the joys of my life at that time!

It was probably more stressing for the medical students and nurses, who were given the job of trying to stick a needle into me most days, than it was for me to endure it. At it's worst, four or five nurses or student doctors would forcibly pin me down whilst a reluctant vein in my arm was teased into cooperation as the hypodermic drew off the required amount of blood. Some times were easier than others, usually when a bribe was involved: 'Just a tiny prick in your arm, David, and then I've got some chocolate for you'...or, 'Let's see what a brave boy can have for his pudding today... something really special and nice as long as he's a good boy now.' To be honest, I never accepted this torture at all well and it compounded the misery of the whole situation. Both my arms were black and blue bruised, too, as my tormentors sought a fresh patch of skin to dig into each time they approached with that little kidney shaped bowl with the plunger of the hypodermic peeping over the edge.

Another miracle my mother 'pulled off' was somehow to get my *radio* fixed up beside my bed! In those days it was no 'palm sized' transistor either. It was a large brown box-shape with the top half being a speaker protected by a sort of thin porous canvas. The bottom would have a line of knobs for tuning, volume and changing stations. Quite why I was allowed such a luxury I never really worked out. Actually I don't really

Always loved my radio

remember listening to it much either. Ungrateful little sod! Except of course for my nightly favourite fifteen-minute serial—'Dick Barton, Special Agent.' Dick and his two companions 'Jock' and 'Snowy' were saving the world from one threat or another. Each episode ending with a cliffhanger situation, usually one of our heroes in great peril and the only way we'd find out the outcome would be to listen tomorrow night. Above all, was *that* theme music (Devil's Gallop) which played the programme in and out each evening and will be forever imprinted into the minds of folks of a certain age: '*Dum, diddle um, diddle um, diddle um da,da,da, da,da,da,... da,da,da, da,da.*' Great stuff. Always loved my radio ever since.

One day a nurse let out a piercing and sudden scream on the other side of the Ward from me. She dropped a large glass container of some sort that smashed onto the floor and shouted at the top of her voice: 'Quick, quick, oxygen, oxygen!' There was a lot of panicky running around by many people and I recall a large blue cylinder being wheeled towards someone's bed opposite mine. It was obviously very serious. Never relished emergencies of any kind and, like most folks, have been involved in a few along life's highway.

Another time, as it was Christmas, we were visited by Father Christmas himself and a gentleman wearing a large shiny chain around his neck. (I found out later that it was none other than The Lord Mayor of Bristol, as if I could have cared less!) Anyway, this gentleman reached into a bag and gave Father Christmas a package which he handed on to each child with all the requisite 'ho, ho, ho's' and tickles under the chin.

Now I distinctly remember my gift was one of those 'kaleidoscopes' in the shape of a Toblerone bar that you looked into, shook, and all the dazzling colours rearranged themselves into different mosaic patterns after each 'shake'. So far so good. Quite how I managed to shake it in such a way as to break it and get glass splinters in my eye I know not, but I did!

By now it was about Boxing Day as I recall. I found myself being wheeled across to the Bristol Eye Hospital, which, fortuitously, was situated just across the road from the Infirmary. (I seem to remember it was through a tunnel under the road.) The upshot was that some unlucky eye doctor had his Christmas revelry interrupted in order to dig a number of glass shards out of my eyeball!

So much for the Lord Mayor's Christmas present, which very nearly permanently blinded me in one eye. In these days of instant litigation over anything, my Mum could probably sue the City and County of Bristol for zillions in damages. As it was, the latest disaster to befall yours truly was shrugged off by one and all with a 'cluck' of the tongue and a 'what a shame...must have been his own fault though'. So, there you are.

The first black people I can ever really remember seeing properly were a couple of black nurses on Ward 20. I remember they had a different smell when they bent over me. (Get locked up probably if you said that today; all I know is they smelt different to the other nurses, and that's a fact.) One told me she was 'from Africa' and that sort of fascinated me. In hot weather they would push our beds out onto the large balcony outside Ward 20. This was a real treat as the Infirmary was built on a slight hill and one had a marvellous view across the tops of the buildings and church spires of Bristol. On the horizon were some hills that I assumed to be in a foreign country, probably

Africa. Would have shattered my illusion if I'd known that the hills of my foreign land were Knowle and Dundry! Never Mind.

On that balcony on a Sunday morning we heard the bells ringing out from (what seemed to be) dozens of churches. That and the smell of cooking rising from below where the kitchens must have been situated, are vivid memories.

The major event in the Ward each week was the appearance of the very man himself, Professor C. Bruce Perry. He would burst through the doors to the Ward with a small army of white-coated doctors and medical students (I think they were distinguished by the 'qualified doctors' in full length coats and the students in short white bum-freezer coats). However, an army it was that swept into the Ward and an army that meant business!

Bruce Perry was a striking and impressive man by any standards. He was almost mongoloid in the shape of his head and features. A great booming voice which blotted out all else and a brisk 'no nonsense, don't you even think of contradicting me', manner. He would come to the side of my bed, the orange tubing of his stethoscope seeming to stand out. The great crowd would gather around and little me, the patient, would be looking around at a sea of nervous faces peering back at me. 'Examine this boy's heart!' Prof Perry would boom at some individual he had chosen to toy with, 'and then, be so good as to tell the rest of us what you find.' A sweating face would bend low over my chest and listen through his stethoscope. 'Before you say anything, dear boy,' boomed the great man as the hapless student was about to open his mouth, 'you've forgotten to percuss! What kind of doctor are you going to turn out to be!' (Whatever the hell percuss meant, it had been forgotten.)

The rest of the group would seem to know that this was all part of 'The Bruce Perry Show' and be smiling at their colleague's discomfiture (probably with relief too that it wasn't them who were on the 'hot spot' at that moment). At some point Prof Perry himself always had a listen to my heart and, as much as to say, 'I'm only kidding with this big bully stuff,' he would squeeze my hand or give me a friendly little prod in the tummy, or even a 'wink' that was always just between the two of us.... What a man! What a great doctor! I wouldn't have had a life at all but for him. Thanks, Professor Perry.

(xii)

As much as anything, having to stay permanently in bed was not easy or natural for a young boy. This was especially true as, once the aspirin poisoning was finished with, I felt more or less OK and ready to resume the helter-skelter sort of life I had prior to the onset of Rheumatic Fever. Well, there was no chance of that as bed rest was the treatment that was prescribed and no amount of pleadings of 'when can I go home' seemed to cut much ice with anyone. I would pile on the emotional pressure, especially on my long-suffering and ever-reliable Mother who must have had enough to worry about without having to prop me up. She had to run a failing business, look out for the interests of her other offspring and, at the end of a day's work, catch a bus into snowy Bristol Centre most nights throughout that awful winter. And all in order to listen to my moans and groans. Unconditional love, eh? My Mum doled it out in spades. After about eight or nine months I was sent to Winford Hospital for 'convalescence'. Winford was a collection of what appeared to be converted army barrack huts (probably were!). Now designated a hospital, it was used for patients who were over the worst of their illness but still needed to be 'hospitalised'—yep, like me! The other feature was that in the children's ward we had school lessons. It was strange. The teacher stood in the middle of the ward by a portable blackboard and easel and you sat up in bed with a tray arranged in front of you to do your writing and your sums. (As a matter of interest, sums didn't come any easier to me whether I was horizontal or vertical!) Such lessons took up most of the morning. Then it would be lunch. ('Dinner' to us. 'Lunch' was something posh people did 'out there' somewhere.) After dinner was rest time. It never struck me then—it was somewhat ironic to insist we rested when, in fact, we never got out of bed! The difference was, on reflection, we had to remain quiet and go to sleep. They were jokers, weren't they—we were getting more sleep and rest than Rip Van Winkle! They meant well though and full marks too for trying to ensure we got our lessons even if, at the time, it was not much appreciated.

We were a noisy lot whenever we were allowed to be and I recall much communal singing and shouting at times in the day. There was one song that was a special favourite that we all sang daily with real gusto. I remember the words to this day...

There is a Winford Shell
Far, far away
Where we get bread and cheese,
Three times a day
Eggs and bacon we don't see
We get sawdust in our tea
All through the day

The nurses are so barmy
The Sisters twice as bad
Early in the morning
We hear the nurses shout
Get up you lazy So and So's
And clean your lockers out!

Winford was about as inconveniently situated for my visitors as it could have been (on the Somerset side of the River Avon to the south of Bristol— we lived in Westbury on the Gloucestershire side of The Avon to the north of Bristol). I was there for about six months I think, perhaps less. They gradually let me get up for short spells and I found walking again—a very wobbly and strange experience.

At this point I may as well deal with my other childhood illnesses. It seemed that once the 'streptococcus' virus had got a taste for you that it hung on like mad. About a year later I had a second attack of Rheumatic Fever and found myself back in The Infirmary for another couple of months, this time in Budd Ward. It was a repeat of the first occasion... bed rest, aspirin poisoning and, something new, penicillin injections! The last named were fun—a needle in your bum every few hours that eventually turned your 'gluteous maximus' into a very painful pincushion. I was never very happy either about always having to display my naked bum to female eyes. It was embarrassing but somehow not altogether unpleasant: remember I *was* approaching a certain age....

Just when you thought old 'streptococcus' might have finished with me, he popped up again a few years later when I was about 12. This time he slung me a dose of Meningitis. No fun, trust me, waking up one day with your head lolling over to one side of your body where it was sort of cemented-on to you (or that's how it felt as you couldn't move it for love nor money). This time it was Southmead Hospital in Bristol where I ended up and (thankfully!) into the care of Dr Beryl Corner who was, and I use the word advisedly, an 'eminent' paediatrician. She it was, I later learned, who established in that very hospital one of the first, if not *the* first, specialist premature baby units in the world.

Good old Beryl didn't mess about with me either. Within hours of receiving this very sick boy with his fevered body and cemented on head, she had wielded the lumber puncture needle, pushed it into my spinal cord and drawn off the poisonous pressurised fluid which was trying to push my brains out.

That just about tidies up my childhood medical history, and they say it's only in old age that one bangs on about one's complaints! As a matter of fact, old 'Strepto' wasn't quite finished with me even now. Watch out for his next thrilling appearance a little before my eighteenth birthday... the bastard!

Mum's and Dad's Wedding 1926
Auntie Dorrie, Not Known, Not Known, Father, Mother, Uncle Sonny, Uncle Allan, Nanny Webb,
Auntie Sis, Auntie Margie, Granny Hamilton & Uncle Bert.

Allan, David
and Jill 1942.

Stoke Bishop Primary School,
in the old building 1947.

A rare family picture,
Mother, Father, Jill and Me,
Saltford, Nr. Bristol 1946.

Stoke Bishop Primary School,
in the new school building at
Cedar Park 1950. Doug
Silverthorne on left.

Direct Family Line

Siblings-
Edward Dutton
Edna Dutton
Doris Emily Dutton

Married-
Catherine Mary Webb
  W Allan W Dutton MD
  Gillian Mary Dutton
  David Hamilton Dutton

Eve Wood
  Faith Dutton
  John Dutton

Olwen Cockroft
  Peter Timothy Dutton

William J Dutton
1905-1958

Timothy F Dutton
1882-

James Dutton
1848-1901

John H Dutton
1818-

Mary Pennyman
1816-

Emily Hayward
1850-

James Hayward 1809-

Sarah 1813-

Nellie E Ridgway
1884-1919

Willy Ridgway
1864

Unknown

Emma Ridgway
1845-1901

Ellen Denham
1864

George J Denham
1832-1910

Charlotte Lippett
1832-1900

Siblings-
Stanley Hamilton Webb
Dorothy Clara Webb
Allan Hamilton Webb
Herbert John Webb
Marjorie May Webb

Married-
William James Dutton
  W Allan W Dutton MD
  Gillian Mary Dutton
  David Hamilton Dutton

This is me folks

Catherine Mary Webb
1905-1985

Herbert John Webb
1879-1947

John Webb
1848-

Richard Webb
1823-1886

Sarah Skidmore
1821-

Mary Bruton
1850-

Llewellyn Bruton
1823-

Anne Webb
1821-

Clara E Hamilton
1885-1958

Allan Hamilton
1849-

David C Hamilton
1806-

Mary Ann Flaxman
1804-

Elizabeth Williamson
1848-

James Williamson
1802-

Catherine Durie
1819

Chapter Two

The Webbs

I DON'T REALLY remember my maternal grandfather 'Pom Pom' Webb. I have just a very flimsy, faded sense of his being there during those first few years as he died when I was four. His family was from Gloucestershire and he was a major influence in my mother's life, as she revered him. I got the feeling that being his first child, the eldest and a girl, she had been, in some ways, his favourite. Mother always spoke of him with clear affection and respect. From what I gathered he was an artist and a dreamer—an intelligent man who was never successful in a business or financial sense but who nevertheless brought up, presided over and guided his brood of six, happily through their childhoods. He was obviously loyal and steady and his marriage to my grandmother (Nanny) was a happy one. He was no wanderer or philanderer and all his children always spoke of a happy childhood within a warm fug of a family life. The Webbs made up in love, between them all, what may have been lacking in material assets. 'Pom Pom' was something of a wise old bird and mother frequently prefaced a remark with, 'As my father always used to say...' So, my mother was the eldest of six... Catherine (Mum, also known as Kitty by her family), Stanley (Sonny), Allan, Dorrie, Herbert (Bert) and Marjorie (Margie).

All the Webbs had a marvellous sense of humour, each of them being funny in their own special way. They all visited our house and we visited theirs frequently throughout my childhood and I got to know and

A picnic in the woods with Pom Pom and Nanny Webb with their children Uncle Bert, Auntie Margie, Uncle Sonny and my Mother Kitty.

love them all. I would be hard pressed to nominate the wittiest and funniest of The Webbs. There was always laughter with all of them. If you twisted my arm I would have to say Auntie Margie probably edged it. In later life, like one or two of the others, she became a hopeless moaning hypochondriac, but her brilliant dry sense of humour never deserted her, as in: 'The doctor asked me when I went in how I was. I said you tell me, you're the doctor!'

Uncle Sonny was so named because of his permanently sunny disposition. He was a 'commercial traveller' selling shoes around the country so he was away quite a bit. He was a soft and kind person and, as far as you can describe a man as 'sweet', then that's what he was. Always smartly dressed in a suit and never a bad word about anyone. A creature of habit, he loved to go up the pub for a regular pint (not to excess). He married a girl from London (Ada) and it was said that she married Sonny on the rebound, but I'm not sure. Ada was a large domineering lady who definitely wore the trousers in the marriage. She was jolly and kindly herself but she kept Sonny on a fairly short lead. The story goes that 'the lads' (his brothers and my father) called round one Saturday to collect Sonny on the way to see Bristol City (All the Webb males and my Dad were 'City' supporters, not 'Rovers', please note). Ada was on the prowl and as Sonny headed down the path to slink off with the others to football, Ada nabbed him and in her London accent barked: 'And where do think you're going.... oh no ya don't, you haven't finished cutting the grass out the back!' Without a fight or a whimper Sonny turned round and headed for the lawnmower!

They lived all their married life in the same house in Sea Mills, Bristol. (In fact, their son Michael still lives in that house nearly seventy years after his parents must have first moved in.) They also had a girl, Valerie, who is exactly the same age as me (apparently Kitty and Ada were the objects of a little parallel teasing as they carried their bumps around in early 1940). Cousin Valerie inherited her father's sweet nature and has a distinctive laugh and a lovely manner.

The last time I saw Uncle Sonny was visiting him in hospital after he had had a stroke. As I took my leave he raised his arm and smiled. 'Up the City,' he said. I know I had a tear in my eye on the way back to my car.... He was a lovely man, honest.

(ii)

Mum's brother Allan Hamilton was named after his maternal grandfather (the Allan Hamilton who came down from Scotland and opened a photographer's studio in Bristol at the end of the 19th Century). Like the rest of the Webbs, Allan was witty and intelligent. As a boy he had been renowned for bolting his food down at record speed—an unfortunate trait which gave him a lifetime of gastric problems, ending with his having a large part of his stomach removed in his middle age. He had been something of an athlete in his youth and had joined a photography business when he left school (not his grandfather's), earning a living as a photographer for the rest of his life. Eventually he ended up as manager at Bromhead's Photographic Studios which were situated at the bottom of Blackboy Hill. Poor Bristol had a legacy of unfortunate street names which linked it to its slave trading past.... 'Whiteladies Road' is another. True, Bristol's prosperity was built to some extent on the Slave Trade of previous centuries, but the notion that its present citizens are in any way responsible for the business of their forbears, who marched to the tune of an entirely different set of social values, is illogical; further, that they should be called upon to apologise for Bristol's part in The Slave Trade is, to me, an altogether ridiculous notion. Be that as it may, my Uncle Allan would have not given any of this a single thought as he snapped, developed and framed countless thousands of photographs down the years as he looked out of the window up Blackboy Hill or down Whiteladies Road!

His marriage turned out to be a tragic one. He married Daisy Leaman who, contemporary pictures show, was a slim, pretty, athletic and stylish girl. They had no children but Daisy had several miscarriages. It was said that it was because of this that her mental health problems began although she had had a previous unhappy love affair, so perhaps that contributed too. I wonder, even now, whether mental illness is much understood. Back then there didn't seem to be much effective treatment. Auntie Daisy was given electro convulsive therapy that seemed to make her worse, if anything. These treatments were done at Barrow Gurney Hospital, universally known amongst the sympathetic Bristol public as 'The Loony Bin'. She and Uncle Allan would frequently turn up at our house at the weekend (my mother was a great support) after Daisy had had 'a treatment'. Daisy would be trembling and weeping and smoking one cigarette after another. Uncle Allan was more and more her carer as time went on and she descended further and further into her illness. Looking out for Daisy took its toll on Uncle Allan over time. He was always stressed and nervous, chewing his fingernails and forever easing another cigarette from his cigarette case. Every adult seemed to have a cigarette case back then. Another custom of smokers was to drop their cigarette ends into the bottom of their teacups or saucers. This seemed to be perfectly acceptable and I can still hear the 'sssssh' sound of a cigarette end dropping into tea dregs in a cup... or shreds of tobacco floating in tea that had slopped into saucers. Nice!

Uncle Allan's patience was always thin and he was frequently irritable as in, 'Can't you keep that boy still Kitty, he's always fidgeting, is there something wrong with him, he must have "St Vitus' Dance" or something!' Never did quite know what 'St Vitus' Dance' was but it didn't sound so bad. I remember whenever I went out to play with my friends around this time I would jerk around like a demented puppet for their amusement... 'Wos smatter wiv you Dave?' they would ask. 'My uncle says I've got "St Vitus' Dance" and this is how you do it!' Then they'd all join in too and a crowd of us would all go up Crow Lane doing the 'St Vitus' Dance!'

(iii)

Daisy and Allan's relationship was touching too... she called him 'Daddy' and he called her 'Diddy'. When Daisy was well or at least not too bad, they would love to do what then was a principal recreation for the lower middle classes at that time—they loved to go out for a ride in the car.

Uncle Allan had a little grey Hillman Estate and it knew its way everywhere within a 50-mile radius of Bristol. 'Diddy and I had a lovely ride out, up towards The Cotswolds. We watched some cricket at Stinchcombe, didn't we dear?'.... 'Yes, Daddy, and I had an ice cream.'.... 'It's lovely all up through there and on the way back Diddy wanted to spend a penny, didn't you dear?'.... 'Yes Daddy.'... 'And we'd just come through Wootton-Under-Edge and there was no toilet there, so we stopped out in the country and Diddy went into a field and "went" behind a wall... I said when she got back in the car "she-wouldn't-under-a-edge-but-she-would-under-a-wall!"'.... or, 'We had a little run out to Cheddar, didn't we dear?'.... 'Yes, and you bought me some strawberries, didn't you Daddy?'.... 'Never knew they made berries out of straw, did you Diddy!' And so on.

Auntie Daisy was not the sharpest knife in the box and she'd say daft things even if she hadn't been daft.... 'I don't know why they don't just print more money, then we'd all have plenty,' to which Uncle Allan (sort of exasperated) would say, 'Yes, but Daisy dear, it's not just as *easy* as that, you just *don't* understand!'

The poor soul was ever more sad and desperate as her illness progressed. One day Uncle Allan came home for his lunch (which he did every day of his life) to find Daisy slumped on the toilet seat having drunk half a bottle of bleach straight down. Allan had (Webb-like) loved her, cared for her and done his best.

After a year or so Uncle Allan got together with an old friend Win, herself fairly recently widowed. They had a dozen or so tranquil and contented years together in Win's house in Weston-Super-Mare. It was fitting he should enjoy some calm after the turbulence of his previous life with poor Daisy. He saw out his time pottering in their small garden, watching his favourite sports on TV (golf and tennis). Sweet Win would shop, cook and care... it was perfect. Now and then his brother Sonny would come down to stay for a weekend and they would walk along the Weston-Super-Mare Prom, sit on a seat in the sun near the Grand Pier and do the *Observer* crossword together. (It took some doing *The Observer* crossword—still does!) Allan would tackle it with my mother too when he came over with Daisy in earlier times... all the Webbs were good at difficult crosswords. It's always seemed to me to be a useful 'barometer of cleverness' being able to do hard crosswords...'nuff said, I'm no good at them at all!

It was marginally disappointing that Win, when she died (she outlived Allan by a few years), didn't leave any money to the next of kin—me, my brother and sister and all my cousins! Win had no relatives at all and she and Allan had combined their assets when they got together, which must have amounted to a considerable Estate, one way or another. Uncle Allan was the only Webb who had piled it up, partly through thrift, partly through circumstance. Anyway, I must confess I was hoping not to be overlooked when it came to 'the Will'. It was my one and only chance really in this life to get my hands on some real brass. Anyway, Win dealt one off the bottom of the deck when she left the whole lot to her next-door neighbour! To be fair, she had once told me that the neighbour was a very 'helpful person'... I bet she was—bloody hell!

(iv)

Three boys, three girls in their family—my grandparents kept it even. Dorrie was the middle of the three girls. There are pictures of her as a bridesmaid at several early family weddings... she and her younger sister Margie seemed to perform regular bridesmaid's duties for their older siblings. These pictures show Dorrie to be a lovely young girl wearing the lacy dresses, bonnets and pointy shoes that were the wedding fashions of the day. All three of the Webb girls were good looking by any standard, but perhaps Dorrie was the very prettiest pick of a pretty crop.

She left school at fourteen and went to work as a hairdressing apprentice at the same business, I think, as her older sister Kitty... a business situated close to Bristol Bridge in the City. At some point she met her future husband Leslie Neller. Where and how this occurred is unknown to me but Les was not a Bristolian, his family being originally from the Birmingham area.

It was soon evident that Leslie Neller was something of a wanderer, unlike the Webbs who were basically 'stay at homes'. It was also said that Uncle Leslie had a somewhat jealous nature and he was possessive towards Dorrie. If true, to my knowledge this never affected the marriage as, by all accounts, it was a happy one. I think the Nellers moved around several venues in the first years of their marriage as Les changed jobs a few times. By the start of the war they were in the small Somerset town of Chard and had a two or three year old son (my cousin John). Two more children were to follow quite soon (my cousins Tony and Wendy). The house they had in Touchstone Lane in Chard was large... it needed to be, as at one stage in those war years it housed all of the five Nellers, Pom Pom and Nanny my grandparents, yours truly and my sister Jill who had come down from bomb-threatened Bristol and Auntie Margie, the youngest sister who was pregnant with her son Robert (cousin Bobby Kent who was born at Chard during this time). Margie was especially sheltered by the rest of her family as her husband John Kent was in the Army in the Far East 'fighting the Japs'. It must have been quite a family cauldron bubbling away in that house in Chard. I was really only a toddler and only have a blur of memory. It would have been certain though that Nanny, Dorrie and Margie would have been major players in presiding over a reasonable ordering of the domestic scene.

Dorrie was closest to her younger sister Margie and they must have had a little sisterly time together in between the pressures and tribulations of being young mums. Truth was they were little more than girls themselves. One summer evening they both went for a walk around the country lanes (which were numerous there). Feeling a little adventurous as darkness fell the two girls decided it would be fun to make their way home across the fields. Soon it was pitch dark and they were somewhat disorientated. They came to a stile which Dorrie clambered over first, only to scream once on the other side as she stood straight onto the back of a large brown cow! This frightened the giggling sisters to death but they eventually got home to recount their adventure. When Dorrie had long gone to live in Australia her sister Margie would often wistfully repeat this story as, somehow, it encapsulated all her feelings and memories of her beloved lost sister.

At some point Leslie Neller survived a bombing raid on Filton Aircraft Works and when the War finished his wanderlust soon reasserted itself. The late 1950's was the era of mass emigration to Australia. The 'Ten Pound Poms' programme was promoted by Australia and Britain. What an attractive proposition it must have seemed to Uncle Leslie... a land of opportunity and promise for him and his young family beckoning. It offered an escape from Britain, tired and war weary and still largely 'on the ration'. The days when different foodstuffs came off the ration were red-letter days just after The War. We had had just about everything on the ration for a number of years. Each person had their little brown ration books with coupons inside entitling them to so much meat, sugar, butter or whatever. In fact, in the absence of sweets it used to be a 'sugar spread on butter' sandwich that satisfied our cravings for sweet things. That and condensed milk. For some reason there was no shortage of this thick ultra sweet glutinous substance which you twirled around your spoon as you dug into the tin. It was delicious too! You can still obtain it in the shops today—probably make you sick though! Another food memory from those years was powdered egg. Anything which tasted or looked less like anything to do with eggs you would have been hard pressed to find. But we ate it.

Soon the Nellers were all signed up for their great adventure. The weekend before they left for Australia there was a large, entire family gathering at Hamilton's Photographers' Studios in Staple Hill which was now in the hands of mother's brother Bert and where Nanny was now living too, 'Pom Pom' having died a few years before. I recall tumbling happily around on the floor with my cousins Tony Neller and Bobby Kent, blissfully unaware of emotions that must have been swirling around the adults. It was 1949 or 1950. It was to be the last time our whole family was entirely together. It was, sadly, to be lots of 'last times'. Most poignant, it was the last time her mother and her brothers and sisters were ever to see Dorrie again. Part of the Webb family effectively died as The Nellers set sail for Australia.

(v)

Herbert Webb (aka. Bert or Bertie) was in many ways the most talented in the family and yet the most blinkered. Uncle Bert (as he was to me) was highly gifted both artistically and cerebrally. His ability to draw with simple pencils was marvellous and he could produce remarkably accurate likenesses, especially faces. He possessed an excellent singing voice and sang in a trio called 'The Three Nomads' who performed in a semi-professional capacity for several years. The highlight of his singing career was an appearance on the fledgling television service of the day in a programme featuring Entertainment

Acts from different towns and cities. This was a competition to find the 'Top Town', as the programme was called. I recall the excitement amongst the rest of our family as everyone found somewhere to watch television (these were the days when by no means every household possessed what was often known then as a 'goggle box') and Uncle Bert's keenly anticipated appearance at the appointed time. The programme was not recorded but made 'live' in Manchester and 'The Nomads' sang a song that had no meaning whatsoever but was a catchy tune. It went....

Quanta la gusta, la gusta, la gusta
Quanta la gusta, la gusta, la gusta
When are we leaving, where are we going, what are we gonna do?
We're on our way to somewhere, the three of us and you.
When will we be there, what'll we see there, what'll be the big surprise?
There may be senoritas with dark and flashing eyes.
We're on our way, we won't look back
And if we stay, we won't come back.
How can we go, we haven't got a dime
But we're going and we're gonna have a happy time.
Quanta la gusta, la gusta (etc.)

(They don't write 'em like that any more.)

So, there was my Uncle Bert, in his prime, dead handsome in a cream tuxedo and a dickie-bow tie, singing out of that little black and white screen. All the family gathered around their goggle boxes gasping and muttering with pride and pleasure. In another time, Uncle Bert might have been quite famous. By the standards of the day 'The Three Nomads' were good. Incidentally I'm pretty sure that, in spite of Uncle Bert and The Nomads turning in a good performance, Bristol lost to Blackpool in that edition of the programme. Shucks!

Starting in his grandfather's photography business and seeing it decline, Uncle Bert tried his hand at running a grocery shop... the previously described 'Table Delicacies' on Staple Hill High Street. This failed as Bertie's heart wasn't really in the faggot and sausage making business (which, when you really 'hold that thought' was just as well). He found his calling when, some time in the mid 1950's, he went to work for the Bristol Aeroplane Company at Filton. I'm not really sure of the exact nature of his job but he was rapidly promoted and his technical mind and draftsman's skills happily combined into a successful mix. In the days before computers

Bertie's fast moving brain seemed just the job. He worked at Filton for the best part of thirty years and found fulfilment through his work.

Yet in many ways he was a very limited and unambitious soul, for all his talents and knowledge (Bertie was a real 'anorak'). He never really wanted to go anywhere or do very much. He was a genuine prototype Webb stick-in-the-mud. It was always something of a family joke that Manchester (where he had gone to take part in 'Top Town') was the very furthest he ever travelled. I believe he never even went to London (120 miles from Bristol!). He went on holiday to the same place in Devon every year for over thirty years and he kept a tight regime of habit and custom with his own little branch of the family.

He married Edna Bonning, known to all as Bonnie. If ever a name suited anyone it was 'Bonnie'. She was a person of consummate sweetness and patience. She stuck by Bert through all the difficult years of shortage and business failures. She cared for him and practically nursed him as they grew very old together in their little house in Downend. Bertie became something of a grumpy old man as his age increased and Auntie Bonnie was always present to placate and administer to him. Uncle Bert lasted right up into his mid nineties, dying in the house he would not leave, clinging on to the very end to the familiar things that gave him comfort. When Bert died, Bonnie, a nonagenarian herself, seemed in robust health and it was thought she might have had a few years of contentment left. It was not to be, and as though Bert and Bonnie had somehow survived for so long together only through their mutual dependence, dearest Auntie Bonnie had a stroke within a week or two and herself expired.

Bert and Bonnie had two children (my cousins Margaret and Philip). Philip Webb inherited many of his father's talents and he too has had a highly successful career at The Bristol Aeroplane Company, on the technical side. Philip Webb is also a custodian of the Webb sense of humour, being an extremely amusing and engaging bloke... as in, at the very infrequent gatherings of the Webb cousins about every ten years: 'Oh, hello, I believe we are related.' Or, when riding in the passenger seat of your car and pointing at the dirty windscreen, 'You can get these in clear glass you know!'

Their daughter Margaret is an apple that never fell far from the tree. Amiable and reliable like her mother, she married Barry Jenner... a 'rock-steady, true blue' Englishman, Bristolian and ardent Bristol City fan (in that order probably!). Together they always did their stuff for Bert and Bonny, remained tight and close with Philip and his wife Marion and Philip and Marion's son Ian and his thriving young family.

So, that was my Uncle Bert... probably the cleverest of a clever brood. A contradiction of a fellow nonetheless!

(vi)

Marjorie May Webb (aka. Margie)—Auntie Margie to me, youngest of the Webb children—was born in May, hence the middle Christian name. Pulled along through her childhood by her loving pack of older siblings in that large white house on Ninetree Hill, just off Stokes Croft. She adored her father, would run his errands, listen to his musings, watch the antics of her brothers and share the girly secrets of her two sisters.

All the good humour and wit that went on in that house cascaded down to Margie and she must have soaked it up daily. Pretty and cheerful, she left school at fourteen and what she did at first is unknown but by her late teens she was working in a photographer's shop in Bedminster. I believe she had started hairdressing like her sisters but had not much liked it.

Margie was completely daft about animals right from the beginning. In a family not really noted for its concern about animals, Margie was forever feeding her guinea pig or changing her mice or worrying about a stray cat or dog. She started in this way and it never changed... looking out for her animals was as important to Margie as looking after her family.

A young man working with her in that photographers was a John Kent. He plucked up his courage one day and asked her out (always somewhat shy, Uncle John) and next thing she's 'courting' as they used to say. John was part of a huge family that came from the Bedminster/Ashton area of Bristol. Shortly after the War started she and John were married. By now, with John in the Army, they were together a very short time before he was posted to the Far East where he was to be on active service throughout the war in Burma. He did not return home to England until the war ended. Fighting the Japanese in the jungles and river deltas of Burma must have been an almost unspeakable experience for the soldiers who went through it—that's what it was literally to Uncle John because he would never talk about it afterwards. Like most little boys I had a fascination with wars and fighting and especially the Second World War... 'Did you ever kill a Jap, Uncle John?'.... 'Did you have a bayonet, Uncle John, did you ever *use* it?'... 'Did you ever *see* any *dead* Japs, Uncle John?' Uncle John would smile and deflect my blood lust with a packet of biscuits or a tube of wine gums or reach for the dog lead for 'walkies' (he was pretty daft about animals too which was just as well, living with Margie).

Occasionally, when you asked him about the war in Burma, he would nod knowingly towards a small locked tin box he kept on a shelf in the living room. 'One day,' he would say somewhat mysteriously, 'we'll have a look in there.' 'What's in there Uncle John, what's in there?'.... 'We'll see... eventually.'

All this did of course, was to inflame our curiosity and we would imagine it contained gory photos of Japs with their stomachs sliced open by bayonets and their entrails liberally scattered about (or similar!). Uncle John had the last smile though, as years later after he died I saw the photos from that box—a collection of what amounted to 'holiday snaps' of Uncle John and his soldier mates frolicking at the side of a river, jumping in, splashing, having piggy-back races, gesturing happily at the camera—all taken when they were on some sort of leave or rest period! So, what Uncle John actually *did* experience he kept to himself. No soldier fought the Japanese in Burma for several years without the very deepest of emotions and feelings being engaged. With Uncle John these were strictly private and personal. I had, and have, enormous respect for him, even now.

(vii)

Margie and John did have enough time before he sailed off to the Far East to create their first born, Robert (my cousin Bobby Kent). John wasn't to see his son for several years as he was 'long gone' when Bobby made his appearance in 1941.

I don't think Auntie Margie was exactly enamoured with the whole idea of childbirth. Like the majority of women, I suppose, it was an experience to be endured but certainly not exactly enjoyed. Put another way... Margie hated the whole messy business! This, then, must have been her frame of mind when the midwife handed her the tiny blood-flecked bundle wrapped in a large towel. 'What is it?' Marge asked the smiling nurse. 'It's a little boy, Mrs. Kent'— Marge peering distastefully into the towel. 'No, I asked *what* is it?'

As a matter of fact Marge and Bobby became very close during those first few years when it was just them. When Uncle John returned he had some difficulty in establishing a close relationship of his own with Bobby. One can only speculate as to the cause; probably the separation of his years abroad had interfered with a natural bonding process of some sort or maybe there was some jealousy at play. The outcome was that John and Bobby never really got on too well from the start. This grew to almost silent hostility in later years. Things were very different when their second son Peter (my cousin Peter Kent) came along. If Bob was Mum's boy, then Peter was to become 'Dad's'.

The Kent family took a while to stabilise after John's return. For several years they lived in a large, cold flat above a shop on Staple Hill High Street (virtually next door to Uncle Bertie's grocery shop).

God, that flat was cold! I remember we would stay there at times after we had visited our Grandmother. Our cousins Philip and Margaret Webb would come in and we would play in this huge living room. It was heated by a small open fire which fought a losing battle trying to heat the room against its large windows, vast recesses and lofty ceiling space. The grown-ups would huddle around the fire chatting and occasionally letting out yells of 'stop running in and out of that door you children, there's a terrible draught'. If it was a Sunday we would gather at the window as it was a wonderful grandstand to watch the Salvation Army Band and Parade which occurred right outside. With banners fluttering, brass band blaring and drum thumping, the good folks of The Sally Army would march by in their dark uniforms with red piping—the women in bonnets, the men in peaked caps, most of the marchers with bibles clutched in their hands. We cousins would press our noses to the cold glass of the window whilst Margaret and Philip would point out local people they knew who were swirling by below.

The bedroom in that flat of Auntie Margie's was cavernous and deadly cold. We would pile coats on top of the blankets to be warm. Our breath condensed as we exhaled and it used to make me laugh to see my sister with steam coming out of her mouth. Mind you, it wasn't quite so funny if she emptied her bladder up my back in the middle of the night. What with the sub-zero temperature of the air in that room and the freezing pee of my sister spread up my back, staying the night at Auntie Margie's was a degree or two less than something I exactly relished!

I seem to remember going over to Auntie Margie's for longer periods on my own to play with Bobby, he and I being close in age and interests. My cousin Bob was a bright boy, brighter than me. We used to play a board game called 'Dover Patrol'. We'd play it for hours. There were little cardboard boats of different types that could be moved around the board; there were destroyers, torpedo boats, minesweepers, submarines and several other types of naval vessels. It was a game of strategy and tactics. Frustratingly for me, Bobby always won! I used to keep a simple diary in those days and a while after I found in one I had written at the time an entry: 'Went to Staple Hill to see Auntie Margie. Played "Dover Patrol" with Bobby... I BEAT HIM!' So, that was obviously quite an event! Mind you, we used to play football too out in the lane at the back and I would invariably beat him pretty easily, much to *his* frustration. There was a grumpy old lady (probably not grumpy at all but worried to death about the two hooligans outside playing football and threatening to spoil her beloved vegetable garden). Anyway, her name was Mrs. Crew and she would stand guard outside watching us play football. There was only a small stone wall around the perimeter of her beautifully maintained little garden. Fairly frequently I recall the ball would land plop amongst her lettuces. Quick as a flash she would rake the ball towards her with a long washing pole, grab it and whizz

inside her house clutching the ball to her tiny bosom. Somehow we would carry on; usually Bob had more than one tennis ball or occasionally she would throw it back with what we would have called then 'a good telling off', but probably today, by the deteriorating manners of our times, 'a bloody good bollocking'!

The Kents eventually got a council house a mile or so away in Mangotsfield. John obtained work at The Bristol Aeroplane Company at Filton. It seems that Uncle John was contented to come and go across Bristol every morning for the next thirty years or so. He was a loyal and long serving employee. Whatever thoughts he had about

Uncle John in Burma.

the contrast between picking his way through the morning Bristol traffic and crossing The River Irawaddy under artillery fire, he kept them to himself. Life fell into a comfortable routine—he liked his tea on the table at five o'clock, Bristol City one Saturday and Bristol Rovers the next, quality time with his younger son Peter, visiting his own elderly mother down in Ashton, walking the dog and generally keeping a steady hand on things.

Meanwhile Margie had started to work at a local hospital (Manor Park) a few nights each week caring for geriatric patients. Margie never obtained any formal nursing qualifications. She was really at the least desired working end of the health care system... long tiring nights of toil, much of it concerned with the waste and leaking body fluids of old, sick and frequently demented folks. Not for everyone! Margie kept it up for many years and must have eased the discomfort of hundreds of poor souls down the years—always with that Webb phlegm and humour never far away to assist her through the woes and tragedies that abounded. 'How was work last night, Margie?'.... 'Fine, we've got this one old girl who thinks she's Queen Victoria'... 'Really, how do you deal with her?'... 'Well, I go up to her bed, curtsy and say "Would your Majesty care to sit on the commode now?", then I leave her to it and when I go back I curtsy again and ask her "Is Your Majesty kwite ready to have her bum wiped now? Good, please roll over Ma'am".' Nice work Margie!

Not that things were all tickety-boo at home. Bobby had several bouts of illness (a burst appendix nearly killed him when he was about 12). Bob's relationship with his father maintained its steady decline and Margie felt the stress of always trying to keep the peace between them. Peter (who in later life turned out to be a truly lovely fella, possibly my very favourite cousin) was becoming a 'problem' too. He somewhat dismayed his parents: he wouldn't go to school and he was desperately withdrawn and shy. Margie and John tried every which way to get him moving. Half the Educational Psychologists in South Gloucestershire were mobilised, but the little bugger wouldn't go to school and he wouldn't talk to hardly anyone except his Dad and (sometimes) his Mum. It's quite a story really how old Pete got over this distinctly unpromising start in life and ultimately became a successful businessman (owning a fishing tackle shop) and an all round good egg and happy family man. Trust me though, he did!

Bobby weaved his own rather bewildering course. He gained a place at Grammar School (Kingswood), did OK at school but not brilliantly and left too early. He was a good rugby player and a lifetime love of that game developed from his schooldays. He went through a slightly tearaway phase on the fringe of the biker scene. Next thing you know, he's designing kitchens (great draftsman, Bob) and with a business partner providing the more practical 'building them' side, he's soon piling it up in the bank account. By the mid 1970's it's all booming—about twenty blokes employed. Whilst still living at home in his parents' council house, our Bob soon gets a taste for expensive things—a boat (no less), not a small one either, one which happily sailed the ocean wave with Captain Bob and his mates back and forth across the Channel just for fun. A couple of classic motor cycles, off to The Isle Of Man for the 'TT' races... cousin Bob was certainly revving it all up. By the time Maggie Thatcher came along in the early 1980's with her 'Right To Buy' for council house tenants (at huge discounts below market value), our Bob seized the moment and was one of the first to get his cash out.

Good in one way—Margie and John could live rent-free in the house. Bad in another—it was now Bob's house and his circumstances were to change dramatically within a few years. First, he thought it would be nice to have a wife. Where better to get one, without a lot of fuss and bother, than from amongst the queue of eligible foreign ladies from the Far East, Africa and elsewhere who sought to meet and marry Englishmen through the medium of advertising themselves in relevant publications and contact mags. This was just before the advent of the internet which has taken over all these sorts of arranged introductions. So, Bob got himself a Philippino wife.

Some of these things work out well but Bob's didn't. His new wife, Maria, turned out to be a volatile and difficult person who could have a row with herself if there was no one else around. Bringing her into the house to live with Margie and John turned out to be an instant disaster. Once Maria was in the door, then everyone else was going to get pushed out. At this point, as the impossibility of the new domestic arrangement was becoming daily more evident, Uncle John, one morning, went for a shower and dropped dead from a heart attack right there and then, just like that. Margie lived on for a couple more years in that house becoming more and more unhappy as Maria took over the territory almost completely and Margie hating her probably more than any mother-in-law had ever hated her daughter-in-law in the whole history of The Universe. There was compensation for Margie in the baby girl (Vickie), her first grandchild. Bob and Maria went on to produce two more children, Johnnie and Susie (balls over brains, Bob!). Margie doted on her grandchildren, investing most of what was left of her wonderful 'karma' towards them in the years before she died.

Bob's kitchen business went belly-up in the recession years of the early 90's. He went severely bankrupt. His marriage had gone rotten years before. He had put his house on the line too to shore up his ailing business and 'wallop', he lost that as well. Bob turned out an excellent father though, virtually raising his two older children on a shoestring but with love and care. It looks as though it may turn out well with Vickie going on to University, Johnny shaping up well and the youngest Susie as bright as a button by all accounts. Margie and John would be proud.

Margie ended up in a purpose built little bungalow for elderly people. She steadily went 'do-lally' but remained a familiar figure out at the shops getting tangled up in the leads of her two tiny Yorkshire Terriers. When she sat down, calmed down, puffed away at yet another of the zillions of 'fags' she worked through, she was often as amusing and adorable as always. Such interludes were rarer and rarer. Margie had always, like her father, been a champion worrier (all the Webbs were to be honest) and as physical incapacity gradually overwhelmed her she became a real toxic sort of person—no-one knew quite what to do with her.

Last call for Margie was a residential home. Pete and Bob and the grandchildren visited (as did my sister Jill who brought much comfort to the Aunt she loved). All did their best to jolly her along. There were flashes of the Margie that used to be from time to time. Eventually she had just had enough and, we were told, one night just slipped peacefully away. I hope so.

The Webbs died in the order they were born—first Kitty, then Sonny, Dorrie, Allan, Bertie and Margie. Great how nature arranges things sometimes. I loved them all—The Webbs were the strongest bricks in my wall, without a doubt.

Hamilton Coat of Arms and Name History

Origin Displayed: Scottish

Spelling variations of this family name include: Hamilton, Hamelton, Hameldon, Hamildon, Hamylton, Hambleton and many more.

First found in Renfrewshire, where they were granted lands by King Robert the Bruce of Scotland.

Some of the first settlers of this family name or some of its variants were: David Hamilton settled in Boston in 1651; Mathew Hamilton settled in New England in 1685; William Hamilton settled in Grenada in 1774; Charles, Henry, James, John, Joseph, Mathew, Patrick, Robert, Samuel, Thomas and William Hamilton all arrived in Philadelphia between 1800 and 1860.

Mother aged 11 (1916).   **Mother aged 14 (1919).**

**A Webb family fishing picnic in 1926 with my
Father and Mother, Uncle Sonny, Uncle Bert,
Nanny, Auntie Margie and Grandfather Pom
Pom.**

Great Grandmother
Elizabeth Hamilton circa 1890.

Great Grandfather
Allan Hamilton circa 1890.

The Webbs all together for the last time on the eve of Auntie
Dorrie's departure for Australia in 1949. Uncles Allan, Sonny and
Bert, Auntie Margie, Mother, Nanny Webb and Auntie Dorrie.

The entire Webb family with their spouses at the wedding of Uncle and
Auntie Bonnie 1938. Mother, Father, Auntie Ada, Uncle Sonny, Nanny Webb,
Brother Allen (aged 11), Pom Pom Webb, Auntie Dorrie, Uncle Leslie Neller,
Uncle Bert and Auntie Bonnie, Uncle Allan, Auntie Daisy and Auntie Margie.

'Uncle Bert, Uncle Allan, Auntie Dorrie and my mother Kitty on Weston-Super-Mare-Beach circa 1931.This happy picture says it all about the Webb family.

Wedding of Uncle Allan, Auntie Daisy circa 1936. Uncle Sonny on groom's right and Auntie Bonnie on bride's left.

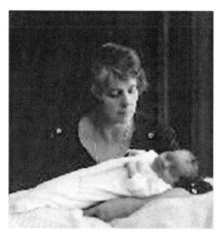

My Grandmother Clara Webb with my infant brother Allan circa 1926.

Chapter Three

The Duttons

BUILT ON THE HILL which rises above Park Row, on the road running along the front of Bristol University, is the huge ugly concrete monolith of The Bristol University Medical School. This building bends around to the shape of the hill before tapering away to a slope that runs down to St Michael's Hill, which now forms the eastern extremity of the whole University Campus. It was built in the 1950's and formed part of the huge expansion of Universities throughout this era.

Before the development began it was necessary to remove large numbers of Victorian dwellings that for a hundred years or so had been home to working class Bristol folks. A quarter mile square area had as its widest street Tankard's Close, into which fed a number of smaller side streets and alleys. The whole patch was known locally as 'Tanks'. There is nothing left of it at all now except one solitary stone bollard marking the end of a pathway that once opened out directly onto the cobbles of 'Tankard's Close'. The inhabitants would have walked down the slope and steps to Park Row to shops in one direction and onto the steep St. Michael's Hill in the other. Their spiritual needs would have been met by the Church at the bottom of St. Michael's Hill (which is still there and in which my parents were married in 1926) and their drinking habits (principally of the men-folk) taken care of by numerous pubs, the one most adjacent to 'Tanks' being named 'The Robin Hood'.

It was here in these little damp houses with their outside toilets, arched brick alleyways, tin coal bunkers, open fires, wash tubs and iron stove kitchens, that many members of The Dutton Family lived. I'm not sure how it evolved but a whole kinship of Duttons clustered in that small zone. It was where my grandfather Timothy Dutton (who I never knew) grew up with his brother Adrian (Uncle 'Ad'), sisters Cecilia (Auntie Sis), Eveline, Maggie and Lily (aka 'Ninny'), his nieces and nephews Glad, Eveline and May,

Olive, Jean and Vera, Margaret, Donald and Reggie—not to mention his own children Dolly, Billy (my Dad) and Edna. I've whistled through them, probably even missed a couple, but one way or another they were all Duttons and they all lived at some point 'Up Tanks'.

Judging by his actions my grandfather Timothy was a very irresponsible character. He left his wife Nell (b. Ridgeway, my grandmother I never knew but by all accounts a good looking redheaded lady) with his two younger children and sodded off to Canada. Perhaps I do him a disservice, perhaps the idea had been to make some money, establish himself in Canada and then send for the rest of his family. Well, if that was the case it never worked out that way. I suspect I do him no disservice at all and that he was an irresponsible opportunist, but I could be wrong! The actual impact of his defection was to completely shatter his family. Tragically Nell died in the great influenza epidemic of 1919. With no parents the four Dutton children were shunted into an orphanage where they remained until such times as they rejoined other members of their wider family prepared to care for them back in Tanks. Thus my father Billy went to live with his Aunt Lily (Ninny), by now herself married to a solid Bristol bloke (Uncle Joe Palmer) who, effectively became Billy's parents and brought him up.

Poor Edna (the oldest girl), after living a few years with one of the 'Tanks' families, trod the path familiar to many young girls of those days. At the age of fourteen she 'entered Service' to a wealthy family who lived in one of those large houses characteristic of the Clifton area of Bristol. Here, she learned how to serve the correct silverware at dinner and all the rest of the flummery which underpinned that way of life—a way of life rapidly coming to an end, unaware of this as its beneficiaries may have been at the time. We tracked Aunt Edna down in later life (she died in her 90's) to the home of her warm-hearted daughter Glenis (my cousin) in Hampshire. She was by then a sweet old lady who smelled the 'pee smell' of incontinence and had only a fragmented memory of her childhood.

As for my grandfather Timothy, he did return once to 'Tanks' after several years in Canada. One can only conclude that he had done reasonably well judging alone from the fact that he could afford to make the journey. Be that as it may, it created quite a wave of excitement amongst all the Duttons (and no doubt all the other inhabitants!) on the day Tim reappeared, wearing a white suit, a broad-brimmed panama hat, a gold watch and chain and fob protruding out of his waistcoat pocket. A silver handled cane in his hand, he strode up Tankard's Close—quite a dandy! He didn't stay long and, taking Dolly with him, he returned to Canada barely to be heard of again. Years later my brother Allan (by then a successful doctor, himself living in Canada) tracked down Tim's youngest daughter Dolly. She, by then, was as Canadian as maple syrup, and remembered virtually nothing of her Bristol origins. However she was able to direct my brother to our grandfather living in London, Ontario, with a whole new family who knew nothing of his life in England. You never really covered yourself in much glory, Grandfather Timothy; as a father and family man you didn't square up, but you certainly started a lot of significant balls rolling...

(ii)

'Tight knit community' is a cliché used nowadays throughout the media in Britain. Every time there is a murder, or a bad accident, or a horrible crime, the impact on 'the tight knit community' is always bigged up by the TV and newspapers. Local people are trotted out in front of cameras and microphones to testify to the close bonding and brotherhood gluing together the locals in a communal grieving. Whilst not denigrating the fact that stuff happens and much of it extremely regrettable, the notion that everyone in the area of an event lives in a kind of 'Coronation Street' of collective concern and emotion is, to me, so much media-driven drivel. It's stated merely to flesh out a good story. The reality is that people by and large get on with their own lives and those of their immediate family and are not greatly bothered about others. The modern world of family separation, mobility and the pursuit of money and advantage (all normal!) means that 'close knit communities' are mostly fiction. For instance, I have lived with the same neighbours all around for years and we're on smiling and first name terms— but what I really *know* about them, and if I'm honest, actually *care* about them is, as they say, 'diddly squat'!

It wasn't always thus. In and around The Tankard's Close area of Bristol the Dutton family lived and carried on for many years in a 'close knit community', bound by kinship and the stifling geography of the time. To visit Ninny and Uncle Joe (father's aunt and uncle and de facto parents) and then cross over the cobbles to see Auntie Sis (father's Aunt) and her family, were occasions which left their mark.

One thing, my Dad himself was never there! One can only speculate (but not too hard!) as to where he might have been. I would always visit with my sister so a taxi driving neighbour would take us there. My sister adored Ninny and this affection was obvious. Perhaps the fact that Ninny had been childless increased the intensity of the love between her and Jill. When Ninny died in 1947 it set off a grief in my sister which isn't far below her surface even now. Personally I don't really remember Ninny as vividly as I do her husband, Uncle Joe Palmer. He dressed exactly as a working man of the time—boots, baggy black serge trousers and faded cotton shirt, braces and (sometimes) a cap. He always had a pipe in his mouth or in his hand and both he and his house smelled permanently of rich, dark shag tobacco. Only thinking of his house releases its aroma in my nostrils.

At the rear of their house it was clear how Tankard's Close was cut into the hillside above Park Row. Uncle Joe had a superbly maintained terraced garden overlooking the whole of Bristol Centre. At that time it was a grandstand vista across the bomb-damaged skyline. This was about 1945, remember, so nothing had been rebuilt after the attentions of Field Marshall Goering and his Merry Men. I do recall the numerous church spires defiantly protruding. Even when churches were bombed out (and many were in Bristol) it always seemed that the spires remained.

That garden of Uncle Joe's, with the wall at the bottom marking a sharp drop to a lower level of the hillside terrace, was a garden that was a perfect little 'jewel'. It was Uncle Joe's total pride and joy and he grew and tended his flowers and vegetables in the manner of an artist. Spade or paring knife in hand, the image of that man amongst his lettuces, carrots, turnips, cabbages, broad and runner beans comes to me in an instant. He had several trellises of long sticks crossing 'wigwam style' at the top for his beans and the other veggies grew in abundance and luxury in their allotted rows. Never mind feeding just The Dutton family from the produce of that garden, there must have been plenty left over for several other 'Tanks' households.

Over the road Auntie Sis (father's aunt b. Cecilia Dutton) was a truly larger-than-life figure. Large, loud and jolly, she presided over her brood (Olive, Vera and Jean, my Dad's cousins) with barking good humour. Totally in charge of the household she would direct operations from a sitting position. She rarely stood as her mobility was restricted by the large surgical boot she wore on her right foot. Auntie Sis was a victim of a nasty gene threaded in and around the Duttons which caused a birth defect (club foot) whereby one foot was set incorrectly at an angle. The only remedy available in those days was to 'force' the foot straight so as to allow enough balance for walking. This was done by the means of a large heavy surgical boot. This condition was known overall as Talipus and it has always been evident in The Dutton Family. Sis's niece Glad was so afflicted, as was my sister's second daughter Sally and my Dad's brother, Ted's son, Andrew. Treatments for this condition have improved greatly down the years but in earlier times seeing people weighed down and immobilised by an ugly surgical boot was quite commonplace.

So, from her chair, Auntie Sis would grab you when you were in her orbit, give you a giant hug, lunge into your groin with a podgy hand and shout in broad Bristolian: 'How's yer dink'ums my babby!!' It was playful and all part of the frenetic activity that always seemed to be prevalent in that house. I vaguely remember games of hide and seek with one of the hiding places being the coal shed at the bottom of some small steps at the rear of the house. One emerged after hiding in there with a blackened face and coal dust all over—it probably pleased my hard pressed mother when I got home at night after a visit 'up Tanks'! Sis had married a Welshman, Ted Griffiths (aka 'Ampsey') who worked on the railways. He became a greatly revered family figure. He was a quiet dignified man who lived a very long and steady life, dying in the 1980's just a couple of months short of his 100th birthday.

Now, Sis and Ted's oldest daughter Olive (my Dad's cousin) became firm friends with Kitty, my mum, when they started work together as apprentice hairdressers (this would have been the early 1920's). It wouldn't have been too long therefore until young Kitty Webb would visit her new friend at Olive's welcoming home 'up Tanks'. It would have taken the young Billy Dutton, who lived opposite on Tankards Close, an even shorter time to notice the pretty girl knocking about with his cousin Olive and even shorter time again than that for the rascal to make his move! 'Fatal attraction', 1920's style! Poor innocent inexperienced 'Pretty Kitty' Webb never had a chance! Billy was a fast moving charmer who could, as they say today, 'walk the walk and talk the talk!' Don't suppose I can complain too much... I'm here, aren't I?

As for Olive Griffiths, she remained a staunch pal of Kitty's throughout the rest of life's thicks and thins. She courted and eventually married Percy Harding, an industrious and enterprising young man, himself born and brought up in another of Bristol's now largely obliterated old working class communities, Cathay, behind St. Mary Redcliffe Church. This young fellow went on to build up one of the most successful family business dynasties known in Bristol. A business built on butcher's shops and chandlery (provisioning the ships in and out of Bristol and Avonmouth Docks). Bristol was once a major player in a worldwide cargo trade, much of it now having disappeared. Harding Bros—Percy Harding and all his brothers and sisters, successful business people all. Largely through my mum's enduring friendship with Olive (Auntie Olive as she was to me) we sort of always remained attached to The Hardings in a loose way. My sister Jill and Diane, Olive and Percy's daughter, have always been tight. All this though is, as they say, another story...

My Great Grandparents,
Willie and Ellen Ridgeway
and the children. My
Grandmother, Nell Ridgeway
is on the far left. Circa 1905.

The Dutton children in
the orphanage circa
1915. Matron with
(front) my Father Billy
and Ted, (rear) Edna
and Dolly.

"Ninny" Palmer. My
Grandfather Timothy's
sister who mainly brought
up my Father and played a
large part in my sister Jill's
early years.

Auntie Jean's wedding 1940 showing Allan (left) in front of Mum. Michael Harding in front. Percy and Billy behind the groom. Auntie Olive holding Jill's hand (front). Nanny Webb holding me, a few weeks old, right at the back near the railings.

A Tankards Close occasion. The wedding of my Grandfather Timothy Dutton's nephew Reggie Briggs. A gathering of Duttons, Briggs and Griffiths. Auntie Olive directly behind the bride standing next to Auntie Sis who is wearing a large flowery bonnet. Diane Harding, little girl at bottom right. circa 1945.

**My paternal Great Grandfather
Willie Ridgway.**

**My paternal Great Grandmother
Ellen Ridgway.**

BRISTOL

City of my birth

Chapter Four

The Wanderers

NOT LONG AFTER my parents' divorce the hairdressing business mother had clung to and worked so hard to maintain finally went bust. I don't know what the financial outcome was but I think mother emerged relatively unscathed in as far as she was not burdened by debt as a result. She was, of course, left with the small problem of somewhere to live and how to provide for her two remaining children (yours truly and sister Jill... my brother Allan was by now married and had set up his own home).

Funnily enough, those premises in Stoke Lane always remained thereafter a hairdressing business. Not so many years ago I went back there along with my brother and sister. The then incumbents allowed us to have a look around the premises which, we discovered, had altered little in fifty years or so. On that occasion, by way of conversation, I remarked to a lady working in the 'salon' (as they were now known, 'saloons' being strictly the domain of western gunslingers only, nasty rough places, not to be confused with matters of coiffeur!). So, I remarked to her that I had been born in one of the rooms upstairs and I had once watched a man arrive on a bicycle each evening at the edge of the pavement of the road outside and reach up with a long pole to light a gas lamp. She stared back at me as though I was possibly a psycho who had conned his way in to rob the till and ravish her in the process. In short, she couldn't get me out of there quick enough. Now this, come to think of it, had always been how welcome I had been in that 'salon', all the way back to my mother's day!

Back then though in the late 1940's, Mum did her last perm at 121 Stoke Lane and we three (Mum, Jill and me) began several years of wandering from one accommodation to another, not becoming finally settled until I had reached my late teens.

Luckily for Mother at that time she had a friend called Dorothy Furber who was also a hairdresser and who owned a business in Henleaze (posh area of Bristol, immediately very appealing to Mother, well away from 'oiks'and 'Bristolians'!). This Dorothy Furber, with her husband Murray, did not choose to live in the accommodation above their hairdressing shop on Henleaze Road. Enter the desperate Duttons! It must have been a huge relief to our mother. Accommodation *and* a job! We lived in that place for about two or three years. Whilst we were there one Sunday was the day when most of the kids in England (and probably half the adults too) were ablaze with excitement—sweets came off the ration!

There was a large confectioners' shop in Henleaze Road called 'Nivens' and on that Sunday Jill and I (and one of her friends) joined the rapidly growing queue outside that shop about an hour before it opened. Trust me, that queue was several hundred yards long when they eventually opened the doors for business. I recall spending the collection of hot coins I had been clutching in my pocket for hours, within seconds of reaching that counter. I don't honestly remember what I bought but I always preferred sherbet and minty things rather than chocolate or sucky things. So, it was probably things like that. The sight of all those tempting delights stacked up in boxes on the counter and overflowing on the shelves behind was truly a wonderland beyond description!

Although Mother must have been pleased to have a payday each week (she got nowt from father, he was juggling with his next round of irresponsibility by then!), her wage could not have ended up as much at all. The Furbers clearly took a big slice from her money for the accommodation. So, once more the family financial wheels were mainly oiled by the tips mum received from her customers. Of course, like all kids of all time, we did not appreciate that 'money doesn't grow on trees' (a very frequent expression of my mother's).

Friday night was speedway night!

As far as we were concerned it may not have grown on trees but we expected it to grow steadily out of the overall pocket she wore to work every day! Hence, my sister and I were mad on Speedway Racing at this time and Friday night was speedway night! In Bristol this meant Knowle Stadium and the roaring, racing Bristol Bulldogs! It also meant bus fares for two, admission money for two, programme money for two, a hot drink money for two and 'a few pence over' money for two... just in case. It was amazing how our mother always came up with the required amount each week and amazing too, looking back, how utterly unfeeling we were towards any understanding of how difficult it must have been for her to provide it. Any suggestion at all that we might not be able to afford to go to Speedway on a particular week would be met with an immediate tantrum from me certainly, and probably my sister too. What selfish little sods we were. I'm so sorry about it now, fifty odd years too late of course...

We longed for Friday nights to arrive and the start of our trek across Bristol to Knowle Stadium. There was always the last minute battle with mother as she insisted that we 'wrap up warm'. Even though the Speedway season was throughout the summer months, fairly often speedway meetings were abandoned because of, usually, a 'waterlogged track'.

The bus we got to Knowle was one of very many put on especially for the speedway crowds. These buses filled up quickly with supporters, many decked out with the black and orange scarves and favours of 'The Bristol Bulldogs'. One adornment which was unique amongst speedway fans and I never saw again in followers of other sports, was a metal badge worn in the lapel or pinned on to a coat or jacket. This was formed in the emblem of your team (in our case the little face of a bulldog). Two tiny metal hooks were moulded onto the bottom of the badge and in turn hung onto these hooks was a small metal rectangular bar with a year date on. Underneath this were tiny hooks to allow for an additional bar for subsequent year dates... and so on. These badges, so proudly worn, indicated the number of years a person had belonged to the Supporters' Club. The more bars, the longer the membership and the greater the pride! These badges were worn like medals and someone with a badge indicating several years or more was a really proven follower... 1946, 1947, 1948, 1949, 1950, 1951... oh, to have all those bars attached!

By the time the crowded bus chugged, gears grinding, up the steep hill to Knowle Stadium, anticipation and excitement were starting to boil. During those immediate post-war years Speedway Racing was riding higher than high. For a few years it was getting larger crowds than football. It was booming! It was nothing for there to be ten thousand fans at Knowle Stadium for a home meeting. The 'Bulldogs' rode against teams from all over England; enthusiasm for Speedway blanketed the country... The Belle Vue Aces (Manchester), The Wembley Lions, Harringay Racers, Cardiff Dragons, Poole Pirates, Swindon Robins, the Wolverhampton Wolves. Almost every city and town with its own track, team and supporters... or so it seemed. But by the mid-fifties it was largely all

The rider who reached the first bend first invariably won the race

over. Its bubble burst almost overnight. There are theories as to why this should have been: changing tastes and fashions, increasing (slowly!) prosperity offering wider choices of leisure pursuits, even the advent and rapid growth of television coaxing people to stay home. Probably it was a little of all of these. Certainly, not least, there was a growing realisation that the rider who reached the first bend first invariably won the race. What promoted itself as a thrilling and exciting sport was, ironically, both boring and predictable! It was as though countless thousands of followers had suddenly emerged from mass hypnosis!

For a while there, though, a visit to the 'Bristol Bulldogs' was really something. We always headed for a small raised open stand adjacent to 'the pits'. This was the area from which the riders emerged onto the track to race. Here too they attended to their racing bikes between heats. There was a small army of mechanics bustling around the pits at all times, their overalls usually completely grimed with oil and greasy splodges of some sort. The tools of their trade were scattered around everywhere... spanners, nuts and bolts, jemmies, grease guns, oil cans, chains, tyres, mudguards and, invariably, a cigarette on the go not too far away. Considering the presence of petrol all around it was a wonder they got away with this but, in those blissful far-off days before 'health and safety' issues were not choking common sense to death, no-one paid such things much attention.

At the start of a meeting the music would blare out and marching from the pits would come all the track maintenance squads, wearing bright coloured sweaters, black berets, in perfect step and carrying their rakes and brooms like rifles on their shoulders... accompanied always by this song:

> Marching along together
> Singing all along the line
> What do we care for weather
> We'll be there in rain or shine
> Ready to do or die
> We'll march along with a cheery song
> To brighten every mile
> We've packed our troubles in our kitbags
> And that is why we smile
> So, marching along together
> Happy just to be side by side!'

Knowle Stadium, home of
the Bristol Bulldogs
Speedway Team.

Knowle Stadium 1951. The
rush for the first bend. Note the
size of the crowd!

Father, always the master of
the microphone, doing his
stuff. Exeter 1951.

Father with Ken Le
Breton, the legendary
'White Ghost'. One of the
best riders of the time,
killed at the Sydney Sports
Ground, Australia 1951.

Father, England Team Manager, leading out the riders for the Test Match versus Sweden 1952 (wearing the white coat of which he was extremely proud).

England versus the USA 1952. Father leads out his England team.

Manager, Exeter Falcons 1951. Directly behind Father is the 'wizard mechanic' Don Weeks.

It really was a great spectacle. In between races these squads would get busy repairing the track for the next race. The previous race would have left the track rutted and grooved with tyre tracks and scattered with disturbed shale where the riders had extended their legs as they entered corners at high speed and dragged them behind themselves as they exited. Then they'd hurtle down the straight sections of the track. Accidents were common (one of the reasons the crowds kept coming no doubt). Usually they were not serious but enough to stop the race (red lights would come on all around the track). An inquest would be held and the rider thought responsible for the race being stopped was liable to exclusion from the re-run race. Occasionally an accident was more serious. It was a dangerous sport and a number of young men were killed whilst racing, none at Knowle though to my knowledge. All these events we would follow closely in our programmes. We'd keep the scores, read about our favourites, strain our necks to see what was going on in the pits, and chant our battle cries excitedly in unison:

One, two, three, four	or	One, two, three, four
Who are we for		Listen to the Bulldogs roar
B-R-I-S-T-O-L		B-R-I-S-T-O-L
Bristol!!		Bristol!!

Above all, we would become intoxicated by the heady mixture of roaring bike engines, exhaust fumes from the racing fuel or 'dope' as it was called and the pounding out of the popular songs of the day over the loudspeakers:

> She wore red feathers and a hula hula skirt
> She wore red feathers and a hula hula skirt
> She lived on just coconuts and fish from the sea
> A rose in her hair
> A gleam in her eye
> And love in her heart for me

That was Guy Mitchell. Another favourite was Kay Starr's 'Wheel of Fortune'. We loved the part of the song that went 'and the wheel is...spinning, spinning, spinning' and all join in like mad. Then there was Johnny Ray whose classic hit of the day reached its crescendo with 'Soooo lett yerr hairrrr down and gowa right on and cryyyyyyy!!!'

Then there were our very own heroes, the riders! Gods they were in their leathers, visors, helmets and gloves (you hardly ever saw their faces). We all had our favourites. Mine were Dick Bradley (he was always immaculate, never seemed to get mud or shale on *his* leathers!), Billy and Johnny Hole (brothers, both had an immaculate and upright style), Eric Salmon (a real classic rider who 'trailed' his leg almost continuously round bends and down the straight). We worshipped all of them for a while. I think my sister liked a handsome young rider called Chris Boss.

So that was the Speedway. It played a potent part in our lives for a few years. Knowle Stadium has long gone. A housing development covers it all. Where the bikes once opened their throttles as they jockeyed for that vital inside track position at the first bend, housewives now hang out their washing and blokes cut their hedges.   Speedway is well and truly a 'done deal' nowadays. The last lap over. Probably most of the fellows who rode the bikes by now are at their own final pit stops... great days though, great memories.

(ii)

The atmosphere on the bus returning into Bristol from Knowle after a Speedway Meeting was as charged as the journey had been on the way to the Stadium. We were squashed up like sardines but still enthused with excitement and bonded to strangers by the collective enjoyment of the last few hours. There was often some residual singing and chanting to underline who we were and what we subscribed to, our 'Bulldogs'! GGGGRRRR!!

Returning from one Meeting I had not been able to get a seat on the bus (which was not at all uncommon for 'young 'uns'). Mind you, on ordinary buses, my mother had trained me to always give up my seat to a 'lady' if the bus were crowded. Believe me, I was always a Little Lord Fontleroy in this respect and, just in case I didn't immediately spring up like a cocker spaniel, mother would give me push or a nudge or a nod. In these days of equality the custom of giving up your seat to females has, of course, now come to be regarded by many women as almost an insult, so it doesn't happen very much. The entire practice has largely been abandoned. You still do, to be fair, see occasional examples of this old fashioned virtue, the recipients often mostly being the elderly. Nice to see when it happens.

So, back to the night I stood on this bus pressed around tightly by happy humanity on all sides. A man in a smart white mackintosh had his back to me although I was so close I could smell the Brylcream from his curly hair. Remember Brylcream, a pleasant smelling sort of white paste men used to ladle onto their hair to make it smooth, slick and manageable—or so the advertising would have had you believe? As the bus lurched the man in the white mackintosh changed his position so he was facing me and... I was staring straight at, none other folks, than—my Father! There was a moment of disbelief. As the bus proceeded we had a ten-minute chat (sort of surreal, looking back). As we approached Temple Meads Station there was a 'can't stop now son, I've got a train to catch', then a hug (father was tactile), followed by the pressing of a sixpenny piece into my hand. Then he was off, darting up The Incline towards the Railway Station. What the rascal had been up to I know not. In my innocence I was just pleased to see him and passed no judgements. In fact I couldn't wait to get home to tell mother: '...saw Daddy on the bus coming back from the Speedway'.... 'Oh, did you dear, that was nice.' Nothing more, although I think I recall a somewhat weary look in her eye... If you grant him the benefit of the doubt he was there just to see the Speedway. He was, after all, manager of both Exeter *and* The England Speedway teams. So, let's give him the benefit of that doubt. Would have been nice though to have known he was going to be in Bristol that night and to have had a little more than ten minutes of his time. Jill and I had been to stay with him in Exeter on one occasion since he divorced our mother. By then, he was married to Eve and they had two

Father with Faith and Johnny, my half sister and brother.

young children, my half sister Faith and half brother John. I must have been about eleven or twelve. Eve was a lot younger than father and I recollect her being a kind person to Jill and I during our visit although she clearly had her hands full with her two children and Father away a lot. It's almost certain that he had started to give Eve the run-around by then.

There was a great tragedy about their son John. It was discovered when he was less than one year old that he suffered from an incurable eye disease and he was permanently and totally blind. This is almost too sad for me to write about. We (my side of the family) lost touch completely with Eve, Faith and John as my father's blighted life continued to unravel and he left them for good. What is true is that Eve, gallantly and against the odds, cared for her brood with tigerish dedication, although John was eventually institutionalised into a specialist facility for blind people where his mother and sister could visit and stay close to him, which they did right up until he died. John (or 'Johnny' as his mother and sister Faith called him) died very young, in his thirties, his blindness merging with mental incapacity in his final years. Deep down, I ache with guilt about John. Never knew where he was, what had happened to him, didn't even try to find out... never really gave it a thought. It's only in recent time I've understood that it could and should have been different...

During our visit to stay with Father in Exeter I recall greatly enjoying the time when he took me to the stadium where his team, 'The Exeter Falcons' had their track and held their meetings. It was called The County Ground and is nowadays the home of the Exeter Rugby Club. Father was the General Manager of all the events there at that time including the Greyhound Racing. I recall that he did the announcing when it was greyhound racing and he let me sit with him one night perched aloft in a little raised white sort of shed which was elevated above the track that ran some twenty feet below. The position was adjacent to the finishing line of the races. This vantage point afforded a complete view of proceedings. My father was a great communicator and effortlessly commanded a microphone. People have often told me I'm good at that sort of thing too... those genes you see, can't escape them, no matter which way!

My Father was a great communicator

Bizarrely too, during that visit Father took us to the theatre to see and hear 'The Ivy Benson All Girls' Band'! This professional band was famous and renowned during those years. In fact they were described on the billboard outside the theatre as 'Recording Artistes'. There was a large picture too of (probably) Ivy herself blowing a trumpet dressed in an evening gown... I remember thinking how very strange she looked—only men blew trumpets, surely! I found out later that father taking us to the theatre was no act of generous largess but that he had acquired a few freebies from one of his bookmaker pals who had been attending to the trombonist in the band for a number of years! Blow me down, my Dad, eh?

By now mother had picked up another stray. One of her apprentices from the hairdressing saloon (still known as that, not having yet been 'upgraded to 'salon') had been thrown out by her parents for some reason and had nowhere to live. Her name was Stella Wellstead. For a while mother took her in and helped her along although I'm unsure what eventually became of her. What I do know is that she would baby-sit us on the few occasions mother went out (she sometimes played the card game 'bridge' at someone's house). On the one or two occasions this happened my sister would have one of her friends in and I would be with Stella in another room. She must have been about sixteen or seventeen and by then I was around twelve or thirteen.

Anyway, she was the first girl I ever kissed properly. I also began, right there and then, to discover that girls were indeed really very different in many ways... Best leave it at that. It was pretty innocent fumblings... nice nevertheless!

The skids were under us all at that address for sure as The Furbers had decided they did, after all, want to reclaim the flat we lived in above the Hairdressing business. Where next for our little trio? Not my problem, but certainly another major one for our beleaguered mother!

(iii)

When our little 'caravan' moved from Westbury to live above The Furber's hairdressing business in Henleaze, mother took with her a band of loyal customers whose locks she had been perming and waving for donkeys' years. All posh ladies of course with whom she always kept friendly. In some way these 'posh customers' confirmed to mother that she herself was securely anchored to the middle class in spite of all her personal misfortunes that were always threatening to cut her adrift. Hence mother's conversations were littered with remarks such as 'Mrs Sacof, my rich Jewish customer, told me the other day that...' or, 'Mrs Young, one of my customers who lives in that big posh house on Downscote Drive, was telling me all about her son at University...'

It was indeed the aforementioned Mrs. Young who came to our rescue when the Furbers wanted us out, and smartly, from their premises. Mrs. Young had once or twice invited the newly divorced Kitty around to her house to make up the numbers amongst her card-playing pals ('Bridge' or 'Canasta' of course, nothing 'common'). One of regular participants was a chap named Bill Surtees. It's possible that Mrs. Young saw herself as the very 'Queen of Hearts' herself and was intent on a little matchmaking. If so, I don't think mother was swept off her feet! Bill Surtees, frankly, was not exactly an attractive catch. He was a large scruffy, pot-bellied man in his mid-fifties with a fag always dangling in his mouth from which the ash at its tip eventually lengthened until it dropped of its own accord onto the floor where it was usually ground into the carpet with the a quick scuff of the shoe. Or the ash fell onto the clothing and was brushed off with a careless sweep or pat of the hand.

Having said all that, 'Uncle Bill' (as I was soon to be encouraged to call him) was a widower whose three grown siblings had long flown his nest, leaving him to pad around alone in his (as it turned out) messy, untidy but reasonably spacious council house in Dingle Close, Sea Mills. I never really took to Uncle Bill (could have been jealousy of course, a rival for my mother's attentions). He didn't really like me much either, possibly for the same reasons. However, in our hour of need he was able to offer 'The Wandering Duttons' an immediate home. Looking back of course his motives were probably more ulterior than ulterior can ever be. Maybe I do him a disservice. I know he and mother had separate bedrooms in that house and the thought that there was *anything* shifty going on never crossed my mind—mainly because I didn't really know what 'shifty' was anyway. Also mother was always just there only for me and Jill, wasn't she? I remain convinced that Bill Surtees wasn't really very high on mother's desire list. Realistically though I must concede that there may have been some 'hanky' between her and scruffy Bill occasionally, perhaps even a little 'panky' too. However, mainly because I can't bring myself even now to accept or believe it, there was, hopefully, never both 'hanky' and 'panky'.

Be that as it may, we were to stay in that house for about a year. The house, No.21, was opposite some tennis courts and it had a little public lane running just alongside and parallel to its boundary hedge. This was a cut-through for pedestrians from Dingle Close to the road beyond, called Failand Walk if my memory is correct. There was a constant trickle of people using that lane and snatches of conversations, shouting and laughter were always floating across the rear garden. 'Garden' is a misnomer as it was more a jungle, Uncle Bill being an even bigger slob about his garden than he was about his house. However, I soon had a little gang of pals around and was still at the age when building a den was an essential for the games of 'commandos' and 'missions behind enemy lines' which were in full swing when the school holidays came around. The bottom of Uncle Bill's garden soon boasted a fully camouflaged and fortified five-star den. It was big enough to accommodate almost any number of combatants for any war games in progress. When it rained we would huddle in that den trying to avoid the intruding raindrops. There were several of us and I've forgotten their names, although one was called John Parker. He was a little older than me, about fourteen. On one occasion during a rainy spell in the den, I recall John Parker saying in his fruity Bristol accent: 'Jew wank boys?' Without a pause he got out his dick and proceeded to demonstrate as we watched in awe. 'This is 'ow you "get it",' he gasped as he continued to the conclusion of an act with which I shortly became regularly acquainted myself, in private naturally.

It's easy to tease mother about her snobbery. Without a doubt though, underneath the distance she always sought to put between herself and 'the oiks' of Bristol, was a steely determination to protect her kids from any descent down the social ladder. There was an immediate issue focusing around the question of where I was to go to Secondary School. According to the system in operation at the time, I was a natural candidate for a Secondary Modern School. As indicated previously, you took the 11+ Exam... pass and you went on to a successful life and career, fail and you were on the scrap-heap. This is how my mother would have seen it and her view wasn't far from the reality. She was totally determined I would not go to a dreaded Secondary Modern. The situation did not look too promising though. As anticipated I had failed the 11+ miserably and by miles. I recall sitting the exam in The Stoke Bishop Village Hall, a really quaint little building at the bottom of Stoke Hill nestling in the valley where 'the village' is situated.

I remember sitting, chewing my pen and with tears of frustration welling up as others all around me seemed to be getting on happily with answering the questions. This was especially true of the 'sums' questions... it all seemed to be about bloody sums and more bloody sums all the time! Wasn't anything else ever important in this life other than sums? I was beginning to doubt it! So, the scrap-heap for me then. But no! Once again, mother pulled my destiny out of the fire!

This was where our connection with The Harding Family paid off big style. By now The Hardings were wealthy and established as successful business folk with half the butchers' shops in Bristol owned by one or other of the clan. Also owned were a string of cafes and restaurants throughout the seaside resorts in the West of England. The most successful Harding of them all was Percy, the industrious and determined young fellow from the slums of Cathay just behind St Mary Redcliffe Church—the same Percy Harding who once had a pal named Billy Dutton from Tankard's Close back in those bygone days of the 1920's; the same Billy Dutton who introduced his pal Percy to his cousin Olive Griffiths, also from Tankard's Close; the same Olive Griffiths who had always remained close and best pals with my mum, Kitty Dutton. Yes, *that* Percy Harding also owned, almost as a little extra bauble, his very own small private school in the Clifton area of Bristol. Now get this, not only, once Auntie Olive had 'had a word' with Percy, was a place at the school offered to the hapless young David Dutton but, as he was 'family' (well, 'loosely', anyway), it was at an extremely nominal rate for the fees, commensurate with his mother's near permanent impoverished circumstances. In short, a virtually free place at the school owned by Uncle Percy Harding! Whoopee!! She'd done it again! They should have renamed my mum Houdini!

(iv)

After a year or so things were getting a little 'testy' at 'Uncle Bill's'. It has to be recorded that we would have been in a bit of a mess if he hadn't been there to give us a helping hand. However, as the months went by it seemed as though he was increasingly unhappy about his untidy and disordered 'space' being invaded and occupied by the Duttons. That, plus the fact that yours truly (and probably my fiery sister too) were almost certainly thinning his patience. The upshot was that mother announced one day that we were to move on. She had been doing a little plotting with the ever-helpful 'posh customer', Mrs. Young. This lady, apparently, had another really 'posh rich friend', a Mrs. Bailey (one of 'the card school' probably). She, it turned out, owned a house divided into flats in Clifton ('posh' area—mother would have immediately pricked up her ears). Well Mrs. Bailey, who turned out a bit of a shark to tell the truth, just happened to have a one-bedroomed flat available. For a while it looked a good proposition but when we got to actually visit this flat (in St. Paul's Road) our collective hearts fell. The 'flat' turned out to be nothing more than one very large room divided up by partitions (made of not much more than cardboard). Worse, these partitions did not even reach up to the ceiling so there was no privacy at all for anyone. The swiftest way of giving each other anything was to throw it over the top of the partition. Yours truly saw this as a great prank of course and was soon lobbing dirty underpants, wet towels and God knows what else 'over the top'. This was done principally to annoy my sister. Jill was by now a fully-grown girl of about fourteen. She was acutely conscious of not being seen in her bra and knickers or anything as embarrassing as that. It was impossible to preserve any modesty in this pokey little arrangement of spaces called a 'flat'. It was probably better suited to mice or gerbils as a matter of fact. Of course this situation impacted much more on mother and Jill than on myself. Little boys (I was about 11) don't notice discomfort so much, being adaptable and more at home in an upside down environment—*this* young boy anyway!

As a consequence it was a fertile situation in which to torment my sister. She must have hated me so much at this time. I never missed an opportunity of telling tales on her and stirring it up at every opportunity... especially as she had delivered into my hands an extremely potent weapon to make mischief for her. She had *boy friends* and she didn't want our mother to know what she was getting up to! I knew though, you couldn't keep anything secret from the little fella with the big ears!

So, this was our new cramped environment, almost nothing good one could say about it. Steve visited us regularly at this time when he came down from London where he had commenced his teaching career. Within a short time of walking in the door he had christened our new home 'The Hovel', and that's what it was known as ever after.

Mother continued to follow her relentless routine of work and worry. By the time the rent was paid there was little over. Everything, it seemed, was a financial struggle for her to make ends meet and inch through each week towards her next payday. Once again the ubiquitous tips from her customers were the financial lifebelts they had always been for our survival.

My job each night once home from school was to fetch a large bucket of coal from the coal cellar. This dark and dirty hole was situated in the basement of the house. It was reached down a flight of steep steps that descended from the path at the side of the house. Our flat was on the third floor of a four-storey house—all in all a lot of stairs to negotiate and it was by no means easy hauling a full and heavy bucket of coal up four flights (counting the cellar stairs). This was my contribution though and it was sort of pleasing to set the fire and light it before mother arrived home each evening. She would always have a couple of shopping bags and she would be quite out of breath when she staggered in. 'Does anyone know anyone,' she would say, slumping down on a chair, 'who makes a cup of tea better than our Dido?' 'Dido' was always her pet name for me...don't ask!

One Christmas when we were there she managed to buy me a bike. It was second-hand and not the super duper brand new racing type bike I had probably been nagging about having for months... but it was a bike, for goodness sake! So, smart-ass leapt straight onto the saddle and could not be prised off that bike for days. I probably wanted to take it to bed with me.

So incapable was I to ever employ any consideration or common sense to any situation that, a few days after acquiring the wheels I had so longed for, I got the bright idea of riding it down the cellar steps to fetch the coal. Where better to put the empty coal bucket too than to dangle by its handle around my neck as I went! As you may surmise, I survived this suicidal escapade and (just!) escaped with my life which I very easily could have left at the bottom of those steps amongst the coal dust. My bicycle, however, was not so fortunate, as testified to by its completely buckled frame and front wheel! Mother, phlegmatic as always, remarked as I crawled back into the flat with life itself only just slightly flickering within me: 'You were a long time dear!'

Anyway, my randy sister wanted to smuggle her boyfriend into the flat one day when mother was at work. Jill was entrusted with the job of looking after me for the whole day. I think there were another girl and boy involved too who were going to join the little petting party. Their problem was what to do with me, the gobbiest gooseberry on the bush! What would get me out the way and buy my silence at the same time? The panting quartet went into a huddle and emerged with a clever solution.... give him some money for some sweets and send him to the pictures. Sounded good to me, so off I went to The Embassy Cinema ('picture houses' we still called them).

The Embassy was situated opposite The Victoria Rooms just down the road from where we lived. The Victoria Rooms is one of the jewels in Bristol's little crown. At that time it was the home of The Bristol University Students' Union. As a consequence the sweeping and curving stone steps at its front were always swarming with students lolling about and cascading down its steps and spreading all around the large ornamental fountains that adorned the approach to the building, The Victoria Rooms itself. Students then wore cavalry twill trousers and Harris Tweed jackets with large leather patches sown onto the elbows. Then, brogue shoes, university scarves twirled around the neck and sometimes even a hat, worn at a rakish angle naturally. Pipe smoking was commonplace amongst young males too. Females dressed 'sensibly' in long skirts and starched blouses... no cleavages or thighs on display for certain.

Opposite the Victoria Rooms was The West of England College of Art, still there as always. Not least were the statues of King Edward VII and the Boer War Soldier, high on his plinth, thrusting his bayoneted rifle forever towards the traffic heading down Queen's Road.

The Embassy Cinema has long gone now but back then it was one of the very busiest. What the young lovers had omitted to tell me of course was that the film showing that day was the premiere of the latest Charlie Chaplin film 'City Lights'. Hard to believe but Charlie Chaplin was probably more popular than God in those days (well, definitely actually as, in Britain, God's popularity was well and truly 'on the skids' already, even then in the early 1950's). Be that as it may, the queue to Chaplin's latest film was about fifty yards long. I dutifully attached myself and waited patiently as we inched forward. Occasionally a commissionaire would emerge from the cinema and shout down the queue: 'One double at one and six,' or 'Two singles at two shillings!' Then it was first come first served from amongst those nearest to the front. If what you wanted was shouted you darted forward to the kiosk and plonked your 'bobs' and 'tanners' down.

On this day I must have queued for nearly an hour. Eventually my chance arrived and shortly I was burrowed down in my seat, sticky sweets in my palm, the cigarette smoke swirling in the flickering searchlight of the film projector above. One was quickly seduced into the trials and tribulations of the little man with the bowler hat and the cane on the screen in front. What cosy bliss!

So...it must have been about four-thirty in the afternoon when I returned. Mother was not due in until around eight o'clock that evening and Jill and her panting friends had not yet completed their amorous maulings when in walked yours truly! I was about as welcome as Jack the Ripper at an Ann Summers' Lingerie Party. The only solution.... bribe him!

'Daaave,' said all sort of creepy and crawly, 'would you like to have two bob for yourself and we'll pay for you to go to the pictures again?' Mmmm, two bob eh, not bad. 'Make it three and I'll go!' Always a mercenary little sod me! So, off I trotted. Trouble was I had to go again to 'The Embassy' as, although there was another picture house close by, 'The Whiteladies', that cinema was showing a category 'A' film and one needed to be with an adult to gain admission. So, reluctantly, it was Charlie Chaplin all over again, complete with another half hour wait to get in. Still, it was warm and cosy and the thought of the 'lolly' in my pocket was a bonus indeed. Could do a lot with three bob in those days!

By the time I returned home just before eight the two Romeos and the other Juliet had departed, leaving my sister all demure at the door upon mother's return. 'Everything OK, has he been a good boy?' said mother. 'Yes, he's been really good,' said my sister, pinching my arm like a crab and giving me a look fit to shrivel me to dust. All right, so I kept my gob shut at the time, but don't think I wasn't planning to drop into the conversation in a day or two: 'Mum, have you seen that love bite on Jill's neck?' Younger brothers, eh, who'd have them?

(v)

By now mother had acquired a new friend who was to become a staunch support and with whom she went to Southern Rhodesia when I was in my mid-teens (more anon!). We got to know Betty Block through Bill Surtees' daughter Margie. So there was something really positive then that grew from the Bill Surtees' connection after we had left him behind and alone in his jumbly house in Sea Mills.

Betty and mother struck up an instant rapport. She was quite a bit younger than mother, probably about thirty at this time and mother would have been in her late forties. They became close friends over the following dozen years or so. Betty worked for the B.B.C. in their West Of England H.Q. in Whiteladies' Road. She became a stalwart of the then embryonic B.B.C. Television Natural History Unit that became widely acclaimed in later years. What she actually did I am unsure but I think she was a film editor. She was a really cheerful person, always very smartly dressed and with a really infectious laugh. She called mother 'Kit' which no one else ever did— Mother was always 'Kitty' to her own family. In fact mother was known by several names to different people and different groups of people, which is a really curious thing that speaks volumes about her character. What is the conclusion to be drawn from the 'volumes it speaks' actually eludes me even after all these years! To the people she worked with and her employers and often her customers she was always 'Webby'. Steve, as aforementioned, called her 'Mrs. D' or 'Dolly D'. Jill and I usually called her 'Jumpers'. Later when she did voluntary work with 'The Samaritans' it was always 'Catherine'. My brother's kids knew her as 'Nana Jam', my own kids as 'Nanny Bristol'. Her neighbours called her 'Dutt' and way back, when love bloomed, our father always called her 'Jenny Lin' (don't ask!). My brother Allan was really the odd one out in this name game as he called her 'Mother'! All in all she made The Scarlet Pimpernel seem normal! Who *was* she really... good question. Anyway, having Betty as a new friend was a bonus for mother as our fortunes were really bumping along the bottom around this time, by far and away the biggest problems always being financial.

My lifelong love of cats stems from our time at 'The Hovel'. Seems unlikely. doesn't it? Nevertheless, when Jill and Steve walked in one day with a tiny white kitten they had somehow acquired I didn't know it but my fate was sealed... always cats for me, ever since! All three of us knew, as we started to make a cosy place for our new friend and entice it with a little warm milk, that it was not going to be easy to get mother to accept this addition to our hopelessly cramped little partitioned room on the third floor.

Sure enough, when she arrived home from work that night the first thing she said was, '...and you can get rid of that straight away!' Now Steve, as well as being a clever young fellow, was potty about cats and he also peddled a nice line in histrionic persuasion. First he placed Miss Pussy Cat onto the palm of his hand and then lifted his hand close to his mouth. He then affected a 'purry' cat voice, as in, 'purrrr, I know I'm only little, but I'm cuddly, purrr, trouble is I haven't got a home, purrr, and I just want to find somewhere to live and be warm and have some nice love from someone, puurrrrr... please let me stay here....' How could mother resist? The very last thing she wanted or needed however was any additional responsibility. As I recall she did put up a valiant rearguard action. She pointed out how our premises were completely unsuitable: What about the smell and the mess? The cat would be inside all day on its own, who would make sure it was fed and watered etc, etc.... None of this cut much ice with the trio of feline fanciers! So, the kitten came to stay. Our first pet—unless you count 'Pong' the dog we had had when I was very small and do not remember, although older family members always spoke of him with affection. There used to be a picture of him in one of those old family photo boxes that are found usually stuffed into the tops of wardrobes or backs of cupboards in most family homes. He was a big soft looking mongrel with long droopy ears. What to name our little cat though didn't take too long. Steve suggested that since Mrs. D had put up so much opposition, then 'Oppo' would suit him nicely! So, 'Oppo' it was and he became our friend for many months and added somewhat to the domestic scene. When the day dawned to leave 'The Hovel' 'Oppo' went to live at No. 2 The Glen, a home for the aged blind where he became 'Hoppy' and very much loved. I used to go with mother into that Old Folks' Home and watch her talk on her hands to those folks. In fact I used to do it a bit myself. We were relieved when that day of departure from 'The Hovel' dawned, even though it was in some ways to be out of the frying pan and into the fire!

(vi)

By this time I had been attending the school owned by Percy Harding (Uncle Percy to me) for a year or so. It did have the benefit of being situated just around the corner from 'The Hovel'. The school was actually a very large and spacious three-storey house. It had, no doubt, once been a family home in Victorian and Edwardian times but like so many of those grand Clifton houses, its time as a single living family unit was over. The vast majority had each been divided into two or three self-contained flats. Some had evolved to serve a more specialised function, such as The Crescent School, No. 10 Eaton Crescent; Headmaster Mr. Oscar Dahl M.A. (Cantab) and Owner and Proprietor Mr. Percy Harding of Harding Bros. (Shipping Butchers).

This establishment had about eighty fee-paying pupils aged between eleven and sixteen and half a dozen staff. It must have been the rock solid friendship between mother and Percy's wife Auntie Olive (my dad's cousin) which had not only oiled the wheels of my own attendance at this school but also been extended to effect our escape from 'The Hovel'. Quite simply we were offered the flat at the top of The Harding's own house at 4, The Glen, Redland. All this seemed to mark an upturn in our fortunes and in several ways this was to be the case. However as the months ahead unravelled, circumstance and the clash of personalities involved was to turn everything into a cocktail of conflict.

The Curriculum of The Crescent School was as dry as dust. There was no Science at all, no Games or Sports or Modern Language—just a steady diet of Maths (Arithmetic!), Latin, Divinity and English. It has always seemed a curiosity to me as to why Percy Harding was bothered about owning a school at all. It is certain that he had little interest in education for its own sake. As a matter of fact he was all but illiterate himself, which was a shame and for which he can't be blamed. It is to his credit that he largely overcame such a crippling handicap and through hard work and fierce ambition he became such a successful businessman. The other side of Uncle Percy's coin was that he was dictatorial, controlling, without much of the milk of human kindness, ignorant, unfaithful to his wife Olive (one of nature's really wonderful creatures was my Aunt Olive, always treated like a bit of disregarded and ultimately discarded flotsam by Percy; when she should have been cherished and honoured).

So, why did he want to own a school? Don't think there is a satisfactory explanation. Perhaps it was because he'd had virtually no schooling himself and it was his quirky way of somehow catching up. Who knows? The teaching and lessons at The Crescent School were bizarre. For much of the time I was taught by Bill Meredith, a Welshman. Bill was about eighty years old, no exaggeration. One of the canny tricks of the Proprietor and his deviant Headmaster Oscar Dahl (I'll come to him) was to only employ ancients on the teaching staff... didn't have to pay them much—clever, eh? Since my classroom was situated on the top floor of the building and there were several lessons per day, old Bill had to climb up three flights of stairs each time to reach the room; it frequently was a case of not so much what would the lesson be about when he actually reached the classroom but would he even reach the classroom *at all*. Honestly, each lesson was a cliffhanger as we waited to see if Bill would eventually fall through the door. Actually, all Bill's lessons were simple and identical. He talked and we listened. There seemed to be no actual subject he taught us at all, even if it may have said 'English' on the timetable. Bill would just ramble on and on and on. He could talk about almost anything that came into his head. Much of it was about his own childhood in South Wales. He would tell us how he and his pals would play football amongst the slag heaps from the coalmines or have picnics in summer on the banks of the River Taff. One day one of his friends had fallen in and nearly drowned and Bill and his other pals had pulled him out and then they all went and bought sherbet dips for a penny from Mrs. Evans' shop... Really, trust me, Old Bill would churn on and on in this vein for hours. His only concession to actually teaching a subject properly, and I will give him this, is that he *always* had a piece of chalk in his hand... Don't get me wrong, sometimes his tales were quite interesting. Unbelievably, I think some of the things he used to tell us about when he was a boy could well have watered one or two green shoots which grew into my interest in History. Similarly, he had travelled as a young man, even to China. His tales of Shanghai and eating cats and dogs filled me not only with awe but may have awakened my interest in a wider world. That said, much of what he had to say was suffocatingly boring. As my seat was by a window, it wasn't long before my head was down on my folded arms and I was gazing sideways at the tiny park just across the road below. I have the exact dimensions of that park imprinted in my mind forever. If it was afternoon I would sometimes actually doze off for a while. Bill never minded and he'd still be talking when I woke up. I remember a boy called Paul Strange sat immediately behind me and he would reach over and flick my ear hard occasionally. This would help to keep me alert.

One February morning things really livened up when Oscar Dahl himself waddled into our classroom (Oscar was what we would now call clinically obese). On account of his bulk he never ventured to the top of the building (rarely ever left the ground floor if my memory serves correctly). Anyway, this particular day he entered, nodded approvingly towards Bill who was holding his chalk in a purposeful manner as though he was about to actually write something on the blackboard... We all dutifully stood up, something we were always expected to do if a member of staff entered. 'I've come to tell you all,' said Oscar, sweating and panting somewhat after his great ascent, 'that it's just been announced that The King has died.' Blimey, serious stuff! 'We will all now observe a minute's silence,' he went on, his little piggy eyes staring from behind his horned rimmed glasses. So, King George VI had died and there we stood, trying to absorb the enormity of the moment. It was February 1952.

Another almost 'mummified' teacher we had was an émigré Polish gentleman called Karl Kreling ('Kreaky' to us). He was younger than Bill and was probably only in his mid-seventies. He was indeed a gentleman though. He was a mild and kindly man and we all sort of liked him. He looked very much like Albert Einstein with totally wild hair sprouting outwards on both sides of his head and a nose like a duck-billed platypus. He taught us Latin. At least he kept to his subject even if the subject itself was about as interesting as a cup of sick. One thing we all liked though and really raised us from our torpor was when Karl would call for us, in a voice so thickly accented that you only ever understood every fifth word or so: 'Vell,

chillun, ve noww vill decline ze presen tense of ze verby "mitto", to zend.'
We loved this one, especially when it gave us the chance to bawl out aloud
the third person singular...

> Mitto
> Mittis
> Mi....TIT!!

This would create much merriment although it was lost on dear old
Kreaky who would plaintively say something like 'Velly good, chillun, bud
zer is noneed atowl to showt!'

Our maths' teacher was Jack Oxland. He used to live in the house with
Oscar. They both had bedrooms on the second floor where it was forbidden
for us to ever venture. Knowing what I later learned about Oscar that ban
probably did not extend between Oscar and Jack themselves... Jack was a
clever man, wrote the regular 'Bridge' column in *The Bristol Evening Post*.
'Bridge', it appeared, being one of his other hobbies. He was tall, totally
humourless, had a ginger moustache and had no time whatsoever for those
who couldn't do Maths. Just looking at him used to terrify me. Old Jack soon
had me sussed and shoved me into a corner with a couple of other dummies
to do some adding ups and take-aways (come a long way in maths since
primary school!).

So, it's probably fair to say that education at The Crescent School, in spite
of its fancy address and the Cambridge Degree of its Headmaster, was an
experience not exactly at the cutting edge of our educational system as a
whole. It was apparent that, although I was out of the dreaded Secondary
Modern School sink, I was well and truly drowning in a private school
educational bath. The fact that the Headmaster was a twisted degenerate
pervert as well, was, on reflection, not a great help either!

(vii)

To come straight to the point, what used to float Oscar Dahl's boat was
caning young boys, preferably whilst their trousers were hanging down
around their ankles. It can fairly safely be assumed that Oscar himself would
have had rising feelings of pleasure as he leaned into his task. In short, the
man was a sadistic pervert. Hiding behind the cloak of his exalted position as
Headmaster and therefore responsible for good discipline in the school, he
was able to get away with running a singularly unpleasant and unhealthy

regime for several years. I suspect he was extremely cunning about it all and just kept things within limits. These limiting boundaries though were set a great deal wider in those days when corporal punishment was still legal in schools and pain was generally held to be a legitimate means of control. Within this framework, old Oscar had his licence to operate without seemingly any restriction or accountability. It was a disgrace really.

We boys went in fear of 'the whack' as we called it. It loomed over everything and a day did not pass without some miscreant being summoned into Oscar's study and having to bend over at Oscar's command, and no doubt to his pleasure... Oscar had a tariff of punishments and the number of strokes of the cane was linked to the alleged gravity of the offence. There was a sliding scale. The most minor offence (say, not doing homework or losing an exercise book) would qualify for 'two up' (two strokes with your trousers up). Next, would be 'four up' for something like, say, carrying on kicking your tennis ball in the minute play area we had at the rear of the building after the bell had rung to indicate the end of a break. 'Six up' was fairly 'serious', alleged persistent failure or lack of effort in your classroom work or just bad behaviour perhaps.

Now, it was getting interesting as the scale rose to 'trousers down'! No doubt it was beginning to get Oscar really excited.... 'Two DOWN'.... mmmmm, perhaps for a repeat offence or fighting. 'Four down' was a very serious matter indeed—rudeness to a teacher or bullying or something of that nature. The absolute climax came for Oscar no doubt when he had to deal with an offence so serious 'SIX DOWN' was the only suitable punishment to fit the crime.

The ritual for trousers down whackings was usually the same. Oscar would be oily and almost friendly in his approach to his victim. He'd say, 'Look, you've done this "old son",' (one of his favourite means of addressing you), 'you wouldn't expect to get away with it now, would you, and I wouldn't be doing my job if I let you off, now would I? So come on, let's get this over with' (at this stage he may actually slip his arm around your shoulder), 'so, just drop your trousers down and lean over across this chair.' Then, taking his time, Oscar would very carefully and from behind arrange your legs, slightly apart(!), and strike you agonisingly across your bare cheeks with his long thin cane. It hurt, trust me folks, it hurt.

Afterwards, Oscar resumed his oily manner. He would quickly hide his cane away and adopt an avuncular 'now we can be friends again' style as he ushered you towards the door. Your backside was on fire and the tears were still managing to leak out in spite of your gritted teeth and determination to keep them back. It must be said that the whole ghastly procedure was strictly for the boys. Oscar was not the least bit interested in girls and they could have been strangling and stabbing each other daily and right in his full view and he would have walked straight on by. Very single-minded Oscar, always kept his eye on the ball...

I got whacked a few times during my time there—only once, though, going through the indignity and embarrassment of trousers down. I did achieve the ultimate nevertheless—it was 'SIX DOWN'! Someone sneaked on me to Oscar for stealing some comics from the pavement newsagent who used to lay out his wares in front of the West of England College of Art opposite The Victoria Rooms. I'd been getting away with this for a while and was heading for a fall anyway. Oscar did me a favour, really, as I have always respected other people's property and I'm almost certain have never ever stolen another thing. Food for thought there!

Anyway, the whack ruled the school and it dominated our thoughts and conversations. Those who made really frequent visits to Oscar's punishment den achieved celebrity status amongst us lads. A boy called John Norman and another named Michael Linton were regarded as almost Royalty. They both spent more time in Oscar's office pulling their trousers down and up than they ever did in the classroom!

There was one highlight during my time there. We went on holiday to Cardigan Bay in Wales. We stayed in tents and although Oscar's depressing regime of beatings followed by hugs continued, it seemed to omit me altogether. By then, I suspect that something may have been said to Oscar in the background, along the lines of, 'I'd lay off young Dutton if I were you Oscar Old Bean, his uncle does *own* the school after all!'

So the holiday was memorable for the right reasons. It was really the first occasion I had ever been far away from Bristol and it was all refreshing and impressive. We travelled by train through The Severn Tunnel into Wales which seemed a big enough adventure all on its own. I shall never forget the impression made on me by Cardigan Bay with its wide, curved and sweeping white sands. Nor riding on the little narrow-gauge train, the Talyllyn railway, running between Tywyn and Abergynolwyn. So, that was all good at least. The rest of my experiences as a pupil at The Crescent School had been sour, negative and unproductive. My days at this establishment were now numbered, however. We fell out with Percy Harding around this time so the issue of my future schooling was back on the agenda.

It was very ironic therefore that when I eventually left Grammar School (Q.E.H.) several years later and was set on becoming a teacher, it was none other than bent old Oscar Dahl himself who gave me my first teaching job to set me on my career path! Bizarre, life's twists and turns... interesting though how all this was to come about....

(viii)

Things seemed to be looking up when we left the awful 'Hovel' in St Paul's Road. Had we had but a small glimpse into the immediate future we may possibly have thought ourselves better off to have stayed put! Percy Harding and his family lived in a fine house at 4 The Glen, Redland. It was in a road of fine houses only some few hundred yards from the edge of Bristol's famous open space 'The Downs'. It was a prestigious location and in keeping with Percy's position as a successful and wealthy businessman. The house had three floors and then an attic section. Here was a small but compact little attic flat with a tiny kitchen, separate toilet, bedroom and living room. I don't recall how we slept. It must have been mother and Jill in the bedroom and yours truly in the living room (although there may have been a tiny box-room where I slept).

The Hardings were: Percy and his wife Olive (Auntie Olive to me), son Michael Harding and daughter Diane. Michael Harding was a shadowy

Michael Harding

figure who, at that time, was mostly away training to be an Army Officer. He must have been in his late teens or early twenties at that time. Percy had sent him to Clifton College, an expensive Public School. Whenever he did sweep into the house he had the same 'brisk and brusque' manner of his father. Michael was destined, not unnaturally, to become a major player (for many years *the* major player) in the Harding business empire. He certainly inherited most of his father's business acumen, some may have said even ruthlessness. There was a photo of Michael standing on a large sideboard in one of the living rooms of the house. In this photo he looked every bit the handsome young army officer and expensive public school product in his officer's peaked cap, creaseless army jacket with a leather band across his chest. His mother always kept that photo prominently and proudly displayed in her subsequent homes long after Percy had discarded her.

Michael had several mannerisms identical to his father. When he smiled his eyes would almost squeeze closed and his cheeks seem to widen so what you were left with was a sort of squinty smiley leer. Michael's speech was staccato too like his father's, except with Michael his voice came out as an accent forged at an exclusive Public School and layered on top with army officer polish. The whole effect was phoney but maybe that's not fair, whereas with Percy's accent, although by no means broad, he retained the Bristol twang of his origins. Strangest of all Percy had had some childhood ailment which had left him with a partially deformed arm which he carried in an almost permanent crooked fashion. Through some mysterious process of bonding, Michael seemed to carry his arm in the very same manner!

I only ever came across Michael Harding a few times again in my life, one occasion being at my mother's funeral (which earned him brownie points with me for turning up. It seemed he had a genuine regard for his 'Auntie Kitty'). Another time we met was a couple of year's ago at a social occasion at his sister Diane's house. He had softened and mellowed a great deal down the years and we shared a pleasant conversation. We both put on the rose coloured spectacles which always seem to fit much more easily when recalling events from long ago which may not have been so comfortable at the time of their occurrence... 'Yes, I remember you around our house in those days,' Michael said to me, his voice as clipped and military as ever, 'I used to think you waah a noisaay and awkward little bugga!' We had a chuckle about that and took another vol-au-vent from the proffered dish...

Percy and Olive's daughter Diane was always around at that time, however, and she must have thought it fun and a bonus suddenly to have two cousins (albeit second cousins) in the house to share her company. Diane was about nine or ten years old and she mainly attached herself to Jill who became a ready-made big sister. Diane was a cheerful and tactile girl, the very apple of her father's eye, yet she was much more like her mother in temperament. Even Diane could not avoid the displeasure occasionally of her overbearing and domineering father. This displeasure fell much more frequently upon the Duttons, though, as we shall see.

The time we lived there included an intense period of my development and experience. There were good times. Uncle Percy had a large expensive Jaguar car and on some Sundays we would all get loaded in and set off for the day to Weymouth where Percy owned a couple of businesses. Once or twice he took me to Weymouth on my own on a weekday, mainly I suppose for the company. On those occasions he would drive really fast in his powerful Jag. In those motorway-less days it was a real roller coaster of a ride as Percy zigzagged at high speeds around the cars ahead (nothing ever passed him!), braking for the corners and accelerating rapidly along the straight sections. On the return journey it was frequently dark and the whole experience was heightened as Percy altered the high and low beam of the headlights so as to reduce the glare and dazzle for oncoming cars. He did this by pressing a little button situated in the well of the car with his left foot. This image of Percy Harding, sort of crouched in the driving seat with his eye line not much above the dashboard in front of him (he was a small man), his foot periodically clicking down on the 'beam adjusting' button, is one forever etched in my mind. We literally whizzed back from Weymouth on those occasions and I found it always very thrilling.

Another time Percy announced that we were all going to Blackpool for a few days' holiday. Now, logistically getting everyone up to Blackpool must have been quite a business. There was another car in addition to Percy's with some other family or friends. It was the furthest Jill and I had ever been for sure. This was the age when Blackpool was in its absolute pomp as the queen of all holiday resorts, the Blackpool to which the holiday hordes flocked from the cotton towns of Lancashire, the wool towns of Yorkshire, the pits and factories of Northumberland, Durham and the Central Lowlands of Scotland. It was 'Kiss Me Quick' hats, sticks of rock and candyfloss, naughty postcards and end of the pier shows. All the very essence of British vulgarity wrapped in an atmosphere of 'knees up, never mind the weather we're all here to enjoy ourselves and, by golly we will!' Into this very Blackpool drove Percy Harding, leading his little caravan of wide-eyed West Country folks! We were all under firm instructions from Percy to have a good time. To be fair, by and large we did. Certainly we kids did. A highlight for me was a trip to the Blackpool Tower itself. Here in its famous Ballroom couples twirled in their best frocks and best suits to the swelling music of Reg Dixon at the huge electronic organ. This mighty instrument seemed to fill an entire wall space of the giant ballroom. Reg himself was a small, smiling figure perched high on his seat pressing the gleaming keys amidst the coloured and flashing bulbs all surrounding and festooning the monster emitting the crashing, musical crescendos. This was an atmosphere unlike any other we had ever known.

We also went swimming in the giant Derby Baths. These seemed vast, warm and welcoming after the freezing cold Clifton Open Air Baths to which we usually went in Bristol. I ask you, who in his right mind came up with the idea of 'Open Air Swimming Baths'? Shivering even as you got

Enjoying yourself at the swimming baths 1950's style

undressed behind those wooden doors stretched along the edge of the swimming pool, a gap below each door and the floor. Once in the pool, one could observe people's lower legs and feet through that gap and the final parts of the removal operation of trousers, socks and shoes and undergarments. This was often not without a passing interest especially on the female side of the pool. Then, by now blue with cold, one would spend another ten minutes plucking up the courage to get into the icy looking green swell. Would entry to the water be the direct plunge or the bit-by-bit lowering of the torso down the unfriendly metal ladder at the corner of the pool? Either method was excruciating! All this was for *fun*! Enjoying yourself at the swimming baths, 1950's style! To be fair, only a few swimming baths were open air but even the enclosed swimming baths were usually an ordeal with barely heated water and poor facilities generally. Plus of course the ever-present threat of ingesting enough chlorine treated water to burn your insides out!

However, those Derby Baths in Blackpool impressed me greatly and though very old fashioned probably by the standards of today they stood out for me. So, all I had to do now was learn to swim!

(ix)

Everyone returned in one piece from Blackpool, a place to which I never went back again. This, in common with most of its former visitors, apparently. Increasing prosperity, cheap foreign travel and a realisation that in Blackpool the 'sun just don't shine', at least not very often, combined to send the town into steep decline. It is nowadays a mortally wounded place in spite of periodic attempts to apply a tourniquet. It had its day though without a doubt!

Mother somehow acquired another bicycle for me. These wheels began to assist in the expansion of my experience and independence. It was at this time I came to understand and really appreciate the game of tennis. A short ride from where we lived was The Redland Tennis Club where, each year The West of England Tennis Tournament was held. The Club was surrounded by high hedges that cut off the view from the outside. However, if you had a bicycle you were able to lean it against the fence behind which grew a tall hedge. Standing on the saddle of your bike it was possible to lever yourself upwards using a telegraph pole as a support. You were then able to stand (admittedly somewhat precariously) on top of the edge of the thin final panel of the fence, steadying yourself with one hand on the telegraph pole. Now this was not exactly the Centre Court at Wimbledon but it was perfect for me! From this vantage point one looked down over the heads of the seated crowd to the main tennis court on which the principal matches were staged. It was here, slightly wobbly at times, that I watched, worked out and enjoyed the game I never really learned to play but have always appreciated and followed. All the big tennis stars of the day took part in this Tournament, all amateurs then of course. Over at least a couple of years I saw many of the best players and marvelled at their athleticism and skill—Jaroslav Drobny, Frank Sedgeman, Vic Seixas, Doris Hart, and others who's names I can't recall. One very young Aussie stays in my mind... blond, hair swept back and slicked down, bouncy as a rubber ball, with gleaming teeth and a flashing brilliant racquet—the legendary Lew Hoad for certain.

Speedway still held me enthralled at this time and I remember deciding that I would become a speedway rider as a career and make my fortune in the process. An adjacent road to The Glen was Blenheim Road. On this road were two manhole covers set dead in the middle of the road and about thirty yards apart. This was just right for my own speedway track! Peddle furiously between the manholes, down with your left leg, broadside around, rear wheel sliding about so you emerged facing back the other way and ready to hare off again down the road towards the other manhole. Perfect! So, it was here between two humble manholes that I commenced training for my future sporting glory. Pinching one of my sister's scarves and folding it in such a way as to form a triangle of material across the nose and tied behind the neck so two long ends blew out and trailed behind me in the wind. Ready!

The downside of this fairly short-lived ambition was the ruining of about three pairs of shoes in the same number of weeks to the consternation of my ever financially crippled mother. Throw in a couple of badly gashed and scraped knees and at least one near concussion, it's no surprise that my journey to the winner's podium at Wembley Stadium on World Championship Night was put on hold. My proud father would have been looking on, talking into his B.B.C. microphone as he spread the news of his son's achievements around the world, all now abandoned! Instead it was an upset for my worried mother and another of the many bollockings I got from Percy Harding. In this instance probably justified!

More serious is that I began to flirt with a way of life that could have had very serious outcomes for me. With my friend, a lad named Richard Denning, the border between pranks and criminal acts was about to be crossed. After nightfall we would put on dark clothing, creep up to front doors of houses, retrieve the empty milk bottles left outside by the householders which were intended to be exchanged for full ones by the milkman the following morning. Then, from the gate of the house we would throw a milk bottle in a perfect arc to smash to smithereens outside someone's front door—at which point we would run like hell off down the road and hide, preferably where we could watch the wretched folks we had tormented performing angry circles for our entertainment.

I'm deeply ashamed now to confess to even worse. In those days car indicators used to be little 'arms' which were fixed onto the sides of cars. When turning, these sprang out from the side of the car to indicate the direction of turn. What Richard Denning and I did was, with a penknife, lever the little indicator arms out from the slots where they rested and then snap them off. This was truly appalling and grips me with regret even now. One certainty is that, had I continued in this vein, a criminal record would have been quick to follow and my life probably would have followed a very different and much more miserable course. Luckily for me this stage in my life and form of behaviour did not last long. I recall my partner in crime moved away and this nocturnal nonsense seemed to just fizzle out, thank God!

The Hardings had a lovely dog, a golden retriever named Rover. Percy would come into the main hallway of the house and be greeted by a very excited Rover jumping up at him. Dog and man would wrestle playfully with each other for several minutes. Looking back it was nice to observe Percy acting naturally, being so tactile and friendly. We rarely saw him in that mode when dealing with people. The whole 'quid pro quo' of our living at The Hardings was that in return for living rent free we would surrender our freedom to Percy. Trust me, Percy Harding put the control into freak and the freak into control! He was just too much. Most of it fell onto our mother who was always being ordered to do something or other. Some of it she endured, more out of loyalty to her beloved Olive than subjugation to Percy. For instance, Percy held many social gatherings for his business associates and he always wanted mother there to assist until the wee small hours, even though she was exhausted with having to work, each and every day, long hours in the Hairdressing Saloon (at this time she had a job in a saloon just off Whiteladies Road). Mother was told to 'dye your hair Kitty' or 'you will spend Christmas here with us Kitty' or 'Kitty, you and Olive will take the children out for a few hours, it's good for them' etc, etc.

Mother was a great one for keeping the peace and she was not daft. She knew that Percy had a powerful lever on her and that we would be virtually homeless again unless she toed the line and bowed to the dictatorial regime he imposed. However, mother had a saying, 'I can stand too much but not three much'—and she would occasionally dig her heels in. Percy would frequently stand at the bottom of the stairs and yell, 'Kitty, come down here please, straight away!' The tone was unmistakable—he was going to indulge in some bullying. On one occasion mother was thus summoned and told, 'Kitty, Jill and David are to go to church on Sundays along with Diane.' This was mother's 'three much'! 'No, Percy,' she replied, 'I'm not forcing them if they don't want to go'... 'Kitty, I'm ordering you to tell those children they are going to church next Sunday!' Now, one weapon mother could always employ was that she was more worldly-wise and generally more intelligent than Percy (who's strengths were cunning and manipulation). In this instance she responded, 'I expect you've heard of Odette, have you Percy?' ('Odette' was a popular film of the day about the British wartime spy Odette Churchill who had been captured and tortured by The Gestapo.) Well, for certain Percy would not have had a clue who she was. He would have been more likely to think that 'Owe Debt' was something which would appear on a bank statement! So, mother continued, 'Well Percy, I can only say to you what Odette said to her torturers...do what you like but I have absolutely nothing further to say!' With that, mother dramatically withdrew. She won that one though and we didn't go to church next Sunday or indeed, in my case, more or less ever since! This was not the only confrontation she had with Percy, there were others. It was increasingly clear that our position in that house was becoming ever more precarious and untenable. Naturally, though, the actual straws that broke the camel's back resulted from actions of my sister and yours truly.

Jill was virtually a grown woman and Percy sought to run her life for her in his customary tactless and insistent manner. Put simply, she was now past the age when she was going to be dictated to by anyone and she was quite prepared, if push came to shove, to state her case. This occurred one day when she wanted to go out with her friend Sally Ford. Percy told her she was not going out as he wanted her to baby-sit Diane whilst he and Olive went out that evening. Well, this escalated and, to cut a long story short, Uncle Percy did the wrong thing and slapped Jill around the face. Jill didn't have red hair for nothing: next thing, she's picked up a wooden framed clock from the mantelpiece and whizzed it at Percy's head where it connected with a satisfying 'clunk'! If this wasn't enough to make mother look up the section in the citizen's advice booklet she always kept handy and read the paragraph headed 'what to do if you are made homeless', then when my own misdeeds came into the light of day there was to be no alternative whatsoever.

Let's make it clear. I always liked Diane. It's fair to say we liked each other. It's just that things were starting to move just a little past 'liking'. She was pretty and starting to get prettier. I was, as previously disclosed, conscious by now of the things one needed to be well aware of when one reached a certain age! Well, I guess nature 'kicked in' to some extent and

Diane and I started having our own little games of 'hide and seek'. It wasn't much more than a snog, but rather more than cousins usually get up to (probably not second cousins though!). Anyway, I did a little more exploring of Diane than I should, I guess. Well, trust me, the roof not so much caved in as blew completely off when Percy discovered what had been going on. I was immediately in very, very deep doodoo. There was a swing in the garden and I was sitting innocently on that swing when Percy came towards me, steam blowing out of his ears. (To be fair, justified to some extent, although he probably imagined things might have progressed further than was the case.) Never had I seen a face so contorted with rage—a face he pushed to within a couple of inches of mine. I never forgot his words: 'You little bastard, if you ever even touch Diane again, by Christchurch, I'll skin you alive!' Now, curiously, I don't remember being too frightened, but I remember thinking to myself, 'Heck, he *is* a master butcher'—and this being quickly followed by a picture in my mind of being hung up on one of those butcher's meat-hooks with all my skin hanging down off my feet in one continuous piece all the way to the floor. You're right, time for The Duttons to get packing!

(x)

Although Percy spread a permanent stain across that household there were two redeeming features in the shape of Auntie Olive herself and her father Ted Griffiths, who was always known to one and all as 'Ampsey'. He was recently retired from a career on the railways and, in his early sixties, was a frequent visitor to the house where he maintained the garden and did odd jobs. A quiet and dignified man who just got on with whatever he had been entrusted to do, he never raised his voice and was generally a calming influence in what was a sometimes turbulent household. Ampsey often wore a very faded orange jacket, always a 'grandpa cap', black trousers kept up with a belt or braces and usually working man's shoes or boots. His face was crinkled, his smile warm, and he had a wisp of white hair which stood up when he removed his cap. As often as not he was carrying some produce from the garden wrapped in a piece of newspaper—a cabbage, some carrots or onions or perhaps some flowers. Great character, never forgotten!

Auntie Olive herself was a special person by any standard. She inherited her good nature from both her parents and her jollity from her larger than life mother, Sis. (Auntie Sis to me, my grandfather Timothy's sister.) Olive had some unique mannerisms, responding to something said to her by frequently sucking in her breath and letting out an elongated sound such as, 'Weeeelllll, Reeeellly', or 'Ooooohhhhhh, did hee, weeeelllll…' This was always followed by a chuckle, a pause, then, 'Now, what was I doin', you made me forget….' As a young girl she had met and married Percy and had grown very dependent on him as the years passed. This was no surprise with a character as controlling and domineering as Percy, but she had been a good mother and dutiful wife. Olive was not a person of great initiative and the reality was that it was, and had been for many years, Percy, Percy, Percy. Yet Olive remained the very essence of simple Christian goodness. She had her own moral compass and this is what gave her independence from her selfish, driven husband. She preserved much of her essential self and had her own family—her beloved parents Sis and Ampsey, her sisters Vera and Jean and their families, her own special friends Kitty and Dinah and her sister-in-law Eileen. After her divorce from Percy there was none of the fury of a woman scorned from Olive. She could have had a legally backed huge financial and property settlement had she been inclined. This approach probably never even occurred to her. She became a sort of 'retained person' somewhat down the Harding payroll but was provided with accommodation (a small flat in Sea Mills), an allowance for her expenses and to run her car and a few minor other perks. She remained a staunch friend of our mother through thick and thin. In later years Olive built her life around her daughter Diane and son Michael and their respective families.

Once or twice I visited her in her flat in Sea Mills, usually with my two oldest children Jane and Allan. Olive would make us a special little tea party with chocolate rolls, crisps and triangular sandwiches. Her sideboard was covered with pictures of her family with all her grandchildren very prominent. She would love to bring me up to date with news of them all and there would usually be a pound each for my two as we took our leave.

It would be going much too far to say she always loved Percy in spite of all. However, I formed the impression that she always retained some residual feelings for him. On my visits I would ask her about her childhood 'Up Tanks' and the 'old days' generally. She was happy to have a trip down memory lane. I even asked her once about how she really felt about life with Percy. 'Come on Ollie (everyone called her that) it can't have been much fun with him always ordering you about now, can it?' 'WWeeeell, not always bad you know.' 'How do you mean Ollie?'—wondering what was coming next. 'Sometimes when Percy would come home at lunchtimes and there was nobody else about, you know….' 'What Ollie?'….chuckling, more chuckling… 'Weeell, as soon as he came into the hall he would shout "OLIVE, UPSTAIRS, BEDROOM QUICKLY!"' 'Blimey, what did you used to think about that then, Ollie?' There was no hesitation in her reply: 'OOoooohhhhh, Lluvverleeee!!' Like I say, a very special person. I loved her dearly.

These days football matches shown on television are ten a penny, or some might even say fifty a penny. Anyone so inclined can watch at least a couple of different games each night from somewhere amongst the proliferation of TV channels in existence today. Years back a live football match on TV was an event of note. The 1953 F.A. Cup Final is very much a case in point. It must have been amongst the first live games to be shown, possibly even the very first. Possessing a television set back then was still the preserve of the relatively wealthy. The huge boom in the increase in TV ownership was still a few years away—a boom that, when it arrived, was to change the leisure habits of the entire nation. Just now though 1953 was right at the end of the period of television innocence when owning a TV was still a bit of a novelty and overheard remarks such as 'so and so has got one of those newfangled goggle boxes' were commonplace. Well, one 'so and so' who *did* own a goggle box was Uncle Percy! The TV in that house was kept in the smaller of the two living rooms on the ground floor.

There was another large room on the other side of the hallway into which we were not allowed to venture. Naturally, when the opportunity presented itself I soon had my nosy little head around that door! No idea what I expected to see but it turned out to be a snooker room with a full sized snooker table. Now, this was really something. Snooker was a little played game in those days, having been imported originally from India where the officer classes serving The Raj in the Indian Army had adopted it. Uncle Percy's snooker table filled that room. The snooker cues were racked up side by side against one of the walls contained within an open wooden cupboard edged with chrome strips. The 'reds' on the baize-clothed table were tight within their plastic triangular positioning frame. The 'colours' were in their positions down the table and the white striking ball in the 'D'. Everything in that room was immaculate and highly polished like the long sideboard with a couple of large glass ashtrays. The room was only ever used when Percy entertained his business associates so one assumed that on these occasions the gentlemen would go to the snooker room whilst the ladies were left in one of the living rooms to chatter. This sort of behaviour would have fitted well into Percy's notion of 'upper class' behaviour to which he seemed to aspire. So, Percy had a TV and the F.A. Cup Final was shown live that year. I recall feeling quite swanky settling down to watch Bolton Wanderers v. Blackpool. This became one of the great classic games of all time... 'The Stanley Matthews Cup Final'!

Like most occasions that turn out to be significant enough to acquire the title 'classic', they all seem ordinary enough at their start. All F.A. Cup Finals were always important in the English sporting calendar and safe within the nation's sporting psyche. Other events like the Grand National and the University Boat Race come into the same category. What lifted the 1953 Cup Final into the legendary and classic definition was the match winning performance by one of the greatest of footballers, Stanley Matthews. He was famed for his amazing acceleration over the first twenty yards; then with the football seemingly glued to his feet he would tease his opponents into reckless lunges and tackles, eluding them at the final moment in the manner of a matador with a bull. Once past his bemused challengers he'd whip the ball away and deliver an inch perfect pass into the stride of one of his teammates. This skill was known as 'dribbling' and had been perfected by Matthews and is always associated with his name.

At first, in this Cup Final, it was Bolton Wanderers who generally played the better football and were leading at half time. Bolton had their own star player in the figure of Nat Lofthouse. He was in the tradition of powerful goal-scoring centre forwards considered essential for a successful team. These were the days of heavy, laced leather footballs which frequently became even heavier when they absorbed moisture from a damp pitch. Unless these often dead weights were struck with the right timing and method, footballers of the day risked the distinct possibility of snapping toe bones, metatarsals, cruciate ligaments and just about anything else! On Saturday evenings hospitals were filled with limping young men on crutches still wearing their muddy shirts and shorts!

The very footballs themselves could be a distinct hazard. Players like Nat Lofthouse somehow thrived and survived kicking and heading these cannonballs. Nat Lofthouse went on later to play regularly for England and became known as 'The Lion of Vienna' after scoring a hat trick for England in that city. He has been canonised around the Bolton area ever since, even earning that most supreme of accolades... having a pub named after him!

So, Bolton forced the pace in this particular game and with only fifteen minutes to go led by 3-2. 'Cometh the hour, cometh the man,' as they say. The next quarter of an hour was to immortalise Stanley Matthews. He didn't look too much like a honed athlete; bow legged, craggy faced, slightly receding hairline and the baggiest pair of shorts in the kit bag. Wide on the Wembley wing he teased and bamboozled his opponents one after another; then the final lightning-thrusting run to the by-line and the dagger ball delivered into the heart of the Wanderers' defence. It was on a plate for the onrushing Stan Mortenson to score, (3-3). Minutes to go... ball out to

Matthews... a shuffle, a shimmy and a dash. This time the perfect cross for Bill Perry... GOAL! (4-3), Blackpool had won the Cup!! Stanley Matthews ascends his lofty perch, forever now amongst the footballing gods!

Some years later I saw Stan Matthews in the flesh playing at Ashton Gate for Stoke City against Bristol City. By now nearly fifty years old and way past his best he was rather anonymous. Never mind, it was enough to give me a lifetime conversation piece: 'I saw Stan Matthews play, you know...'

The televised Coronation of Queen Elizabeth on June 2nd 1953 brought almost a crowd in to cluster around the Harding's little black and white TV set. Extra chairs had to be carried in from the adjacent, larger and seldom used living room. We took our seats early that day. Auntie Olive made sandwiches and there were some sweets and biscuits. There must have been ten or twelve people gawping at the pageantry and drama unfolding in London. Richard Dimbleby doing the commentary, his rich melodious voice filling in the detail and adding to the pomp of the occasion. We watched all day, quite carried away with it all. I recall the moment of the actual crowning of the bejewelled young girl weighed down with much paraphernalia and looking somewhat crushed... 'Vivat Regina!' crescendoed the choristers of Westminster Abbey. It did seem special and the start of something new. The nation was awash with soggy sentiment surrounding the occasion. There was even a hit song:

> In a golden coach, there's a heart of gold
> Driving through old London town
> With the Sweetest Queen the world's ever seen
> Wearing her golden crown
> As she drives in state through the palace gate
> Her beauty the whole world will see
> In a golden coach there's a heart of gold
> That belongs to you and me

(xi)

It was indeed the start of something new for the Duttons. Percy had delivered our marching orders. The only question was the destination of the new camp and whether or not it might indeed turn out to be a tent! Time for mother to try to pull another rabbit out of the hat...!

In Arnall Drive, Henbury, Bristol there is a plaque on one of the houses to indicate the one-millionth council house built in Britain after the Second

World War. Bristol was typical of most industrial cities after WWII in building new council houses as rapidly as possible to replace the immense housing stock lost by bomb damage. There was an acute shortage and the need was met by the adoption of near revolutionary methods of construction. These entailed the utilising of prefabricated materials so that building houses and flats could be not only quick but as cheap as possible. Thus, often on the fringes or 'outskirts' of cities, there was the development of new 'housing estates'. There was a mixture of designs such as small traditional looking terrace rows often constructed in blocks of a dozen or so with little alleyways cut between them to divide one dwelling from another. Some were built like more traditional semis, each section of the semi often being divided again, top and bottom, to create what became known as maisonettes. One distinctive style was the Cornish Unit. The top outside half of the construction had overhanging cladding of tiling. The tiles themselves were slightly overlapping, making the whole effect not unattractive. Blocks of frequently ugly and cheaply built flats were put up to several storeys height. The simplest constructions of all were small, rectangular units, all prefabricated walls made of artificial material (no brick or concrete) which were assembled on site and became known as Prefabs. Cornish Units and Prefabs were only intended to last for fifty years and although the Prefabs have all but disappeared, the Cornish Units still survive in their thousands.

Housing such as this formed the new 'council estates' with the Henbury Estate in Bristol being typical. Henbury had once been considered almost in the country and was up over the hill from Westbury-on-Trym, a district which itself had once been considered on the very fringe of Bristol. The City had grown relentlessly in the earlier part of the century, forever nudging its perimeters outwards. Now, with the post war explosion of need, it was as though the tide of humanity and housing was lapping over and across the city's traditional boundaries of higher ground to the north and east and across the River Avon to the south and west.

In the 1920's and 1930's it was an outing on a Sunday for people to drive, cycle or even walk out of Westbury, up and over the hill, perhaps through Blaise Castle Woods to the little village of Henbury—once there, maybe to have a drink in one of the two pubs, 'The Salutation Inn' or 'The Henbury Inn'. It was here, by the early 1950's, across the fields and open country adjacent, that the Henbury Estate now spread. This was now home to thousands of former inner city dwellers numbered amongst whom were...the itinerant Duttons!

To be strictly accurate it was now down to just mother and yours truly. My sister Jill, who had shared all the recent turbulence in our home life, now sought some independence and fresh opportunity. She was about sixteen years old and her own education had been bits and pieces with hardly any continuity at all. Jill always carried, too, strong feelings of inferiority and insecurity—the inferiority springing probably from believing she was just not very clever. She had gone to a Secondary Modern School (Bishop Road) and this, in itself, was perceived as failure—especially so in an atmosphere in which 'good education' was constantly held out as the template for success and achievement. Not that mother would have deliberately put Jill down in any way. However, 'getting on' and 'succeeding' were implicit themes never far away from mother's mind or conversations. This, and the gentle but implacable snobbery always applied to questions surrounding jobs, accents, dress, where you lived and what you lived in, who your friends were and what you owned... made up a whole package of 'attitude' which always permeated our domestic life. Both Jill and I took all this in (Allan too probably), if not exactly with our mother's milk, then inexorably and gradually as we progressed through our childhoods. It's not difficult either to work out where Jill's insecurity was rooted. Although she was always much loved, the events and circumstances of her broken childhood had left her unsure of who she really was at all. She knew little about her own abilities or potential and was ill equipped to make good judgements for herself, as was to become clearer over the next few years.

Jill had long wanted to be a nurse and when she saw an advertisement for a residential position at 'The Sunshine Home for Blind Babies' at East Grinstead in Sussex, she quickly applied for and obtained the job. Jill saw this opportunity as firstly a possible stepping stone into 'nursing proper'—and secondly as an escape from all her recent domestic unhappiness and insecurity.

Percy Harding's axe hovering over our necks

Finally, the promise of the freedom and independence she wanted. It all seemed to be just right! Also, she had on her mind no doubt the knowledge that our half brother John was blind and this gave the job a more personal dimension. As it turned out she wasn't in East Grinstead for very long, less than a year I think. Whilst there she did discover a couple of things about herself for sure. First she wasn't cut out for nursing and also, something which was to have a much more lasting impact on her life...the opposite sex!

It transpired that once mother had felt Percy Harding's axe hovering over our necks she had thrown herself upon the mercy of The Housing Dept at the City Council. In those days you qualified for council accommodation by a 'points' system linked to your assessed needs The more points you were awarded meant the greater your need and therefore the better the chance of securing some form of housing. People would build up their points often over a considerable time on the waiting list. Obtaining accommodation in this manner was by no means a done deal once the application was made. Demand always far outstripped supply. This was not long after the War and one can understand the circumstances whereby the entire issue of the nation's housing was plagued by shortage. The sixty four thousand dollar question seems to me to be why has it never improved much over the last seventy years or so? Why is this country beset always by a chronic and institutional housing shortage? What is it about the way our society is structured that it cannot deliver decent affordable housing for renting and buying? They seem to be able to manage it quite comfortably in the U.S.A. or Canada or Australia or indeed just about everywhere else in so-called advanced countries. Like the historical notion of a permanently rising middle class, does it forever have to be 'there's a terrible housing shortage at the moment you know'? *What is it* about this issue in Britain? I've never heard a really convincing explanation. Seems we have to accept it as just one of those things which is, when all is said and done and there is apparently no answer.... 'just one of those things'.

Well, as the jury sometimes says of a rubbish entry in The European Song Contest, the Duttons were awarded 'nil points' when mother sought council accommodation. Our application form was shuffled well down the pack of eligibility. We must have been looking down 'Desperation Row' at this stage. Time for mother to bring into play the trump card, which can move even the most stubborn of bureaucratic mountains in jolly old England. Mother knew somebody amongst 'one of her posh customers', whose best friend was 'on the Council'. This lady (posh probably), in turn, had a word with somebody in the Housing Department who then whispered in the ear of her boss who just happened to be the person who organised the allocation of accommodation in the Henbury area... and guess what, Mrs. Dutton.... dead right—'He's going to give you a ring tomorrow!' That most unique of all methods which keep the wheels turning in this country (most likely most others too) had been utilised once more.... *the back door*! Thus it was that shortly thereafter we accepted a set of keys to the upstairs flat in a Cornish Unit at number 40, Grayle Road, Henbury.

(xii)

Our new abode was to be a relative sea of tranquillity for about the next three or four years. These were certainly transition years for me. It is fair to say that over that time I passed from the last flourishings of childish childhood and into a more serious and thoughtful stage. In short, during our time at Grayle Road I grew up a lot!

By now I was in my teens ('teenagers' as such hadn't been invented for a few years yet) and I had started at my new school, a prestigious Grammar School, no less. How I came to be admitted to Queen Elizabeth's Hospital Grammar School (Q.E.H.), one of the finest in Bristol and undoubtedly the single most significant event in my entire life, is a story yet to be told...

Mother's existence continued as ever. She clearly enjoyed having a decent place of our own and now she resumed the pivotal family role that had receded somewhat during the previous couple of years. Once again all my uncles and aunts became regular Sunday visitors. Mother and I went frequently still to Staple Hill to visit my grandmother ('Nanny') and the large family branch living in that area. In order to get to work Mother was faced with longish bus journeys now at the start and end of each day. As indeed was I, with Q.E.H. being situated in town. However, I would always get home before mother and be able to set the fire and then usually meet her off her bus. Our flat was situated at the top of Grayle Road and as I walked down towards the bus terminus, there was mother coming up the road always, really always, laden with shopping bags. Steve was a frequent visitor at this time and he remarked on one occasion, 'The eternal vision of Mrs. D. coming home from work, struggling up the road with her shopping bags, one we shall all retain for ever and ever'.... prophetic words indeed! As you might imagine by now, although she was generally happier, mother's problem with living in Henbury was the usual good old class problem. Henbury, after all, was filled mainly with people who had been re-housed there from the traditional working class districts of Bristol. Suddenly, mother's worst social fears were realised... the Duttons had landed themselves right in the midst of Bristolian 'oiks'! In fact, she coined a term to apply to her new neighbours.... a special sub division of 'oikdom', a name indicating her fear of how very close now was the threat of being socially consumed... '*Henburyites*!' There were a number of protective barriers still in place between us and the 'Henburyites'. First, as aforementioned, all our large family who came and went and to whom we went and came all still retained their more middle class existences. There was the continual and continuous connection with the posh customers at work who had always sustained her. Now, as additional ammunition, there was the oft-repeated and esteem bolstering statement frequently uttered, 'Yes, my son's a doctor you know, my daughter's a nurse and David is now at Q.E.H.!'

Above all, were the frequent occasions Steve and his University friends would congregate in our living room. Steve was advancing his teaching career in London during these years at establishments like Woolwich and Battersea Polytechnics. During his frequent holidays between terms he lived with us. He had a circle of friends from his days at Bristol University and they would sit around for hours and often late into the night drinking coffee and discussing serious subjects. Mother used to love joining in and being a part of this vibrant group of highly intelligent younger people. I would sit and listen to their conversations too, absolutely enthralled as they spoke of politics and religion, wars and peace, nuclear bombs and economics and just about every other topic under the sun. Their general stance on most issues it is fair to say was liberal and radical, although at that time I had no idea what that meant. I remember a number of those friends of Steve's, who didn't know it but who helped to awaken in me a wider interest and awareness. Matters somewhat above and beyond whether Bristol City was going to advance in the next round of The Cup and suchlike! There was Jocelyn Slade, who later became a distinguished academic in Mathematics at The University of Chicago and always remained a friend of mother's thereafter. Also, Arthur Marmour, a witty Jewish guy. 'Nag' Anstey, Michael Weeks and his sister, whose name escapes me. Also, a Pete Hawkins. He was a very handsome young man, an engineer of some sort I think. I seem to recall mother was a little sweet on him and when sometime later he went to work in Iraq (what was then Persia) they would correspond with one another and he would send her photos of himself and his pals working amongst the oil pipelines. Mother would read me out loud some of his fascinating letters. In one such letter I recall him saying that in order to endure the extreme temperatures in the area he and his pals always consumed up to twenty eggs each and every day. That stuck in my mind as singularly interesting—what was that all about? I've never subsequently got much into a boiled egg without the name 'Pete Hawkins' popping up onto my mental radar... strange, eh?

Steve's seminars, for that's what they amounted to, really registered with me. About the same time Steve, who always teased me because I didn't read any books, bought me for Christmas, *The Complete Works of Sherlock Holmes*. Soon I had whizzed through all the stories of the great detective and can recall most of them with pleasure to this day... 'The Red Headed League', 'The Silver Blaze', 'The Dying Detective', 'The Copper Beeches' and many more. Dr. Watson, Mrs. Hudson, Holmes' extraordinary eccentricities, and always the anxious clients arriving at the waiting room of the house in Baker Street to tell their troubles to the great sleuth. Finally, in all the stories, the pleasures of the 'denouement' when Holmes would explain, by deductive reasoning, how he had arrived at the solution to the case. I loved those stories and they marked the awakening of my interest in wider reading. Hitherto such reading had been largely restricted to 'The Pink'un' and 'The Green'un', Bristol's two Saturday night sports' newspapers! Not that I ever did become a really avid reader of books but, fair to say, since Sherlock Holmes started on my case, I've always had a book of one sort or another on the go.

(xiii)

The local small newsagent's shop on the Estate was owned by a rather grubby looking man called Mr. Palmer. He always had the obligatory fag dangling from the corner of his mouth and he seemed permanently grumpy, sullen and generally resentful towards all his customers. His significance to my life is that he was my first ever employer when I became one of his newspaper delivery boys. It turned out too that long ago in the dim and distant past, Mr. Palmer had been acquainted briefly with my father, Billy Dutton.

Mr. P. and I had not really got off on the right foot thanks to another of mother's 'classics'. Mind you, I should have known a lot better than to fall for it. I had quickly gathered a few pals around me when we moved to Henbury and one of our pastimes was playing table tennis across an old discarded table in a shed behind Dessie Morgan's house. We were always ruining table tennis balls by various means—treading on them, squeezing dents in them, bashing the shape out of them and probably several other ways too. Anyway, it was a Bank Holiday, all shops shut, a wet morning and the Henbury Junior Table Tennis Tournament in full swing in Dessie Morgan's shed. What a time for our one remaining tennis ball to roll out from underneath the small gap at the bottom of the shed door, thence trickle across the little concrete path at the side of Dessie's house and plop down through a broken grill into a drain. Now, a real problem... where the heck to obtain another table tennis ball on a wet Sunday morning Bank Holiday on the Henbury Estate with all shops everywhere firmly shut? 'Why don't you go and knock on Mr. Palmer's back door up at the newsagent's?' suggested my ever helpful mother... OK, now here's the bit which should have set the alarm bells off in my head: 'Just tell him you're Billy Dutton's son and you wondered if he'd be kind enough to let you buy a table tennis ball. I expect

he'll let you have one as he used to be a really good pal of your Dad's....'
Daft and innocent, probably a bit of both, I walked around to the rear of the
totally silent and very, very closed newsagent's premises. It was about 10
a.m. and the pressing need for a table tennis ball cancelled any misgivings
which may have been stirring in my mind about the trap mother was leading
me into.... 'Hello, Mr. Palmer,' I softly called up towards the upstairs rear
windows, 'Mr. Palmer...Mr. Palmer!'—louder and bolder now, and yet
again: 'Hiyaaa, Mr. Palmerrrrr!!' This time the response was swift and
brutal. The window jerked open, and standing there, in a convict style
collarless nightshirt, was a crazy haired and unshaven Mr. P. He had clearly
just got out of bed. He bawled down: 'What the bloody hell do you want?!!'
Gulp...this didn't look good; mother hadn't prepared me for this reception.
'Sorry to disturb you, Mr. Palmer, I know you're closed,' I bumbled out to
the twitching figure framed in the window, 'but my mum said, you used to
know my Dad Billy Dutton and that you would be kind enough to....'
(Uttering these last few words, I knew without a doubt, they were going to
take me straight off a cliff.) '...be very kind enough to...to..... sell me a table
tennis ball?' There was the kind of tension-filled pause which probably only
lasted a few seconds but seemed an age during which the full enormity of my
indiscretion hung just above my head like a scimitar. 'YOU WHAT!!' yelled
Mr. P, his whole body incandescent with fury. 'YOU STUPID, STUPID
LITTLE BUGGER, HOW DARE YOU WAKE ME UP ON A SUNDAY
MORNING! PISS OFF, OH, AND TELL YOUR CHISELING FATHER HE
STILL OWES ME FIVE QUID!!' Well, that was it, tail well between the
legs and the end of the table tennis tournament for sure! Also, the
reaffirmation of a lesson I should have learned a very, very long time
before... always keep your eye on Kitty Dutton!

Somewhat surprisingly, a few months later, Mr. P took me on as a
paperboy. As I don't think forgiveness was much in his nature, it was probably
from his point of view a question of needs must. However, I think it turned out
well for me from two perspectives. It was good discipline for me to get up to
that shop every morning at 6.30, rain or shine, in order to heave a heavy green
bag of papers around a three-quarter-mile circuit. Paper round completed, just
enough time to get home and guzzle down a plate of creamy porridge mother
always insisted I devour, before scrambling to the bus stop in time to catch the
bus into Bristol for school. The newspaper preferences of the Henbury
inhabitants were not difficult to discern from the contents of that heavy paper
bag I lugged around morning after morning... about one hundred copies of *The
Daily Mirror*, by far and away in those days the most popular choice for people
in the Henbury area. Even then, when most papers were 'broadsheets', the

Mirror was a tabloid... 'FORWARD WITH THE PEOPLE' it proclaimed as its motto at the top left-hand corner of its front page.

Delving into that bag containing the papers one would have found that there were just a few copies of *The Daily Express*, some *Daily Sketch's* (a publication now long gone), perhaps a few *Daily Mails*. There was one, just one, copy of the communist paper *The Daily Worker* and again just one copy of *The Manchester Guardian*. Every day I'd find the time, whilst trudging round, to digest some facts and opinions from both front and back pages of most of these publications. The cumulative effect of this daily imbibing of information was that I was becoming really rather knowledgeable, in a general sense anyway. Stood me in good stead though, as I was to start encountering some really very smart lads at Q.E.H.

(xiv)

I've only ever had three real fights in my life (so far!). At the moment it stands at one win, one loss and one draw. If you scratch anyone hard enough you'll reach a point at which they're capable of some violence. That's human nature. Having been brought up by a very passive mother and in a completely non-violent family must have rubbed off to a large extent, as I've never really felt very inclined to hit people. Not to say, of course, that I don't have a temper and can occasionally show it although this has never often been the case. To be honest, the time I felt the most angry surges were during the early years of my teaching career. There is nothing like truculent or defiant teenagers to really wind you up. It's basic really to being an effective schoolteacher to be able to control large groups of youngsters and to impose your will onto them. Without this simple truth schoolteachers may as well pack up and go home. In my early days of school-teaching, before it became illegal to say 'boo' to a pupil, let alone clip one around the ear, there were occasions when anger and frustration led me to thump someone. I'm not especially proud of this but it was not at all uncommon in my own schooldays and the first years of my teaching career for teachers to employ a little physical force in the cause of good order and behaviour. Nowadays, such measures have all been abandoned in schools, probably for the best. Yet casting an eye around the present disorder prevailing in a large number of our schools, to my mind, it's still only a 'probably'.

The most serious fight I had as a youngster was whilst at Henbury and was with the same Dessie Morgan who featured before as an opponent across the other side of the net of our improvised table tennis table. He was just one of the gang but, as in every group of boys, there has to be a pecking order and there has to be a leader. Dessie was of stocky build and had greasy straight black hair and he was what was once described as swarthy. He also turned out to be very strong and agile and, more to the point, unlike me, totally fearless! I knew I'd bitten off more than I could chew when immediately after the initial threats and squaring up phase had passed, he plonked me hard, straight on my nose. As many others have found, being hit hard on the nose can cause a rush of involuntary tears. This was the case in this particular skirmish and it was quickly obvious to the other kids standing around watching that Dessie had now established his

...the iron laws of natural selection weren't going to make any exceptions

position as top dog and that David Dutton was, in future, just a bit part player. This was all somewhat humiliating but the iron laws of natural selection weren't going to make any exceptions, so it was time to bow the knee! I had definitely lost that one!

Earlier, in my Cedar Park Primary days, I fought a draw with a lad named David Warren. It's possible I had been edging ahead in this bout but it was in the school playground and a couple of soppy girls went and fetched 'our sir', Doug Silverthorne, and he broke it up before much damage was done on either side. Later, in my Q.E.H. days came my greatest victory when I took on and clearly defeated 'Tich' Houlson. His nickname should give the clue as to why I fancied my chances in this encounter. This contest occurred one Saturday afternoon during the time I was boarding at Q.E.H. whilst mother was in Africa. 'Tich' and I clashed over whether one of those plastic footballs we used in the yard had or had not gone across the goal line to signify a goal. We swore at each other and then I looked down at 'Tich' and he looked up at me and the next thing I had punched him on *his* nose and he retired to what we called 'The Washhouse' to swill the blood away down a sink. Best not to mess with me again 'Tich'! Sweet triumph! That was the end really of my formal fighting career. Although, as indicated, it was not completely unknown for me to hand out a clout or two later in a few classrooms dotted around the Birmingham area (Birmingham, location of my first sixteen years in teaching).

Back in Henbury, 1954, the end game of the years of childish childhood was underway. There were some final flourishes. Very close by was the Blaise

Castle Estate with its acres of woodland. This was the perfect venue for some final flings at 'soldiers' and 'cowboys' and, let's face it, just plain mischief.

Every Council Housing Estate has its problem families. They are often large families with lots of kids bearing anti-social attitudes and they are usually trouble to some degree or another. One such infamous family on the fledgling Henbury Estate was 'The Tanner Family'. There seemed to be dozens of them spread around and over several generations. You came to recognise them and, if possible, to avoid them. Several of the Tanner family were in their late teens and early twenties and were employed as building labourers around the Estate, some of which was still under construction. In particular, a whole rank of shops along Crow Lane was gradually springing up. Now, young lads, incomplete building sites and school holidays are a potentially volatile mixture. My encounter with Dennis Tanner and a few of his mates amongst the half constructed shell of the building destined to become The Co-operative Society (Co-op) on Crow Lane, Henbury, marks for me a significant finale to my years of aimless childhood.

It was a hot day, towards the end of the long school summer holiday. Nothing much to do. 'Hey, Dave, coming out for a "muck around" down Crow Lane on the buildings?' Might as well, though such forays had by now lost much of their adventurous appeal. Into the shell of the downstairs section, messing around in a pile of sand, workmen working on scaffolding a couple of floors up. 'Hey, you lot!' came a shout from above. All looked up. Dennis Tanner, one of the nastiest from the whole Tanner litter, plus several his pals were all lined up, grinning and leering, and directing a waterfall of coordinated pee downwards to splash on our heads and into our upturned faces! In the scramble to escape that cascade of poisonous liquid a tiny switch was thrown somewhere in my head, not even consciously perhaps. That was enough of all that sort of thing for me—as it worked out, pretty well forever!

(xv)

It was less than a year after she had gone to East Grinstead before Jill appeared back over the horizon. Clearly things had not worked out with regard to her nursing ambitions and, such as it was, she seemed pleased to return to our little fold. To this very day she keeps up with some of the people she met during those few months in Sussex. This illustrates an interesting aspect of her character. She has an absolute talent for holding on to people and never letting her friends go (with one or two notable exceptions). This has held her in good stead down the years. As a matter of fact loyalty is a characteristic well spread amongst the members of our family... it's principally a 'Webb' legacy.

So, back in Bristol, Jill got a job at 'Boots the Chemists' as a shop assistant. This was just about acceptable on mother's little barometer of class. She'd never describe her daughter as a 'shop assistant', oh dear no. Although, 'my daughter works in Boots the Chemists' would just about pass social muster.

My relationship with my sister was always teetering on the brink of hostility. Mother had a job keeping the peace between us. I teased Jill mercilessly as I had always done and she, for her part, never lost the opportunity to register her disdain for her younger brother and chief tormentor. Jill was always hinting at her true feelings about me, as in, 'I hope you get killed in a bus crash on your way to school today!'... 'Now, now just take that back Jill straight away,' our hapless mother would plead, poised, cigarette in hand, trying to do her usual ten things at once before she left for work herself. 'Come on now, take it back, or I'm not going to let him go to school after you have said such a thing.'... 'Won't!' said Jill, 'hope the little sod gets crushed!' By this time, yours truly would be trying to push past mother who was firmly blocking the stairway. 'No, he's not going till you take it back Jill, come on now or we'll all be late.' A bit of a pout and a defiant glare from my sister who would eventually mumble after a few tension-filled moments, 'OK, take it back.' Peace having descended temporarily and mother having stepped aside to gather up her belongings, I would dash off to the bus stop—but not before my sister had whispered into my ear as I brushed past her on the stairs and just out of mother's earshot: 'Don't take it back really, hope it still happens...' Ah well, brothers and sisters, eh?

As always, money, or the lack of it to be more precise, was a continuing problem. Whenever mother could cut a corner in the budget she would do so. She simply could not afford to spend much on food. There was a lot of mashed potato—with egg on Monday, sausage on Tuesday, fish-cakes on Wednesday and faggots on Thursday. Friday night was different, though—it was my very favourite night. Friday night was *tripe* night! Tripe, the lining of a cow's stomach, cooked slowly in milk and onion, lovely! Tripe was cheap and plentiful in those days. Offal, that is, liver, pigs' kidneys, brawn, chitterlings and sweetbreads, generally was fairly frequent on our menus. I've always loved this kind of food although these days you practically have to have a licence to be allowed to eat most of it. Times change!

Weekends were usually the time for visitors and Betty Block started to appear regularly on Saturday afternoons. She had a sister who had emigrated to what was then Southern Rhodesia and was always talking about her sister and what a marvellous life she had in Africa with sunshine and servants and a wonderful lifestyle generally. It must have all sounded very attractive to our responsibility-laden mother. Not that I knew or cared much about Rhodesia. I might have been somewhat more interested had I known that it wouldn't be too much in the future before mother herself would go there. The notion that she would ever, ever leave me was, naturally, unthinkable...

Steve and his troupe of youthfully wise and clever chatterers and debaters were frequent visitors. On one memorable occasion they were joined by a Nigerian friend, a colleague of Steve's, down from London. Well, the appearance of a black man walking down Grayle Road caused a real flutter amongst the locals. Amazing as it seems, this was Britain in the early nineteen fifties, yet the sight of a black person was still a rarity. This was especially so, it seems, right in the heart of white working class folks on a council housing estate in jolly old Bristol. 'Yer, Dave,' said one of my ever-shrinking gang of friends, 'we saw a "blacky" goin' into your 'ouse—woss 'is name then, Mr Fuzzy, Wuzzy? Ha,Ha,Haaa!'

During these years too my mapping and awareness of the opposite sex continued. The lady who lived in the bottom half of our Cornish Unit was Welsh. She had a niece named Dilys who came to visit. Dilys was about my age and it wasn't long before we became friendly. She was a very pleasant girl and we got on well. We would sit for hours on the front doorstep of her aunt's flat and there was, eventually and inevitably, some kissing and hand holding. Unfortunately, it was clear from the outset that Dilys and I could never make it up the aisle, principally for two reasons. First she had a Welsh accent thicker than coal dust and secondly, poor blighted soul... she wore glasses! One thing though, when she went back to Wales she used to write to me and I would reply. They were decent length letters too and for a few months pretty regular. The point being, that I discovered through this little first relationship with dear Dilys that (a) I could keep up a correspondence and (b) writing could be a pleasurable activity that I took to quite readily. Eventually Dilys drifted from my radar.

Enter then the one girl who did really get to me. Her name was Ione Greenland. Slim and pretty, she had a bicycle which she would wheel alongside as we walked hand in hand down to the shops. Amongst the woods of the Blaise Castle Estate were several caves, well known to us local youngsters. One of these was called 'Giant's Cave'. On one occasion Ione and I took some food and sat at the entrance to Giant's Cave. As it was raining we drew back a little within the cave entrance where we had a really good 'snog'. Anyway, this little fling must have fizzled out after a while and, thinking about it, I think she and her family moved away.

Mother never really felt settled in Henbury. Amongst other things she was worried about the bad influence living there may have on me if I got too mixed up and involved with the local kids. After all, they all went to Secondary Modern Schools and they might as well have had leprosy as far as mother was concerned. So, over a period of time she must have been gently lobbying and string pulling via the, by now, tried and trusted methods of cultivating and cosying up to as many influential people as possible. All done, truthfully, in the nicest possible way. The upshot was that she managed to get us a transfer from Henbury to a prefab. A prefab... one of those temporary sort of tin dwellings built abundantly after the war. Nothing special about that, one may think. Indeed, nothing special as an actual dwelling at all. But that's not the point. This prefab was situated in *Henleaze*! Henleaze, one of the posher districts of Bristol. No 'oicks'. In one leap, mother thought, she had solved everything. It's hard to argue that she wasn't right again...

Mother (pretty Kitty) about the time of her divorce 1948 aged 43.

The very closest of friends all their lives. Auntie Olive and Mother on Weymouth beach. circa 1970.

Father Bill Dutton and Percy Harding. circa 1946.

Mother in her prime, aged 47.

Auntie Olive having fun on a cruise. circa 1960. 'Ooooh, luverleee!'

Me at Staple Hill aged 7.

Diane Harding.

Bristol, Background of My Childhood

Isambard Kingdom Brunel's masterpiece, The Clifton Suspension Bridge.

The Tramway Centre Bristol. Here I caught a thousand buses!

The Victoria Rooms. In my day, home of the Students' Union. Edward VII stands guard.

The Cabot Tower, memorial to the Cabot brothers, the fifteenth century discoverers of Newfoundland.

Blaise Castle, Henbury. The perfect place for childhood games.

Part of Bristol Docks. Note Cabot Tower in the background. From here they 'Set their foresails for the New World'.

Sheffield Coat of Arms

Clevedon Coat of Arms

Birmingham Coat of Arms

Weymouth Coat of Arms

Chapter Five

Q.E.H (Queen Elizabeth's Hospital School)

Getting a Foothold

MUCH OF MY LIFE has been fashioned by my becoming a pupil at Queen Elizabeth's Hospital School, Bristol. Getting into this prestigious Grammar School 'by the back door' was a crucial event that forever shaped the rest of my life and for which I have always been truly thankful.

As indicated, it looked to all intents and purposes that I was about to be dumped on the Secondary Modern scrap-heap once our association with The Hardings had begun rapidly to uncouple. Not that I was going anywhere educationally anyway in Oscar Dahl's unhealthy little toxic institution of a school.

Three factors combined at exactly the right time to create the circumstances under which I was admitted to such an august school. These were, firstly the indefatigable and fiercely burning love and ambition of my darling and amazing mother. Secondly, our connection to my 'brother' Michael Stephens (Steve)—who had been Head Boy and one of Q.E.H.'s star pupils in the recent past. Finally, the willingness of the then Headmaster Eric Gillett to bypass the entry regulations and take a chance on such an unpromising looking prospect as David Dutton.

In the end I think it was simple... mother and Steve asked for and made an appointment with Mr. Gillett and put our case to which he must have listened carefully. Then, hey presto, next thing it's running in all directions getting the money together to buy my blazer with its badge proclaiming *Dum Tempus Habemus* ('While We Have Time'), tie, grey trousers (always, always grey), black shoes (always, always black), school cap (essential item, the Q.E.H. cap being dark blue with a hexagonal shaped splodge of yellow on top), long dark blue and yellow scarf to be entwined stiflingly around the neck with plenty left over dangling temptingly to allow for others, friend and foe, to garrotte you at will. Not to mention the correctly coloured rugby jersey (what *was* 'rugby', I was shortly to find out), rugby boots, rugby socks, white shorts and vest (for 'gym') and white 'daps' (Bristolian for 'pumps', 'trainers', 'gym shoes'). We Bristol kids had a joke at the time... 'yer, wos the fastest fing on erf?'... pause... 'seasy, diarreal wiv daps on!' Not to forget of course a satchel, fountain pen (this was a biro-less world folks!), ruler, pencils, compass and set square (both useful tools for a lad not much yet past adding up!). Most of these things, certainly the clothing, only obtainable from 'Marsh and Son. Bespoke Tailors and School Suppliers, Whiteladies Road, Bristol'. Now all this lot must have cost a very pretty penny, several hundreds of pounds probably in today's money. How or from where mother obtained the money to pay for all this I have no idea. For certain though, had it been necessary she would have stolen it. She knew, even if I had no idea of the significance, that she had successfully circumnavigated a zillion obstacles to 'get David into Q.E.H.' and this alone must have given her immense relief and satisfaction. It should be fairly clear by now that my mother was a remarkable person. Of course I've always known it but it's never struck even me in its complete totality until these thoughts and words all came together. Truly, a remarkable woman.

So I began my first day at Q.E.H. in January 1953... well equipped in one sense, disastrously ill equipped in most others...

(ii)

Q.E.H. (or The City School as it used to be popularly known) was founded from moneys bequeathed in 1586 by John Carr, a wealthy local merchant, 'for the education of impoverished young boys and orphans born and yet to be born in the City of Bristol'. Opening in 1590 it received, from Queen Elizabeth 1st, a Royal Charter whose wording included that 'our royal assistance and pleasure' was that 'boys in their boyhood years may be properly educated and nourished'. So, thereafter, benefiting from further bequests, the school offered the chance of a good education to boys from disadvantaged backgrounds. The school always largely held to this ethos but by the time David Dutton was to squeeze through the eye of a needle to join this venerable and celebrated institution, it had evolved into a place where admission was through an entrance exam or scholarship with preference always afforded to those with more difficult circumstances of one form or another. The common denominator though was that the entry was still very much a selected one and the selection process, by definition, always threw up the brightest and the smartest. Cream, as always, coming to the top. This may not have been *exactly* what its founders had in mind but it was along the right lines, as they say. The upshot being that it was some clever boys who became boarders at Q.E.H and plenty of other clever ones who travelled as day boys from all parts of Bristol each morning to that imposing and castle-like building snugly planted into and dominating the lower northern slope of Brandon Hill.

Atop Brandon Hill itself is the slender, some may say somewhat elegant, tower raised as a monument to the Cabot brothers (John and Sebastian) who sailed from Bristol on their New World Discoveries at the end of the 15th century. The Tower is a famous Bristol landmark and from its top (had it been built then!) one could have seen the whole panorama of those little wooden sailing ships, all 'ship shape and Bristol fashion', slipping their anchors from Bristol Dock, nudging their way down the muddy and tidal River Avon towards the Bristol Channel and then turning their foresails towards the Atlantic and the largely unknown. Brave guys.

What Bristol's reputation lost on its association with the slave trade roundabouts it gained on the early explorer swings. Its connection to the Cabot Brothers in particular and other early maritime exploits is proudly trumpeted in all the modern promo literature about the City... and why not? Mind you, you probably won't find too much about Samuel Gist (bless him), one of Q.E.H.'s benefactors who made his pile from the slave trade, as did many more 'Samuel Gists' of those days. Bristol has had to hide its embarrassment about such things in these politically correct times. Not sure why really as these generous ancients, as observed elsewhere, danced to an entirely different social hornpipe.

The boys who boarded at The City School wore its very distinctive uniform and were always familiar figures around the Bristol streets. A long outer gown, yellow stockings, a white cravat band, short buckled breeches and, when inside the school, replacing the gown with a bum freezer short ordinary serge jacket. The dictates of changing attitudes and customs mean that this splendid uniform is now worn only by a few boys for special occasions. More's the pity, most former pupils of my generation and before would probably say. Generally though, this whole school uniform business in Britain has become a ghastly charade... in their school uniforms most boys manage to appear like menacing scarecrows and many of the girls as though they are setting out to audition for a porn movie. They seem to manage perfectly well throughout most of the rest of the world without this brand of nonsense.

The school was still dominated by a great deal of watered-down Public School attitudes

Back to January, 1953. The daily realities of existence for boys once within those walls at that time were not strawberries and cream by any means, fortunate though they may have been to have gained admission. The school was still dominated by a great deal of watered down Public School attitude which extended not only to the actual physical conditions but also how people, boy to boy, masters to boys and boys to masters actually related to each other. Bullying, as we have it now identified, was prevalent. The weakest were picked on and preyed upon. Anything outside the ordinary usually drew unwelcome attention. Would you think that a not very clever boy, amongst mostly scholarship and entrance exam 'hotshots', slightly built, who entered the school not with a large intake in September but on his own half way through a school year, might qualify for some nastiness? Correct, I did!

(iii)

The first year I spent at Q.E.H. was not a very happy one. That year is right up there in the running for first prize in the worst year of my life competition. First shock to the system was getting used to Q.E.H. ways. Right off the bat there was the vocabulary of the place. It was strictly surnames only. Certainly the Masters (always Masters, never teachers) would not dream of addressing a pupil by his Christian name. It was always 'Dutton' or 'You, Dutton' or 'Boy' or 'You Boy', or not infrequently, simply 'You'. We boys addressed and referred to each other by surname. This is one reason why nicknames really flourished at Q.E.H. Using a nickname was much more comfortable often than using a Christian name... examples abounded everywhere.... 'Flob' (Guest), 'Domer' (Swann), 'Granny' Gilbert, 'Grumpher' (Steeds), 'Inky' (Wills), 'Susan' Stallard, 'Sailor' (Williams), 'Jammy' James, 'Ram' Cockram, 'Slug' Jennings, 'Perp' Pritchett, 'Smart' Baker, 'Umpeter' Northover, 'Oola' Garnett, 'Clara' Weale, 'One-ball' Stewart, 'Nat' Lewis, 'Birdy' Hopes—you get the idea.

There was always a rigid pecking and rank order based on seniority and, often, size i.e. the biggest boys were always first in lines or queues (only within your own year group though... the smallest sized second year always preceded the largest sized first year). On the long, wooden dining tables it was always 6th Form at the head, then descending down through the year order to the first years at the very end. Since the 6th Formers themselves dished out the food from tin plated dishes set before them at the head of the table there was a built-in system of unfairness of Oliver Twist proportions, whereby the amounts of food passed down the table towards the youngest was barely visible on the plate—the amounts growing very slowly as the year number increased (i.e. a bit more for 2nd years, bit more for 3rd and so on). The results of course were that the older boys piled their plates high and the younger ones faced slow starvation and were left at most mealtimes gazing hungrily up the table as a fourth or fifth sausage disappeared down an older boy's throat. This grotesquely unfair system was always blind eyed by the Masters in charge of the Dining Room. Indeed, the Masters whole approach to the social system they oversaw was very much 'laissez-faire'. Notions such as pupil welfare or a pastoral system were unheard of. The rule at Q.E.H was simple... sink or swim.

Just for a start, the sheer size of the older 'boys' was intimidating in itself. They were, of course, by the age of 17 and 18, fully grown men. To encounter these muscular giants, the Boarders especially, bursting through their buckled breeches and short jackets as they filled doorways, stairwells and corridors, was to know for sure how the Lilliputians felt when Gulliver came to town! The Masters delegated much of their authority to The Prefects. Most of the Prefects were OK but they wielded quite a lot of power and one or two were, in a word, bastards. When I first arrived at Q.E.H., the Prefects held their own 'Detentions'. Miscreants had to report to the gym in shorts and then run continuously around its perimeter whilst a number of Prefects smacked you on the ass with a dap to make sure you kept running. To be fair this practice was abandoned after a short while. It was something though that this sort of thing was condoned. It would have done Heinrich Himmler proud.

Another charming feature when I arrived at Q.E.H. was that many of the cubicle toilets had no doors to them... the 'bogs' or 'trows' as they were known were gas chambers all on their own with the stench of urine and fecal matter always a joy to the nostrils. If you wanted to do a 'no. 2' as it was sometimes coyly referred to, you looked first for a cubicle with a door. If successful you hoped that there was still a lavatory chain and that the bowl would flush (by no means always the case). If all the cubicles with doors were occupied then it was a sit down job in full view of any passers by. Not nice really and, again to be fair, doors were eventually placed on all toilet cubicles. So, these were some of the customs in place at Q.E.H. at that time and which everyone experienced. Frankly, all this was secondary for me. Much more difficult to cope with was being so far out of my depth and behind in almost all aspects of learning and classroom performance. This exposed me to mockery and some actual physical bullying. Looking back, a sad and unhappy time.

(iv)

So, for a while back then it was somewhat grim stuff. I wasn't at the school for many days before I noticed at breaks in the schoolyard that I was being stared at and clearly referred to by a few clusters of boys who never seemed to do much else at breaks than hang menacingly around, clowning about, pushing and shoving each other. These were boys from a year or two above me, not from the fifth or sixth forms who were long past their own time of playground feuds and thuggery.

'Wos yer name, fag?' said one well-built boarder who stepped across my path as break ended and we gathered around the large set of black doors by which you entered the building at one end of the orange tiled yard—a yard that stretched the entire length of the building at its rear to a depth of about forty yards backing up to the first of the massive walls which formed the first partition between the school premises and the steeply rising edge of Brandon Hill beyond. Passing through a door at the foot of this wall there was a set of steep stone steps leading up to an area known to all Q.E.H pupils since time immemorial as 'The Upper'. During my time at the school this area, which formed, in effect, a giant ledge into the hillside, held a collection of huts that were used as classrooms. One of these huts was The Art Room, I recall. This symbolised somehow the very fringe nature of a subject like Art at an establishment like Q.E.H. where the curriculum was tightly tied to the academic and the traditional. Why bother with Art when the important things were Maths and Science (can't argue with that) and Latin and Greek (draw your own conclusion!). The Arts generally were very poorly served in those days, virtually out of sight, in fact relegated to The Upper at any rate. Along the boundary of The Upper was the second huge wall almost a third of the way up the side of Brandon Hill and which formed the southern perimeter of the entire premises.

Back to bully no.1. (I could disclose his name and those of his persecuting pals. However as these days they are mainly friendly old white haired gentlemen whom I encounter most years at the annual Old Boys' Dinner, it is probably wiser they remain anonymous!) So, 'Wos yer name, fag?' ('Fag' equals Public School term for junior pupil wholly existing to do the bidding of older boys... not 'fag' as in many residents of San Francisco.) 'David Dutton' came my shaky reply.... 'OOOOhhh, David Dutton'—other persecutors now joining in—'David Dutton, eh... David Button Dutton, David Mutton Dutton, David Glutton Dutton... ha,ha,ha'— all this being sort of chanted at me... then a push, a trip and a tumble to the ground. Now, this *sort* of thing went on for a while. Worse was to come in the classroom. Q.E.H.'s brilliant secret plan to bolster the self-esteem of its pupils (well the best 5% at any rate!) was to have a public reading every four weeks of 'The Monthly Marks'. All the results from each subject were aggregated and a final monthly position in the Form was worked out. Then, amongst much interest and ceremony, this position was sombrely and formally pronounced to everyone in the Form. Probably won't surprise you to know what this bumper wheeze to encourage incentives (!!) always led to... correct... perm the same names for the first three or four positions each month, ditto for positions four or five to ten and eleven, then again ten and eleven to fifteen or sixteen. Now as all *these* names were called out there was broadly smiling and approving nods around the classroom. As the sword of failure cut deeper when the list of the lower positions was read out of course, gloomy faces and lowered eyes were the order of the day. Noses were rubbed firmly and publicly into the trough of humiliation. You've guessed it, folks! The last position each month in the Form was always, always... David Dutton! That in itself was bad enough but the accompanying giggles and stares from one's Form mates as the sound of the name 'Dutton' crackled across the room was a tough one to try to smile through. (I've always hated my name being called out aloud in any context as it always sounds harsh with its double 't' in the middle.)

In short, with the exception of History and to a lesser extent Geography, my previous years whilst in Oscar Dahl's painful educational wasteland and earlier overcoming the ravages of rheumatic fever were now being ruthlessly and microscopically exposed in the Q.E.H. brains' laboratory.

QUEEN ELIZABETH'S HOSPITAL
BRISTOL

TERMINAL REPORT   Summer Term, 19 53

Name _Dutton D. H._   Form _II B_   Age _13.0_

Position _28_   No. in Form _28_   Average Age _13.3_

SUBJECT	POSITION	REMARKS	MASTER'S INITIALS
Divinity	.	Good work. notebook fair.	*illegible*
English	28	36% Very weak. He must make a big effort.	*illegible*
History	28.	He is outclassed in the form. 36%.	*illegible*
Geography	22:	46% with more effort he could improve.	*illegible*
Latin	28	Far behind the standard of the Class: he has made some efforts.	*illegible*
Spanish			
French	28	10% V. poor indeed. Slight progress. Position unreported.	*illegible*
Greek			
~~Science~~ Physics	27.	Very fair.	O.H.W.
Chemistry			
Biology			
Mathematics	25	His algebra was fair (58%) but the other was very poor indeed. He could do much better	W.G.L.G.
Art	27	His work is quite good at times.	N.M.
P.T.		Quite satisfactory.	A.B.T.H.
Music			

Form Master _His attainments and his work-habits are far below the standard of this Form. Staying in II B next year will give him a chance to get the grounding he has missed_   *illegible*

House Master _He does not exert himself enough._   R.H. MacBurnon

Head Master _He will have to stay another year in II B. If he works hard he will yet do well._   EBW.

NEXT TERM BEGINS ON _15th September_   AND ENDS ON _18th December_

At the end of that academic year it would have been no surprise whatsoever had E.B.P. Gillett shown me the door... Well, he didn't, and for that he earned my eternal gratitude. What he decided in fact was that I should stay down and repeat the second year. The following was his remark written on the foot of my school report in July 1953... 'Staying another year in 2b will be best for him. If he works hard *he will yet do well.*' (My emphasis.) From the depth then, that man, who subsequently attracted much unfair criticism over his stewardship of the school, expressed faith in me and offered out hope. Thank you Mr Gillett, it was the turning point of my life.

If he works hard he will yet do well

(v)

There were some improving straws in the wind as time went on—three or four straws, as a matter of fact. Amazingly, I was cornered one morning at break by a group of lads from about two years above me. Their 'leader' was named Louis Roll, accompanied by some of his pals, amongst them Micky Bachelor, 'Smart' Baker, Dicky Connor and a couple of others. Louis Roll had a large shock of curly hair and an open friendly manner. More importantly, he and his gang had what would now be known as street cred around the Q.E.H. yard. By chance Louis Roll had been a pupil a year or so in front of me at Stoke Bishop Primary some years before and he remembered me from there. More important by far was that Louis and his mates (all day-boys) were huge speedway fans and guaranteed regulars at The Bristol Bulldogs every Friday night. 'Is it true that you're Bill Dutton's son?' he asked, a slight awe already flickering across his features. (Remember my errant father was at that time very well known amongst the speedway 'cognoscenti', being manager of The England Speedway team and as such, something of a minor celebrity, not that celebrities had really been invented back then!) Well, Lou and his pals were well impressed, I can tell you! Thereafter, this group started to call me 'Bill' and afford me that totally priceless commodity amidst the jungle warfare of the schoolyard—respect. This of course did not go unnoticed amongst my regular tormentors. In short, this unexpected assistance from my distant Dad had come to my aid at an apposite time! The attention towards me of Louis Roll and his cinder track followers, although they probably did not realise it, had to some extent called off the bullying dogs who had been making coming to school each day something I had come to fear and to dread. So that was good.

Also, another boy with whom I had been a bit 'palsy' at Stoke Bishop Primary also turned up in the year above me at Q.E.H. His name was Robin Thomas and he was always friendly towards me. Importantly, he was in the same Form as one or two of my 'betes-noir'. Robin too had a lot of street cred, being an extremely promising prospect in both cricket and rugby. He was therefore on the Q.E.H. 'gold standard', as being good at sports was the quickest vehicle to acceptance and popularity at Q.E.H (more about this later). In short Robin Thomas, knowing me and clearly befriending me, was 'grist to the mill' in my improving situation. Robin later became the very longest serving of my friends and we still buddy along together after well over half a century. It helped too that I was gaining something of a reputation for myself as a good yard footballer. The games, played with a plastic ball on improvised pitches spread all across those orange tiles, were one of the great enthusiasms of Q.E.H boys. The skill levels were often extremely high and each break and lunchtime, as the classroom doors opened to release the straining hungry hordes, it was only seconds until at least a dozen matches were in full swing. There was no avoiding, though, Q.E.H.'s rigid hierarchical approach to everything... the biggest, strongest and oldest always commandeered what were held to be the best pitches—namely, the two pitches at either end of the yard (one alongside the Gym and the other at the 'Shoe House' end).

The Wembley of pitches though and most sought after was the middle pitch with one goalmouth being the larger of two small caves set into the Upper wall and the other goal being a protruding wall of the main building, the lower window of which was covered with wire mesh and was indeed The Boss's Office (E.B.P. Gillett was known by all as 'The Boss'). Quite how the very head Honcho of the whole establishment endured without much complaint the constant thwacking of a large plastic ball against the meshed window of his very own study was, even then, something of a puzzle to me and indeed remains so even now, but he did! Be that as it may, you didn't get to play too often on the favoured middle pitch until your seniority rose. In fact, if sometimes it was all clear some of the younger boys might start a game on one of the best pitches only to be cleared off by the arrival of bigger and older boys who would crisply order, 'Clear off, you lot, you're hogged!' (*Hogged* being the universally used word at Q.E.H. that established precedence.) So, being seen as a good yard footballer gave me another nudge towards acceptance.

A couple of the Masters too showed me a little kindness. Tony ('Daddy') Hills was our P.E. teacher and he seemed to like me, and also Mr. Martin (never knew his Christian name, but his nicknames, not to his face of course, were 'Doc' or sometimes 'Holy Joe'). He was our Divinity teacher and was responsible for quite a long flirtation I had with God in my middle teen years... he persuaded me to join a Sunday Bible Group for young people that he ran called 'The Crusaders'. Doc Martin had been a missionary in China and, in truth, he was a gentle and well meaning man driven by his convictions which he always made clear but did not try to thrust too firmly down your throat. I responded to his kindness and interest in me at a time when these commodities were in short supply within the Q.E.H. hurly burly. So I did start going to his bible class on Sundays; I did for a while read my daily key notes which all good 'Crusaders' were called upon to do each day; I did wear the little enamel shield-shaped Crusader's badge with its little cross of St. George and, crowningly, I did go with Doc Martin and his followers to a Billy Graham Crusade in Harringay Arena, London in the summer of 1955. So, I had a go at it all; but deep down there was the nagging certainty that it was all bullshit. This opinion has never varied since those days and I am thankful to have discarded all the whole bag of religious crap pretty early in life. Frankly it has saved me a lot of trouble and freed me up for a lot more interesting things. Sorry, I don't 'do' fairy stories. Nevertheless, old Doc Martin gave me an appreciated helping hand when I needed it. So, by the time I was getting into my *second* second year at Q.E.H. things were on the up. It was about this time too that David Dutton metamorphosed into Harry Dutton... interesting!

QEH The original school at
the bottom of Christmas Steps
1820.

QEH School. 'That imposing
and castle-like building snugly
planted into and dominating
the lower northern slope of
Brandon Hill...'

Cabot Tower. "There
was a good view from
our dormitories at
QEH straight out over
the two 'upper' walls
onto Brandon Hill..."

"The Incline, that stretch of
sloping approach road to the
imposing facade of Brunel's
distinctive Temple Meads Railway
Station... forever imprinted onto
the minds of all Bristolians... just
there, just permanent"

Dum Tempus Habemus Operemur Bonum

Chapter Six

Q.E.H.—The Harry Years

STAYING 'DOWN' A YEAR certainly carried some stigma in a school like Q.E.H. and some of the shame clung to your name more or less for ever. I recall being at a 40th. anniversary reunion of the 1952 intake (would have been in 1992 folks!). Finding myself sitting beside a 'boy' who had been in the 'A' Form from that year (each year was sub-divided, Q.E.H. style, into an 'A' Form, containing the brighter ones and the 'B' Form the less bright, all relative of course, but all nicely hierarchical and Q.E.H. fashion!). Anyway, by the time a few glasses of red had slipped down I was talking amicably with this fellow who I did remember but with whom I had not been especially pally at school...turned out he had had a high flying academic career in the U.S.A and was a fully made up Professor of Quantum Physics (or some such) at a pukka Ivy League University...'blimey, you've done well' said I. 'Mmmm, things did kinda work out', his original Bristol accent now well overlaid with a transatlantic 'twang'...'and what's yer surname bud, I know they called ya Harry'....'Dutton', I offered, as he kindly 'sloshed' another red into my glass. 'Oh, yeah, I gotcha now fella,... *you stayed down* didn't ya?'!! So, there you are, once branded with the Q.E.H. pigeon hole branding iron you sure stayed branded!

Back to 1953...I felt immediately more comfortable in every way among my new Form mates. Just as a start and for the very first time the measure of my progress was proclaimed by not coming bottom of the dreaded 'Monthly Marks'! Mind you, I still SOMETIMES came bottom but now had a few serious rivals for the position....step up to the plate please the following 'thicko's with whom I jockeyed each month for bottom spot....Colin Thorne....Robin Bown....Bert Wilsher...George 'Inky' Wills..... Williams B. and a couple of others. The important thing for me was that, although still amongst the limp, lame and lazy (by Q.E.H. standards), I was beginning to hold my own and to show actual improvement and progress in most subjects

(I wish I could report that one of them was Maths, but alas no, numbers remaining forever a closed book, if I may put it that way, as they had been right from the get go if you recall!).

I'd always been quite good at History and Geography and these two were now edging towards the very good end of the spectrum, whilst French, Art, 'Divinity' (!), English (Language and Literature) were all now within the definitely improving quadrant. Science was still limping along behind but was not yet quite terminal, leaving really only Maths still choking to death. The main thing though was that I was emerging on more or less equal terms with the others and, it's fair to say, that the more relaxed I became the more the old 'Webb' sense of humour began to bubble a bit. Before long I believe my form mates regarded me as 'a good laugh', especially when twisting the tails of most of our Masters. In a word...I was getting popular!

As time went on my new pals discovered my middle Christian name is 'Hamilton' (my maternal grandmother's family had all been 'Hamiltons', the Scottish connection one may say. Not that it ever really meant much to me but has always given me a second team, Scotland, to support if England is ever knocked out of any competition or if Scotland is playing another country other than England. We've even got a tartan you know, but whether my somewhat tenuous connection permits me to wear it would probably be well disputed by purer sons of The Highlands and Glens!) So, 'Hamilton' slid towards 'Hammy' (where many may say it should have stayed(!). This 'wobbled' around for a while.

One of the most crowded places at Q.E.H. was always in front of the large mirror attached to the wall at one end of The Wash House. Here, adolescence, puberty and testosterone all mixed into a cocktail of combing, preening, patting, quiffing and pouting as nature and burgeoning sexuality barged all else to one side. At this mirror throughout the 1950's at Q.E.H. hairstyles were teased into 'Toni Curtis forward peaks', 'Elvis Presley greasy forehead flops' and even Bill Haley 'kiss curls'. In my time the most handsome peacocks of all with the most notable coiffeurs were Dick White, Chris Wide and Barry 'Pancho' Coombs but there were many other popinjays around as we slowly turned from boys to men. Not least...'Hammy' Dutton who always managed to squeeze into a spot somehow and somewhere to admire his reflection! Indeed, SO frequently was I to be found adoring myself that (tongue stuffed into cheeks) my pals started to call me 'Handsome Hammy'...well, the 'Handsome' fairly rapidly fell into disuse (!) but the 'Hammy', I suppose perhaps from repetition or maybe misunderstandings or indeed, who quite knows (or cares!), started to emerge with increasing frequency as 'Harry'... and there it has remained ever since. If it had taken a couple of years to change my name completely, it was to take a couple more to make a bigger dent into Q.E.H. and for Q.E.H. to make an even bigger and long lasting dent in me....

(ii)

To be seen to be good at Sport was a distinct advantage at Q.E.H. Being good at sport was even more highly regarded than being brainy, certainly amongst us pupils. King of the sports by a mile at Q.E.H was Rugby. There was a certain amount of snobbery about this since 'rugger' was the sport of The Public Schools and Grammar Schools and Q.E.H. adhered to this custom. Making Rugby the main sport was important in symbolising that a school was superior and distanced it from all the other schools which 'they' (inferior souls) attended. 'They', of course, practised that other ball game, football. So Rugby, great game though it undoubtedly is and was, became essentially a socially divisive agent in the context of Britain's educational system. Put another way, Rugby was considered a game for those occupying a superior niche in society. You attended Q.E.H., Q.E.H. was a superior school therefore you learned and played the game which differentiated you from the rest...simple! Rugby itself was just another factor in the game which this country really plays best of all...'class'!

Therefore, every eleven year old arriving at Q.E.H. was immediately deposited upon a rugby field to see how well or otherwise he could shape up to this very rough and fast moving game, the outcome of which nearly always being the triumph of the biggest and the swiftest.

The success of its Rugby teams at Q.E.H., it seems, has always been of paramount importance. It is a barometer of the school's achievement, status and success just as much as, if not more so, than any other empirical measurement. At every Old Boys' Annual Reunion Dinner, no part of the Headmaster's Report on the School's activities draws more of an approving and swelling 'hurrah' from the assembled Old Boys, Older Old Boys and even Older Old Boys than the news that 'The 1st XV won most of its matches this season, including...beating the Grammar School!' (Bristol Grammar School, just up the road from Q.E.H. and perceived always as the deadliest rival and success over who, to every Q.E.H. boy was, and still is, the gold standard of achievement).

Having said all that, I never ever really got on with Rugby. I was a natural ball player and became one of the very best exponents of yard football at Q.E.H and later elsewhere. After Q.E.H. I achieved a good measure of success playing soccer, becoming vice-captain of the soccer team at Teachers' Training College and later having two seasons as a semi-pro with Redditch Town in the West Midlands League (as it was known then). It was Cricket which was to be my vehicle of success at Q.E.H., more of which later. However rugby was never to be my 'lady'.

Not that I got off to a very promising start. The very first occasion I participated in a Games Afternoon, as it was known at Q.E.H., at our Eastfield Road Playing Field, was to virtually kill off most of my prospects and interest in the game for many subsequent years. The game to which I was assigned on that first occasion was being refereed by Fred Cook, the Music Master. By the time I made my late debut on the rugby field most of the selection process of abilities had been decided...the best players in Game 1, next best Game 2, next Game 3 and then 'The Left-Overs' Game! Now Fred was reffing Game 2 and since I had never previously even touched a rugby ball let alone taken part in a proper game it was a mystery why I was pitched in at such a relatively elevated level. The only thing I can think of is I must have LOOKED the part, what with my brand new boots and socks, not to mention crisp new shirt straight from the shop window of Marsh's of Whiteladies' Road. Thus, clueless, I took up a position on the pitch and began trying to work out what would be required should the ball come anywhere near me, which I was fervently praying it would not. Damn! Sod's Law! Within a few minutes someone threw the ball at me...I caught it (good start), then looking up and seeing a whole pack of ferocious looking large boys crashing towards me I did the one seemingly sensible thing...I lobbed the ball directly to them, turned around so as to be going the same direction as the onrushing human juggernaut and ran away as fast as terror itself! A sharp blast on the whistle, everything ground to a halt. Then dear old Fred Cook, a mild mannered and decent chap, teacher of music, much happier with playing his Mussorgsky records to bored and philistine little boys in the choir stalls at the end of the Q.E.H. Dining Room, this same Fred Cook uttered the words which determined my whole rugby playing future at Q.E.H. and indeed, at the time, possibly my entire future...'Go and join The Left-Overs' Game, Dutton, you don't have a clue!' Head bowed and chastened, not even a sweat stain on my shirt or a little mud on my shorts, in fact still *looking* immaculate, I made my way towards, by Q.E.H standards, the very pit of humiliation...'The Left-Overs'!

Well the 'Left-Overs' game was in the care of the Maths' Master, that Q.E.H. legend, Mr. W.A.G. Moore (Bill, but universally known as 'Wag'). To be blunt, Wag didn't have a clue either about rugby and was perfectly happy for the rejects in his charge to more or less do anything to pass the time away. I recall when I joined his little band of oddballs, Wag was involved in an animated discussion with two boys on the exact number of miles it was to The Moon from the Earth. This was going on as all three of them wandered around in the centre of the pitch. My fellow players in that game were 'Domer' Swann, a very large boy with an enormous dome shaped head (to enclose his very clever large brain), his pal 'Granny' Gilbert who was always at Swann's side. 'Granny' was born middle aged, bespectacled (perfect for rugby) and always jabbering away about his Physics' homework (or similar). Then there was a boy called Jackson who only had one hand (we understood that his father had been a butcher and his unfortunate son had sliced off his own hand in an accident with the bacon slicer some years before.) Anyway, these were the days before prosthetics and instead of a hand he had a large metal hook, the claw of which he could somehow open and close in order to grip things. Not perhaps the perfect accessory for a rugby game.... Then there was 'Grumpher' Steeds, again a very large lad bursting through the largest shirt and shorts that Marsh's could provide. 'Grumpher' was a lovely lad who just wanted to be left alone to collect his Bristol City Football Club programmes and do his Meccano. His pal was 'Susan' Stallard, a somewhat effeminate boy who had suffered from a childhood ailment, polio I think, which had left him with a withered arm. 'Susan' was a witty and engaging boy who loathed any form of exercise but who was perfectly happy to wander around a rugby pitch discussing world affairs even at such a young age. 'Bert' Wilsher was a 100% Bristol lad with a 100% Bristol accent, whose main claim to fame at Q.E.H. was that he had drilled a hole, with a compass, through his two front teeth through which, cobra style, he could deliver, with deadly accuracy, a jet of spittle over a distance of several yards. You never knew when Bert would fire off a little stream which would fly through the air with considerable velocity. You just learned to steer clear of him and, of course, always make sure that he sat at one of the front desks in every classroom... Amazingly, when he left Q.E.H. old Bert made a fortune with his ice cream business in and around Bristol. He probably got his front teeth sorted out too, he needed to!

Several other players graced the 'Left-Overs' each week. There was Coline (rhymes with 'towline') Thorne, whose speciality throughout a game was to make dozens of mud pies which later became distributed for a general mud pie war amongst just about everyone before Wag faintly blew the final whistle.. This would have suited George 'Inky' Wills, an indescribably scruffy and unwashed boarder who, as his nickname suggests, had a mostly blue face and body (sometimes 'royal', sometimes 'navy' depending on which colour ink he was using at that time). There were others too whose names I have forgotten but all rejected and damaged individuals in one way or another...after all, they couldn't play rugby now could they?!!

True, somewhere in amongst the misfits there was an actual rugby ball, at which someone would occasionally take a swipe or have a hack. This was just incidental and secondary to the fact that none of the 'Left-Overs' were much interested in what they were supposed to be there for each week. As long as they were left alone to make their own amusement for an hour or so, then all was equal.

It didn't take long for me to adopt my fellow 'Left-Overs' attitude to the great game and thereafter rugby and I effectively parted company. Strange in a way with my brother being so brilliant at the game. Takes all sorts...

(iii)

Eric Berkley Parnall Gillett was The Headmaster throughout my time at Q.E.H. He was never known as anything other than 'The Boss' to one and all. For a man who had such an influence on the course of my life it is sobering to recall that I only ever spoke directly to him, or him to me on fewer than a dozen occasions. 'The Boss' was a remote but very much respected figure. It is fair to say that most of us boys treated him with a mixture of awe and a degree of fear. Not that he was the least anything like that cane wielding monster Oscar Dahl at my previous school. 'The Boss' did use corporal punishment but it was rare and not at all what Q.E.H. was about in that sense. Corporal punishment was very much the norm in all schools during this era, it was really a matter of the degree to which it was used. It's fair to say that this degree seemed very limited at Q.E.H., although the ultimate sanction of the cane was always there if required. Many, surveying the current decline in manners and public behaviour that pervades in early 21st. Century Britain, no doubt, will mourn the passing of the use of the cane in schools. If only it were as simple as a few whacks on the behind and a good clip around the ear being enough to mend our wounded country then all would be well and all forgiven. Sadly, in my view, the rot has gone too deep now. Be that as it may, the mere appearance of Eric Gillett on any horizon around the school would immediately send droves of little (and bigger!) boys scuttling into straight silent lines waiting to enter classrooms or just about anywhere else. We were always lining up at Q.E.H. One seemed forever to be steadying oneself against the boy in front of you whilst being shoved by the boy directly behind you. These lines had a living, moving identity of their own. You sort of fused with the boy ahead and the boy behind fused with you and 'the line' acquired a physical dynamic of its own as it swayed backwards and forwards and from side to side. Lines weren't moving snakes like this though if 'The Boss' was approaching. Indeed no, the line was motionless, separated, orderly and patient. Sometimes if the approach of 'The Boss' was not seen by the majority, a tom tom of early warning was passed vocally around like lightning...'Cheese-it Boss! Cheese-it, Boss'. To hear those words was to scatter instantly towards where you should be and to be seen to be doing only what you should have been doing, and silently too! Not that Mr. Gillett LOOKED particularly 'Headmasterly'. He was quite a small man in stature. Whilst at Oxford (Classics' Scholar, naturally!) he had gained a Blue for boxing and his many bouts had left him with a flattened nose. He had a habit of almost closing his eyes when he spoke and a very distinct mannerism when holding a conversation of spreading one hand out 'fan like' across his mouth and lower jaw with his index finger resting alongside his upper cheekbone and eye socket.

The timbre of his voice was especially distinctive; very slow, deep toned and modulated. It was also very easy to imitate and there was not a Q.E.H. boy of my generation worth his salt who was not able to do an impersonation of 'The Boss's voice'!.... as in, 'Oooow kaaay, yooo boooys, fiind yooor deeesks and siiit doooown quieeetly'. He almost always wore a dark blue pinstriped suit, to be honest I wonder if he possessed anything else as it's all I can ever recall him wearing.

He had a reputation for personal bravery. This rested to some extent on the occasion on the playing field at Eastfield on one summer's 'Sports Day' when he grabbed the megaphone being used to announce the results and led a charge of other Masters and sixth formers against a gang of youths (as they would be known today) who had wandered onto the Playing Fields from the nearby Southmead Housing Estate (uugghhh!). These youths were starting to create some trouble and disturbance seeking to spoil, what they themselves probably perceived as, posh boys from The Grammar School at play. That old 'class' thing again, slips in everywhere! Anyway, 'The Boss' did his reputation no harm at all on that occasion and upped his respect score amongst us all.

Mr Gillett was a very fit man. Testament to this is that he lived somewhere near The White Tree and he would always walk to school each morning. Now this was a considerable trek along The Downs, then down Blackboy Hill and along the full length of Whiteladies Rd. towards the Victoria Rooms and thence down into Berkeley Square. This would have been some two to three miles in total. As I travelled to school each day on the bus from Henbury, we nearly always passed 'The Boss' each morning striding purposefully along with a rolled umbrella in his right hand. On one occasion, I obtained a lift from a neighbour in his car and as we drove across The Downs I said 'There's my Headmaster, Mr Gillett'. Before I could prevent him, and to my extreme embarrassment, the driver pulled in beside the swiftly walking figure. I would have never DREAMED of approaching him in a thousand years...'Can we give you a lift?'...said my well-intentioned neighbour, turning the handle to lower the car window. I shrivelled up as small as possible into the well of the car...'Nooo, thaaaank yooo veery muuch' droned that distinctive voice 'I prefeer to waaalk'. So, that was Mr Gillett and one of the very few times we were close up, as it were.

I recall too that he was our Divinity teacher when we were in 5B. By now, after five years in the school, we were battle hardened veterans who knew it all...not quite all of us knew it all though... There was a time when, during yet another tedious lesson reading from The Bible (which is ALL we seemed to do in Divinity, figures I suppose!), a boy named John Shaw asked 'The Boss' what all good interviewers in the modern day media would call the hay-maker question.

John Shaw was an interesting boy in himself. He was a giant in stature and already looked about sixteen when he arrived aged eleven at Q.E.H. During my time at Q.E.H. John Shaw bestrode the athletics' and rugby field like a Colossus, setting new record after new record each year in nearly every athletics' 'field' event, shot and javelin to be specific. Indeed, some of the records John Shaw set over fifty years ago still stand. John was indeed a mighty fellow. He was also, thankfully, a gentle and friendly soul who only showed his teeth on the rugby and athletics' fields. Anyway back in the classroom and E.B.P.G.'s Divinity lesson. He was droning on reading some stuff from The Old Testament....middle of lesson....up goes John Shaw's hand...'Yeees?' says 'The Boss'...'Please sir, what's CIRCUMCISION?!'. A sharp intake of collective breath around the room...was John taking the piss out of the great man, how would 'The Boss' react?

Truth is, that, big as he was, old John was naive and he just didn't know what the word meant, as simple as that. Well, without faltering, 'The Boss' enunciated without a hint of embarrassment or fudge 'Weeelll boooy, ittss the rooolllinnng baack aand seecuuring oof tthe skiiin at tthe tiip oof tthe peenis, beecause iin hhoot countriees oone caan ooften geet saand oorrr griit stuuck iin   thaat part oof yoour boody, maaking iit extreeemely uncomfoortable. doo yoou seee?'. Well, most of the rest of us were choking on our suppressed laughter. Old John himself went a bit red and gulped a bit then shrank back into his little desk, looking about as comfortable as any giant squeezed into an area designed for a pygmy! Lovely fella John. After

Q.E.H. he had a very distinguished career in the Police, rising to considerable heights within The Gloucestershire Constabulary. Deputy Chief Constable, or very close!

Among the very few direct encounters I had with E.B.P.G. was after the G.C.E. exams. He saw each boy in the year individually to review their results. I had managed to achieve the magic number of five passes which was the lowest number really acceptable to be allowed to pass on into the sixth form. Trust me, this was a considerable achievement after all that had gone before in the earlier years of struggle. Naturally, I hadn't passed Maths and I asked Mr. Gillett how many marks I had actually obtained in the Maths' Exam. I swear this was the only time I ever saw the man smile as he replied, 'Weel Duutton. I'mm noot alloowed too reeveal thee aactual maark, buut, I wiil teel yoo, iit waas aa siingle fiigure aand onne oof thhe lloweest weeve evver hhad reecorded aat Q.E.H.!!'

A couple of years before this though came one of the great shocks of my Q.E.H. days. It was when my mother was in Africa and I was a temporary boarder (more about this later). One day, I was scratching away at a piece of work in the classroom, minding my own business (or, more likely, minding everyone else's business!) when a messenger entered the room...'Mr. Gillett wants to see Dutton in his study immediately!' Oh God, what had I done, a wave of nausea and fear engulfed me and made my very knees shake as I approached the 'Holy of Holy's'... 'The Boss's Office'. I meekly knocked the door 'Coome inn', that familiar voice intoned through the panels of the black door with its metal ring handle which one twisted to enter. I remember the distinct feeling as I crossed the threshold that my world was about to disintegrate. No need to worry though! There, standing beside 'The Boss' and apparently in friendly, almost jovial conversation, and wearing his familiar white mackintosh, stood none other than...my father!!

(iv)

My elusive father had pitched up at Q.E.H. on a passing visit through Bristol. Without an appointment he must have climbed the broad stone steps rising steeply to the imposing heavy black main entrance doors. It was in front of these doors that school team photos were always taken. Generations of Q.E.H. boys down the years have lined up there, in their respective cricket and rugby teams, their backs to these doors, all neat and tidy and about to enter a forever frozen moment. A moment which thereafter may always hang upon a wall, sit on top of a desk, nestle in an album or at the bottom of a long forgotten box in a cupboard or attic. No moment was prouder for a Q.E.H. boy than being in a school team and to be summoned from his classroom on a summer morning to get changed and report to the steps for a team photo. No prouder moment for *this* Q.E.H. boy at any rate! It marked a defining moment of acceptance and belonging.

My father had only been a fringe figure for a few years prior to this. I had not seen much of him at all. This is hardly surprising as his hurly burly life twisted and turned its way through a few more disasters. As mentioned previously, by the mid fifties, the popularity of Speedway Racing was in dramatic freefall. After reaching some dizzy heights during the golden years, Father had ended up as General Manager of The Wessex Stadium in Weymouth in Dorset. As such, he was promoter of the Greyhound Racing there and team manager of 'The Weymouth Scorchers' Speedway team. In truth, by this time the Public had really had it with Speedway Racing and Father spent the remaining years of his life blowing on its embers in that doomed Stadium on Radipole Lane (which, apart from anything else, was situated too far outside of the town to ever be economically viable even if events had been put on for free). These days the Stadium has undergone significant redevelopment and is now proud home of the Weymouth Town Football Club. In my Dad's day it was, frankly, not much use to anyone.

I'm not too sure of the details of Billy Dutton's love life during this period. However, by the first time I visited him in Weymouth, which must have been in the summer of 1954, he was shacked up in a bungalow with a young girl called Sheila, I'm not saying that my Dad was not interested in gardening but what I remember about that bungalow is that the grass in the garden was growing higher than the roof of the bungalow itself! Once you entered the front gate it was a question of beating your way through the thick stalks of pampas grass in search of a front door. Once inside the bungalow there was the kind (and swollen-bellied Sheila), very fed up with the fact that Father was hardly ever at home. To be fair to him he was working extremely hard at this time in his life trying to keep a sinking ship afloat. He was also seriously buckling his health into the bargain. It is likely that the catastrophic illness which was to kill him within a few years was probably already lurking. What eventually became of Sheila and my unborn half sibling I shall never know…

On that day he rolled into Q.E.H. and was busy charming Mr. Gillett. As I fearfully entered The Boss's Study none of the unpleasant realities of the wretched fellow's existence were evident, although I probably would not have grasped their significance even if they had been.

'Whyy dooon't yoou haave a liittle waalk aroound the driive wiith yoour faather Duutton?' intoned The Boss. So, there it was, me and Dad walking a few times around and around the drive that looped the front banking of the school just inside the large pair of wrought iron main gates set into the outer wall on Jacobs Wells Road.

Can't really remember what we talked about but I know he gave me a ten shilling note, a not inconsiderable sum back then. Such an amount would buy quite a number of 'dandelion and burdocks' from Mrs Barnes' little tuck shop just a few yards up the hill outside the main gates of the school. Q.E.H. boys always packed into there on their way to and from school. 'Ici On Parle Francais' somewhat bizarrely proclaimed a notice stuck on the window of the little door which opened straight onto the counter of the tiny premises. Mrs Barnes herself was a tubby and kindly lady who wore a faded apron but a smile that never faded. This was amazing considering the constant heaving crush of boys of all shapes and sizes thrusting their pennies and halfpennies towards her. Yes, you could purchase a halfpenny dandelion and burdock too! This was HALF a glass of the bubbling sweet liquid as opposed to a FULL glass which cost a penny. Once you emptied your glass, Mrs Barnes would swivel around and dip the dirty glass into a small sink, give it a rapid swipe with a very suspect looking tea towel she had draped over her wrist. Then she plonked the clean glass back on the counter ready for the next order! Today's Health and Safety Police would swoon and pass out were they ever to encounter such an establishment as 'Ma Barnes' (as we called it).

We, of course were completely oblivious to such modern day notions of what constitutes good hygiene. Like most youngsters of today would be probably if they were not so cossetted and protected. Bring back Ma Barnes, never did me any harm... as far as I know!!

(v)

Throughout my Q.E.H. years I made many good friends, some of whom have lasted me a lifetime and who all, to coin a phrase, have a special place in my heart. Barry 'Pancho' Coombs, Robin Thomas and latterly Robin Bown have all remained pretty well hitched to my wagon as the years have rolled along. I suppose my best pal throughout my Q.E.H. years was Keith (Ram) Cockram.

Ram and I were in the same Form and were both good yard footballers. Some say that Ram was the greatest of them all, definitely during my time.

He certainly had a good footballing pedigree and captained his Junior School, Bedminster Down, when they won the Bristol Junior School's Trophy in 1951.

Ram was really the quintessential Q.E.H. boy whom the founder of the school John Carr may have had in mind when, back in the sixteenth century, he endowed his school 'for the education of impoverished young boys and orphans'. Ram was born and brought up in The 'Dings' area of Bristol close to The Old Market, one of the poorest areas of Bristol. His mother died when he was four and he was brought up by his grandmother ('ar Gran', Keith never lost his Bristol accent or his idiomatic speech). His father was a shadowy person in Keith's upbringing and yet was a familiar figure for dozens of years selling newspapers from his pitch at the bottom of the 'Incline', that stretch of sloping approach road to the imposing facade of Isambard Kingdom Brunel's distinctive Temple Meads Railway Station. This station is an architectural gem. The view of it from the bottom of 'The Incline' forever imprinted onto the minds of all Bristolians whether arriving late or early for their trains, whether strolling or dashing, whether greeting or saying farewells...Temple Meads Station, just there, just permanent. At the bottom of 'The Incline' proffering his copies of 'The Evening Post and 'The Evening World', croaking his unintelligible 'Pote 'n Wud, Evnin' Paypa' was Ram Cockram's Dad!

By the time Keith arrived at Q.E.H. he was a very streetwise eleven year old having had to learn to look after himself growing up in the streets around The Old Market where most folks 'knew a thing or two'. Keith was singled out whilst at junior school by virtue of both being brainy and disadvantaged. He found himself getting a scholarship place as a boarder at Q.E.H.

He told me of his first night sleeping in the school in the same dormitory as all the other new arrivals, many of whom were crying for their mothers and their

Me with my pal 'Ram' Cockram.

familiar home comforts..'never bothered me 'Ar, I never had a mother anyway'. Being bright and good at sport Keith soon established himself at Q.E.H., although he felt the weight of the school's traditions to be a considerable embarrassment at times. None more so than the wearing of the boarders' uniform....the breeches, yellow socks and gown. Every Sunday all the Boarders walked in a crocodile down Park Street to The Lord Mayor's Chapel for morning service. This was prior to being allowed home for the rest of the day before returning to the school in the evening. Keith could not bear the embarrassment of being seen amongst his old pals and associates back in 'The Dings' 'dressed like a bleedin' girl, they'd all die laughing at me Ar'. In order to by-pass this perceived shame Keith would have a small bundle of his own clothes concealed under his gown as the Boarders made their way down the steep slope of Park St. before the curious gazes of locals and visitors alike out on the Bristol Streets on a Sunday morning. We had to sit in that lovely little Chapel (yes, me too during the time I was a Boarder), sing a couple of hymns, listen to some bible readings and endure the usual sort of boring sermon which, in total, amounted to nothing much that I could ever discern at any rate. Emerging into the bright sunshine from the cool shadowed interior of the chapel was always a shock. There was a general milling around of gowns and yellow stockings as bearings were obtained and the rapid dispersals homewards began.

It was at this point that Ram found his own little secret doorway in Denmark Street alongside the stage door entrance to The Bristol Hippodrome. This was a quiet and deserted place on a Sunday morning after the comings and goings of the 'stars', all the lesser 'darlings' in the cast and no doubt the fans ('stage door johnnies' as they were called in those days) who would have been swirling around the night before. Here then, Ram Cockram would discard his boarders' uniform and put on the clothes he had concealed in the bag he had secreted, replacing his uniform back into the same bag. Now, his appearance 'normal', he would either walk or catch a bus from the adjacent Tramways Centre to 'Ar Gran's 'ouse', near Old Market.

Keith had no parental guidance and Q.E.H. was totally bereft in those days of any kind of Careers' Advice or assistance whatsoever. As a result Keith left Q.E.H. at the first opportunity and after one or two rather ordinary jobs he did a stint in the Fire Service and eventually he held a job in an engineering firm for many years. Not a failure then by any means but a great deal of potential wasted really. These days he would have stayed into the Sixth Form and undoubtedly gone to University and then who knows.

Ram had a wicked sense of humour. On one summer's occasion, there was a roll call of boarders at our playing fields at Eastfield on a Saturday afternoon. These compulsory attendances were hated by boarders and the majority were not much impressed by the fact that this particular occasion was the annual clash with arch rivals Bristol Grammar School. The deal was that the Boarders were required to remain until one innings was completed and then they were free to go. Q.E.H. batted first and collapsed disastrously within about an hour and a half to around 80 for 9. This was thanks chiefly to the skills of their demon one eyed (literally) spin bowler Bill Redwood (who later went on to play rugby for Bristol and England). All the Boarders were sensing an early release from their compulsory tedium and when the game reached this stage they were milling expectantly around the gates in anticipation of a mass early breakout. Bill Redwood stood on a hat-trick and Q.E.H.'s no 11 advanced to take his guard at the wicket. Now this no.11 was none other folks than one Harry Dutton who by this stage of his Q.E.H. career was a regular member of the School Cricket 1st X1 (as a bowler you may surmise!). The cunning Redwood ambled up to tweak his magic, I shakily concentrated as best I could. Then across the cricket Square floated the unmistakable Bristolian voice of Ram Cockram from amongst the dense black gowned horde pressing at the exit gate...'miss it 'Ar, please!'. This I did, though unintentionally, in spite of later suggestions to he contrary! Before the bails had hit the ground a huge cheer went up from the mob as it burst through the gates and headed gratefully and speedily off down the path which led to Westbury-On-Trym or along the track beside the field of The Clifton Rugby Club and thence out onto The Eastfield Rd.

Once Q.E.H. was done with I sort of lost touch with Ram for most of our working lives. We met again in more recent years and swopped memories over some pints. By then he had grown into a large inactive fellow with early arthritis and some mobility difficulties. He had a very matter of fact view of Q.E.H., acknowledging that he had benefited from the start it had given him in life in spite of his distinctly unpromising beginnings. 'I always liked the place 'Ar, did a lot for me, I just wished someone had told me what would have been best for me before I left but no-one seemed to care, so I just went me own way like'.

So, that was my good pal Ram. A year or so ago he went into hospital for a minor procedure and (according to the Docs) had an aneurysm of some sort and died right there and then on the operating table. Such a bastard this life at times.

(vi)

Two of the Masters I encountered at Q.E.H. made lasting impressions. One of them was possibly the very worst teacher I ever came across and the other probably the best. 'Piggy' Hoggett, the psychopath from Yorkshire, signs in as the worst and handsome, urbane, witty 'Archie' Preston was a great guy and one of the best. Archie was one of the finest natural communicators I've encountered. Something of a contrast between these two then! 'Piggy' took us for Geography and Archie for History. To experience a lesson with first one, who frankly terrified us, and then the other, especially on the same day, was to board a roller coaster of educational extremism, unusual even within the thick walls of Q.E.H., where many odd things went into the general mix.

'Piggy' Hoggett succeeded a Master named Mr. Thatcher as Head of Geography. This Mr. Thatcher always struck me as a somewhat irascible character and I remember being quite pleased when we learned that he was to be moving on to another post in the Southampton area. Since Geography was one of my stronger cards in what was still overall a pretty weak hand, I thought that a new Master would be an improvement. Not since the lookout on *The Titanic* wasn't really concentrating could there have been such an error...

'Piggy' Hoggett was wonderfully named with both his appearance and his surname exactly encapsulating his swinish nature. He had a squat build with a perfectly square shaped head and close cropped hair and the most perfect little piggy style, squinty glasses you ever saw. When he spoke it was in the flat nasal manner of 'the northerner' (at least that's how a northern accent always strikes the southern ear)....'Naw, boyse, tuday, weere, gowin' to consider agricultchur on the faw main islands of Japan, tek owt your exercise boooks and pay clowse attenshun!'. Trouble was that old 'Piggy' was just a time bomb waiting to go off and it wasn't long before we were all cowed by his towering temper tantrums which could kick off at any moment. Seriously, it was horrible when he started screaming and shouting, almost foaming at the mouth. He was nuts of course but we weren't really trained to think that nuts really could have been nuts in those days. Today probably, a teacher like 'Piggy' would be escorted away trembling from the classroom before he could get his chalk out of his pocket (except he wouldn't have any chalk, as using chalk nowadays would no doubt be a Health and Safety issue).

Mostly then, in Piggy's lessons you just made yourself as small as you could and prayed that his attention never focused on you. It was never long though before something lit his fuse. We boys got to know some familiar trigger phrases. When Piggy said something like 'I doo my best to bee veree reesnable with yoo booys, but yoo alwaays let me down'. Whenever you heard him say something like this you knew he was about to detonate and you squeezed yourself into as small, tight and frozen a form as you could. Didn't really matter though really as literally *anything* could send his voice into a grunting screech and distort his snout with fury. Things came to a head with old Piggy though one day when he finally completely freaked out. The penny dropped with his employers too that day that he really belonged in a straitjacket and not in the classroom.

It happened like this. Brian Winsen, a day boy in our class, had not only not completed his homework but, an even more serious offence in the view of a madman, he had *ruled the margin in his book in ink and not in pencil*!!....'I downt beeleev it', said Piggy...'No matte 'ow reesonable I am, boyse like yoo disobaaye'. By now, he's hovering over Brian Winsen in the manner of a boxer about to deliver a knock out. Piggy momentarily restrained himself and strode to the front of the classroom where he stood incandescent with rage. He beckoned George 'Inky' Wills to the front and said 'Wills, gow to the 'edmaster and tell 'im to send me the biggest cane 'ees got in order to beat a boy!'.

George Wills, as aforementioned, an indescribably scruffy and inky boarder with wild hair and little squinty glasses of his own, set off towards 'The Boss's Office'. A total and expectant silence enveloped the room as we anticipated the drama ahead (perhaps, even then, a very deep down stirring in me of pleasure in the fact that it was not me who was going to get 'bashed'. At that age I didn't recognise 'schadenfreude' in myself but it's always been there throughout my life as a matter of fact if I'm honest!)

Anyway, after about ten minutes George re-entered. 'Well, boy, what did the 'edmaster say?', demanded the Pig. Now, in one of my best ever Q.E.H. moments George 'Inky' Wills went to the very top of the popularity poll and became thereafter, simply, a legend. Fixing 'Piggy' with a level stare which seemed for a moment like the duel of the squinty glasses, George said bravely and calmly 'The Headmaster says you can't have the cane Sir and you have to stop being silly and he will be coming up in a few minutes'. There was a mass exhalation of breath from the rest of us. What drama! No one ever did such straight talking, especially to a Master and especially publicly puncturing the Pig's hot air balloon in such a manner. Good on you 'Boss', good on you George 'Inky' Wills!! Stopped the nutter in his tracks!

Anyway, 'Piggy' never really recovered from this humiliation and, as indicated, he was shortly exited from the school, to the funny farm perhaps or who knows where. Maybe even back to Yorkshire; Leeds to be precise, perhaps they would understand him a little better there....

One thing I should have mentioned though about old Piggy. He did successfully implement and practise the unfashionable teaching method of 'learning through terror'. What Piggy hammered home, you learned, trust me! To this day I can recite the names of the four main islands of Japan, without a pause and straight off the bat. 'Hokkaido, Honshu, Shikoku and Kyushu'! Piggy taught me that! Perhaps there was a method in his madness after all!

(vii)

Tony 'Archie' Preston (never did know how he acquired the nickname 'Archie') was in his twenties and a handsome fellow. He had straight long black hair which flopped over his forehead and regular features with an aquiline nose and slightly deep set eyes. His manner was always brisk and business-like and he had a line in classroom management and communication which was unique. Quite simply with a blend of wit, mannerisms and approach he made the content of his subject (History) not only interesting but fun. He also had a brilliant skill to swiftly cover the blackboard with sketches, plans or maps to illustrate whatever he was explaining. This would be Archie on the system of European Alliances before the outbreak of World War 1...'So Archduke Ferdinand got 'bumped off' by a fed-up student called Princip... so those Austrians were very glum about this, they turned to their pals the Germans and said... we'm in a lot of bother and the Germans said, well don't fret pals 'cus 'we'em with you', plus our friends those Eyeties, 'cus we'em all in The Triple Alliance together'. Well, those Serbs weren't going to put up with that, so they turned to their mates The Russkies and said... 'help us out will you pals' and The Russkies said 'no problem, we'll get those Froggies from France to pile in too'. Well, The Frenchies called up their pals in Britain and said... 'hey, come and help us and The Russkies sort out these Germans, Austrians and Eyties'. 'We'em with you' said the British, 'we're all together girls anyway in The Triple Entente, so naturally we'em going to help each other out. Sorted!'

Now, such a delivery was somewhat racy and would be impossible in these politically correct days but we lapped it up. Such a description delivered in such a manner would be backed up though with accurate board work and references to the text-book. Archie never tried to mess with the facts he just weaved them into a cocktail that was readily and easily digestible. Add in his natural wit and balanced friendly manner and you had one extremely effective teacher. Archie certainly accelerated my own interest and enthusiasm for History. To be fair he was pushing at an open door as far as I was concerned but I never forgot his little sayings and tactics in the classroom and shamelessly incorporated them into my own style when I started teaching.

an iron fist inside the velvet glove

Not that Archie was a 'pushover' by any means as far as discipline was concerned. He generally maintained good order through the respect we had for him and the excellence of his lessons but he was quite capable of occasionally showing that there was an iron fist inside the velvet glove. He had a habit of cracking any miscreants on the top of their heads with the edge of a foot ruler. Since I got cracked once or twice I can testify to the fact that it hurt in a very special way and nearly always made my eyes water.

Archie was 'human' too. We had evidence of this one summer evening when the word flashed around the Boarders in the long dormitory that 'Archie's out on The Tump (what we called Brandon Hill) with *a girl*!!'. Now there was a good view straight out over the two Upper walls onto Brandon Hill from our dormitories at Q.E.H. Within seconds every bed was empty and bodies scrambled to the narrow ledges beneath the recessed dorm windows in order to get a glimpse of Archie and his girl friend. Archie was probably just teasing us anyway by walking along one of the paths which circulated around the hill in the knowledge that it would stir up a right storm amongst us testosterone fuelled but sex starved young fellows.

Girls of course were always talked about and thought about but this was a totally female-less environment and we existed on stories about exploits of a sexual nature a few had had during the last holidays or, the lucky few, may have already had a girl friend they saw during the hours we spent at home on a Sunday afternoon. There was no sex education as such at Q.E.H., although our Science Master 'Mac' McClarnon did once refer in a Biology lesson to the fact that... 'I expect you boys know something about how the sperm is passed between the male and the female in human beings!' KNOW about it!! It's just about all we EVER talked about (that and football, rugby and cricket of course.) Anyway 'Mac' McClarnon's casual remark was just about the sum total of our sex education at Q.E.H.

Masturbation (wanking) of course was widespread and also a regular topic of conversation. It was widely believed amongst the boarders that one of the perils of wanking was that you would end up with 'The Doom'. This was simply the belief that if you wanked too much you would go past what would be called today 'the tipping point' and *you would never be able to stop for the rest of your life*! I suppose it turned out to be one belief with a certain amount of veracity if most of the male species look at things honestly!

Other rumours circulated too. It was widely believed that there would be an annual medical inspection given to all the boys by the assistant matron who was the only young female one ever (rarely) saw around Q.E.H. Part of this inspection was to see if you had a normal erection ('Brute' as we called it), so the assistant matron would conduct the inspection topless. Well, this rumour went around and around, never did turn out to be true... which is something of a shame looking back!

Another event that caused a dormitory cluster was a boxing match. Not, as it happens, between any of us boys although fights were by no means unknown amongst lads where establishing precedence was a recurring issue. No, this was the summer of 1955 and somehow we had a radio in the dormitory and we listened deep in the small hours of a July night to the commentary on the World Heavyweight match between Rocky Marciano and Britain's Don Cockell. Eamonn Andrews was the commentator with inter-round summaries by W. Barrington Dalby. In the days when sound radio was (just about) still 'King' it was always Eamonn Andrews and Barrington Dalby who did the boxing commentaries. On this summer's night their familiar voices crackled through from New York, sadly, of course only to tell a familiar tale. The tale of yet another hopeless and hapless challenge from a British Heavy-weight for the premier of all boxing titles. Marciano ('The Rock') was unbeatable, literally unbeatable in his entire career as a professional boxer, one of the greatest of them all. Anyway, Don Cockell found himself looking up at Marciano from the ring floor after about five rounds. Back in the long dormitory at Q.E.H. we slunk disappointed off back to our beds within only a couple of hours before we heard the familiar clap of the hands from Mr. Mansell our 'Marshal'. Mr Mansell lived in the little gatehouse at the main entrance to the school and who (being ex-military) was well versed in dealing with young males in a brisk, efficient and not unkindly manner. When The Marshal clapped his hands at around seven each morning...you had best get on with it boys!

(viii)

Two huge rooms dominate the entire length of the central floor of the Q.E.H. building. To call them rooms is a misnomer. They are in fact high ceilinged Halls in their own right. One is The Dining Room the other named The School Room. These Halls are connected by a short corridor upon which is found The Headmaster's Office, Staff Rooms and two or three other smaller side rooms.

The Dining Room in my day contained four very long wooden dining tables, each running parallel to another to the centre of the room, then a space of some ten yards before a second table of exact similar size ran the remainder of the length of the room, again parallel to its three companions. Overall then four parallel lines of wooden tables stretching the entire thirty or so yards of the Dining Room with a decent gap at the centre. This room was used for feeding, assemblies, music lessons in the choir stalls at one end, even lessons themselves if only a few pupils were involved (generally a couple of sixth formers doing 'Classics' with Syd Bowen, the diminutive and bespectacled Classics Master who always looked frightened to death).

There was a dumb waiter in the central section of the Dining Room in which piles of food in their rectangular tin dishes clanked up and down in the almost impossible task of fully satisfying the hunger of rapidly growing boys. The Dining Room's sense of being enshrined into the history of the school was reinforced by the walls adorned with photographs of entire school populations of yesteryear. All of these photographs were dated and went back in time to the beginnings of the mastery of large group photography. This being somehow appropriate in a school attended, in the nineteenth century, by William Frieze Green (one of the pioneers of moving pictures, folks!). Also adorning the walls were many 'Roll of Honour' boards with the names recorded year by successive year of the notables of the past. I always used to feel a little surge of pride when regarding the board of 'Captains Of The School' and there recorded '1944-1945. M.A.Stephens'. This was my Steve who I thought of as my elder brother and who had been so instrumental in getting me into Q.E.H. in the first place. After a while I stopped going on to others about him being my brother as it was obviously not strictly true. Our connection was all a little difficult to explain. In later life when describing Steve to people and the part he played in the life of my family, I always described him as 'Steve, my 'sort of' brother', This always seemed to just about cover it! So, that was The Dining Room, soggy with Q.E.H. history and the ingrained remains of tons of food grease here and there embedded along the seams of those long wooden tables.

The School Room in my day featured even more ancient year group photographs and Honours' Boards. Also, it was filled with desks, not individual desks but long blocks of continuous desking with lids which, when raised, afforded small amounts of recessed spaces, each space having an owner to store his books and property. In my day it was always the sixth formers who actually held the ownership of these desks although small classes were also conducted and each evening at Prep every boarder would file in to sit at them for the hour and a half of Prep (here, note the aping of the Public School terminology). 'Prep' was always conducted in monastic silence under the control of one Master. However there were an awful lot of illegalities going on in that silence which were not always exactly monk-like. For a start there was a flourishing bartering of foodstuffs (chocolate at a premium, sweets preferably without crinkling wrappers, a close second). Then there was a good trade in 'crib sheets' going on; a crib sheet being a perfect set of answers, diagrams, formulae even complete essays...just about whatever was required to perfect and improve your own efforts. It was the ideal solution for the lazy and the dim and it was never long before I was seeking a crib sheet, certainly when maths or science were on the prep agenda! Besides that, using a 'crib sheet' would then allow time for much more pleasant pastimes. Overwhelming favourite was 'book cricket'. You had two little identically shaped hexagonal metal rolling cylinders. You rolled one and when it stopped the upside surface would indicate a number...1 or 2 or 3 or 4 (no number 5) 6 or 'OWZAT!. The figure shown would just be added to the batsman's total runs exactly as in a cricket scorebook. If 'OWZAT!' came up, then the second hexagonal cylinder would be rolled. On it's six tiny surfaces were engraved all the methods of getting 'out' in cricket...'bowled', 'caught', 'lbw', 'stumped', 'run out' and finally 'not out'. So, there was a one in six chance of surviving the appeal! Otherwise, again as in a cricket scorebook, the batsman's fate would be recorded.

Now, the beauty of this wonderful clever little game was you could keep your own neat little scorebook and indulge your fantasies as you felt... In my scorebook a typical match would be between England and Australia and the England batting line up would be:

Washbrook	Compton
Hutton	May
Ikin	Statham
Edrich	Truman
DUTTON	Tyson
Graveney	

Needless to say, all the England players would have their scores accurately recorded according to the random rollings of the hexagonal cylinders, but somehow DUTTON would always be top scorer! Could this be possibly because when OWZAT! came face up during his innings, then should the answering cylinder *not* come up 'NOT OUT' then the roller of the cylinders would say to himself... 'will have to do that roll again as the desk top was moving' or 'must roll again as someone jogged my arm'. Anyway, as a consequence of this method Dutton usually 'carried his bat' through every innings and frequently notched up double hundreds just for fun!

Dutton would always be top scorer

Now, the same scorebook would show the following when The Aussies batted....

Hassett	bowled Truman	5
Miller	lbw DUTTON	0
Harvey	bowled DUTTON	21
Davidsen	lbw Tyson	43
Craig	bowled DUTTON	15

And so on, and so on—you get the idea!

Trust me, I kept a really full and neat 'scorebook' for my 'book cricket' and played out quite a few Test Series during Prep time at Q.E.H. Come to think of it, that scorebook was by far the best piece of work I think I ever really produced inside those thick hallowed walls!

Once Prep was over, out would come the 'Shove Halfpenny' Boards. These large rectangular pieces of thin smooth shiny board were placed flat onto desktops; they were often crudely marked out as miniature football pitches. The goals at either end were four small nails, their points bent over with pliers as they protruded through the board. Then, with each player having a simple six-inch ruler, one would take it in turns to push his own penny coin at the halfpenny coin which was the ball in this game. So, simple, you shoved at the halfpenny with your penny to score between the goalpost nails. The skill levels were often exceptional and some boys acquired reputations as great players of this simple and nowadays largely forgotten game that gave so much pleasure.

Also in the School Room were notice boards showing the teams for approaching fixtures. There was always a huge crush around these boards when notices were first put up to see if you were picked for the next game. This could be either for The School Team or perhaps The House Team (rivalry between the four Houses at Q.E.H. was always very intense and serious). The Houses were named after four of the school's principal benefactors... Carr's (John Carr, the school's founder), Birds (William Bird), Ramseys (Lady Mary Ramsey) and Hartnells (Samuel Hartnell). I was in Birds. Personally, it was only the posting of the cricket teams which ever involved or interested me. Towards the end of my time at Q.E.H. I was already playing football regularly for a team outside of school altogether.

At the head of the School Room, on one side if the door was the notorious 'LINE'. This was no more than a long crack running along the floorboarding but it was where you could be sent to stand (still and facing forward, often for quite long periods) for any real or perceived piece of indiscipline. This was a horrible punishment, probably considered very effective by the Masters and Prefects on whose orders you stood on The Line! It deprived you of your freedom throughout breaks and dinner times. (Lunchtimes had not been invented in those days!)

On the other side of the doorway at the front of the School Room was the ten foot long triangular Reading Stand, upon which were spread out the daily newspapers (only the best ones of course were considered fit reading for we Q.E.H. gentlemen). Consequently spread along the Reading Stand were *The Times*, *The Manchester Guardian*, *The Western Daily Press* and perhaps, just perhaps, a paper like *The Daily Express* or *The Daily Mail*.

As aforementioned, I think my Dad passed on his paper-reading genes to me as I was always one of the fewer younger boys who went most days to have twenty minutes with the papers. I would read the editorials in *The Times* on most days even at a young age. (*The Thunderer* then was still very much a broadsheet and had only announcements and advertisements on its front page.)

Not totally surprising then when I won my one and only ever prize at Q.E.H. Once a year one afternoon lesson was scrapped and the whole school did a test in 'Current Affairs and Civics'. The test levels were set as appropriate for each year group. There was a prize for each year for 'The W.H. Coward Award For Current Affairs and Civics'. Blow me down, Harry Dutton was becoming a right 'anorak' as he won the prize for his year! The book I chose was a war escape epic called *The Long Walk* by Slavomir Ravitzch. It was about a group of escapees who walked across the Gobi Desert and endured deprivations of all sorts. They later discovered that it was all a fraud. (Not that this reduced my pride in gaining a prize.) A prize at Q.E.H.!! Shiver my timbers!

I remember on that Prize Day (big business in the Q.E.H. calendar), my prize was presented by Sir Peter Scott, artist, author and naturalist, the son of Robert Falcon Scott, the Antarctic Explorer. He was quite the most famous person I had ever met!

(ix)

As aforementioned, rugby was never my 'lady' at Q.E.H. It was cricket that turned out to be my magic carpet and perhaps above all else cemented me into the place. Prior to going to Q.E.H. I had only a nodding acquaintance with the game, which had never progressed much beyond a tennis ball and an old milk churn for some wickets in the back lane alongside 121 Stoke Lane where I was born. The game was not taught or played in my primary school by my recall, so that hadn't helped. Since the only sport at Oscar Dahl's Crescent School had been 'Whacko', by the time I arrived at Q.E.H. I'd never really had much opportunity to play the game at all. Two events changed that... well, one event and one person, actually. The event was in 1953, when we were given a day off school to go to The County Ground in Bristol to see a day's play between the visiting Australian Touring side and Gloucestershire, our own county side. It's fair to say I think that most Bristolians consider Gloucestershire to be their cricket county, although probably those Bristolians born south of The River Avon may have more allegiance to Somerset.

Tom Graveney was my idol

Be that as it may, on this particular spring morning droves of Q.E.H. boys, both boarders and dayboys alike, made their way up The Gloucester Road and thence along Neville Road to The County Ground. This first real game of cricket I had ever seen made a tremendous impression on me. This was the Aussie team led by Lyndsay Hassett and including such cricket icons as Neil Harvey, Keith Miller and Richie Benaud (although they weren't icons then, just young and brilliant athletes). When those Aussies came out onto the field as a team a half an hour before the game and commenced to do some fielding and catching my eyes were on stalks. These fellows in their floppy green caps whizzed the ball around amongst themselves in dazzling style. Don't really recall how this particular match turned out, probably the Aussies won easily as they usually steamrollered most county sides. What I do remember though was that as I made my way home with my socks down and my yellow splodged Q.E.H. cap slipping sideways on my head (it was a school rule for day boys that you always kept your cap on in public), was this... it was going to be cricket for me from now on! I kept the creased up scorecard of that day for a long while afterwards. Indeed, I made many subsequent visits to see Gloucestershire play at the County Ground. In the 1950's they had a colourful and powerful team... George Emmett, Martin Young, Jack Crapp, The Graveney brothers. All these were names to 'conjure with' as the saying goes. Tom Graveney was my idol. Tall, relaxed and elegant, his flowing bat, whether easing the ball through the covers or playing his trademark late cut, was always a joy to the eye. Tom had that priceless asset of all really class players in all sports—he simply always had time to go through his repertoire and the ability to make it all seem so easy.

The person who accelerated my cricket development dramatically was a Master at Q.E.H. called Ken Carr. During regular Games' afternoons at Eastfield, there were a number of cricket games going on around the field—as usual, in Q.E.H. fashion, divided up by ability. The very best players though and candidates for the school teams used to be extracted for practice in the nets. Ken Carr was umpiring in one of the fringe games going on when he must have thought I had some potential as a bowler. He called and told me: 'Dutton, go and report to Mr. Tandy in the nets—tell him I sent you.' Ron Tandy was Head of Physical Education at Q.E.H. throughout my time—and just about through absolutely *everybody* else's time too as a matter of fact, as he taught at the school for around forty years! (Last I heard he was still going strong in his retirement down in Devon—good for him!)

I remember Ron lobbing me a ball and ordering me to 'throw a few down in this net Dutton'. The batsman at that time in 'this net' was a boy named Trevor Brookes. He was really the top gun batter of our age group and he had an unusual style of patting his bat in the crease during the bowler's approach and as the bowler was almost at the point of delivery he would raise his bat perpendicularly as the ball was in the air and then move quickly into his stroke. As a matter of fact, the only other batsman I ever saw adopting this style was the great Graeme Gooch of Middlesex and England. I saw Gooch bat on television countless times in later years and whenever I did so my mind always flashed back to Trevor Brookes and that day in the nets at Eastfield. Nice lad, Trevor. We thought of him as a bit posh, only because he didn't have much of a Bristol accent and it was rumoured that he had been coached in his batting. From this it was deduced he must be from a more favourable background than most of the rest of us.

Anyway, I duly pitched one down to him and it plucked out his off stump! To this day I can hear Ron Tandy's 'Cluck' of approval from behind me. To coin a phrase, 'the rest is history'—certainly true as far as my cricket career at Q.E.H was concerned. Throughout the rest of my time at the school I progressed as a member of the school cricket team. This culminated, in 1957, in playing regularly for The First XI. Apart from the status being in the school team afforded, there were the away fixtures that provided the opportunity to visit some extremely impressive other schools. These were Downside (the second largest Catholic Public School in England after Ampleforth), then Prior Park School, Bath (situated deliciously at the head of one of the valleys overlooking Bath and with magnificent views as you took tea on the terrace), Queen's School, Taunton and King's School, Bruton. Also The Crypt School, Gloucester and Cardiff High School and significant others in Bristol itself... amongst them Colston's School, Bristol Grammar

School, St Brendan's School and Bristol Cathedral School. It's true I was an impressionable young fellow but going to visit schools such as these as a part of *the* Q.E.H. school team impressed me deeply. What a softy I am!

One thing, though—of all the souvenir bits and pieces scattered around and on my desk in my dining room (each item actually leading a little trail through my entire life should anyone ever be interested enough to follow it), the closest to being most valued is my Q.E.H. 1st XI Cap. It's somewhat mangled and sweat-stained, but having said that, it really is all of my Q.E.H story, right there!

(x)

Being both a dayboy and a boarder at Q.E.H. was almost a unique experience. Looking back, it undoubtedly rounded out my perspectives of the school.   Although there was a commonality of overall experience for dayboys and boarders alike, there was also a significant difference between going home each evening to your own family circumstance, as a dayboy did, and living your life almost totally inside a narrow environment and squeezed-up social system which was the experience of the boarder.

It was rare that a pupil would be both dayboy and boarder during his passage through the school. When my mother went to Southern Rhodesia she pulled off yet another of her magic manoeuvres by persuading Mr. Gillett to take me as a boarder during her absence. This turned out to be for two terms in 1955. Although mother was away for a year she had prearranged that, when not living at Q.E.H., I would be looked after as a shared responsibility between my newly married sister, my elder brother Allan (by now the young doctor with a growing family in Sheffield) and my mother's brother, Uncle Allan (as if the poor man didn't have enough on his plate with caring for Auntie Daisy, his chronically mentally ill wife).

It was around the mid-fifties that 'teenagers' were really invented. This was the time of the first rush and infusion of pop culture. Young people elevated by virtue of a little more money in their pockets to a special place in the aim of manufacturers and marketing men. A place just for them, characterised by fashion they could call their own, music they could call their own and, perhaps above all, an 'attitude' they could call their own. In short, the birth pangs of popular culture. These days popular culture has grown like a giant poison ivy to dictate and to dominate what is held to be important in the world. Most of it sucks in my view! Now you would think that the fine young fellows wearing the mustard stockings and the medieval gowns of

Q.E.H. would have been immune from the rising tides of the teenager and his newly found indulgent tastes. Wrong!

One summer's afternoon, along with my pal Ram Cockram and in our boarder's uniforms, we raised our own little flag of rebellion! We should have been going on the bus to Westbury and thence walk to the playing fields at Eastfield. On this occasion we sneaked off the bus at Clifton Down Station and walked back a few hundred yards to the Whiteladies Cinema. There, that very afternoon, we commenced our own lives as 'teenagers'.

The film was 'The Blackboard Jungle' with a young teacher, Richard Daladier, doing his best to succeed in a tough High School in New York. Daladier was played by Glenn Ford (always one of my very favourite film stars) and the part of the leader of his rebellious pupils was played by Vic Morrow.

The plot was peripheral to the effect on the two begowned Q.E.H. boys hunkering down secretively into their seats, aware that they would face considerable retribution if their truancy was discovered. What *was* absolutely central though, folks, were the first bars of the highly amplified music playing across the credits as they flickered across the screen. The rasping voice of Bill Haley, the pumping beat, the potent suggestion of the lyric... the atmosphere and sheer magic of it all enthralled us and fixed us into those seats with permanent exciting arrows...

> One, two, three o'clock, four o'clock rock
> Five, six, seven o'clock, eight o'clock rock
> Nine, ten, eleven o'clock, twelve o'clock rock
> We're gonna rock around the clock tonight

It was around the mid-fifties too that coffee bars became fashionable. Coffee had hitherto been a decidedly uninteresting beverage. The coffee we had always drunk came in a small bottle as a brown syrupy liquid. On the bottle's label was featured a turbaned gentleman proffering a tray on which stood two steaming cups of coffee. Nowadays, even the label wouldn't pass the politically correct standard let alone an actual coffee being named 'Camp'. Whatever next! Be that as it may, coffee was becoming much more fashionable and 'coffee bars' were sprouting up all over Bristol. They served a new type of coffee dispensed by a hissing and steaming machine. Yes, the cappuccino had arrived and coffee bars soon became the meeting places for the young and

coffee bars became fashion-able

trendy. What better as a signal of independence and adulthood than to be able to wander out of school at lunch times and head for a coffee bar? School caps would be stuffed inside of pockets and the tiny 'windsor' knot of your slim jim tie would be loosened. Then, out would come a packet of cigarettes. Now, feeling very grown up indeed one sipped and puffed away. With two of my close pals Robin Thomas and Colin Townsend this became the lunchtime ritual during my final months at Q.E.H.

The nearest coffee bar was 'The Bolero' on Queen's Road. This was little more than a converted cellar where the smoke was soon so thick you could hardly see the person you were talking to. This mattered not. It was the fact that you were *there* which was important. Sometimes we ventured further afield down Park Street to 'The Continental' or 'The Bali'. The outside world was really tugging hard now.

Things really never were *quite* the same ever again! Although I didn't really understand it at the time, the last year or so I spent at Q.E.H. was a process of gradual detachment and preparation for the life ahead.

We sat our G.C.E. exams in the school library, which, for some obscure reason, was situated at the very top of the building. The library was reached by climbing a steep stairwell. Nothing like making all the library books accessible... put them up in the clouds somewhere. Strange! Anyway, we climbed up those stairs to do our exams and I staggered through to passes in five subjects—English Language and English Literature, History, Geography and French. (Here I should offer a belated thanks to a boy named Barry Anstey who sat alongside me in the narrow aisles of the library where the desks were arranged. He allowed me to copy some stuff off him in the French exam—thanks Bar!)

So, I just squeaked into the sixth form to start 'A' levels. Looking back I foolishly quit Q.E.H. after about six months in the sixth form. This was partly because I was finding the actual work hard and partly financial. My mum was home and we were living in our prefab on the Henleaze Road. Frankly, the money problems which were endemic with my dear mother were once again lapping around our feet. I had a paper round but eighteen shillings a week wasn't much of a contribution to the family budget. Besides, I wanted to have a record player and to be able to buy the records of my new idols—Elvis Presley, Jerry Lee Lewis, Roy Orbison and Little Richard. I wanted also to buy a lovely blue flecked woollen Harris Tweed jacket I had my eye on displayed in the shop window of Hector Powe's Men's Outfitters half way down Park Street. In short, I needed a job in order to live a life—a not unusual circumstance really!

Leaving Q.E.H. and not carrying on with my 'A' Levels was probably a mistake but I think I eventually covered over this error of judgement one way or another. Also leaving Q.E.H. was against the advice of my English Master at the time—the legendary Richard 'Gobby' Hall who advised me to remain at school. Old 'Gobby' gave me a piece of advice actually which has resonated with me down the years on numerous occasions. He said, 'You're an engaging fellow, Dutton, but you show too much of your personality too quickly to others.' True, Mr. Hall, without a doubt.

There was one final flourish at Q.E.H. before I left. I undertook an acting role in the school production of *The Critic* by Sheridan. Cast as Mr. Sneer in this Comedy of Manners, I recall getting a few laughs with the few lines I had to deliver. It was quite a buzz prancing around in a powdered wig and breeches and peering at everyone through a pince-nez. This experience ignited an interest in 'performing' which was to develop a lot more in the years ahead. As the Master who directed this production (Richard 'Quiffer' Deighton) remarked, 'You did pretty well Dutton... considering.' Come to think of it, not a bad epitaph overall for my Q.E.H. days.

Me in my boarders' uniform on the beach at Weston-super-Mare. Summer 1955 (hardly appropriate beach wear!)

In my day-boys' uniform going to my sister Jill's wedding, Yatton Parish Church, Somerset. November 1954.

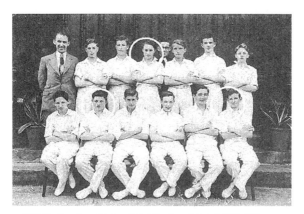

QEH Junior Colts XI (Under 15s) 1955. Me highlighted back row.
Keith 'Ram' Cockram highlighted front row (left) and Roger Gould (right).
The Master shown is Ken Carr who 'discovered' my cricketing abilities.

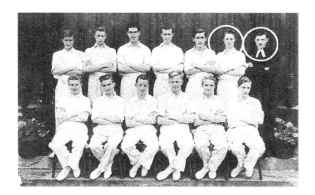

QEH 2ⁿᵈ XI 1956 me highlighted back row next to Keith 'Ram' Cockram in boarders' uniform.

QEH 1ˢᵗ XI 1957. Me highlighted back row. Robin Thomas, my life-long friend highlighted front row.

Q.E.H. May 1954 All those highlighted are mentioned in the text

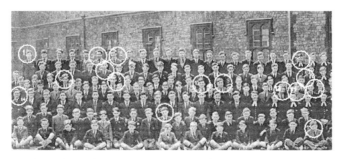

1. Jaques, 2. Louis Roll, 3. Dicky Connor, 4. Bert Wilsher, 5. 'Flob' Guest, 6. 'Nat' Lewis, 7. Brian Winsen, 8. 'Domer' Swann, 9. 'Grumpher' Steeds, 10. 'Granny' Gilbert, 11. Richard 'Feisal' Pratten, 12. David 'Harry' Dutton, 13. 'Susan' Stallard, Fifth figure from right on third row up 'Clara' Weale, 15. 'Beefy' Phillips. Top row, third from right numbered 3 is Barry 'Pancho' Coombs

1. E.B.P. Gillett (The Boss), 2. Syd Bowen, 3. Doc Martin, 4. Ken Carr, 5. Tony 'Archy' Preston, 6. 'Mac' McClamon, 7. Tony 'Daddy' Hills, 8. Fred Cook, 9. Richard 'Gobby' Hall, 10. Mr. Thatcher, 11. Ron Tandy, 12. Bill 'Wag' Moore, 13. George 'Inky' Wills, 14. 'Pelp' Pritchett, 15. 'Coline' Thorne, 16. John Shaw, 17. Robin Bown, 18. 'Birdy' Hopes, 19. 'Sailor' Williams, 20. 'One Ball' Stewart, 21. 'Tich' Houlson, 22. Keith 'Ram' Cockram, 23. 'Beefy' Phillips, 24. Barry Anstey, 25. Chris Wide, 26. Ram Cockram

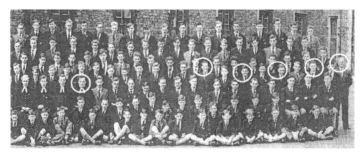

1. 'Jammy' James, 2. Colin Townsend, 3. Robin Thomas, 4. Trevor Brooks, 5. Williams B. 6. Mr. Mansell (The Marshal)

Chapter Seven

Sheffield, Southern Rhodesia and...Clevedon!

MY OLDER BROTHER ALLAN had always been something of a shooting star. In truth, during my earlier years I hardly knew him at all, there being a fourteen year age difference between us. Being our parents' first-born, Allan probably had the best years of their relationship before Father started up his tricks and the marriage hit the skids. By then though, Allan had distinguished himself in his school career, eventually becoming Head Boy of Cotham Grammar School (in those days one of Bristol's most prestigious schools, now no longer in existence). He was an outstanding rugby player who distinguished himself at every level as a schoolboy and went on to play regularly for The Bristol Rugby Club, which, then, as now, was one of the leading Rugby Union Clubs in the country. His blossoming rugby career was abruptly ended by a serious knee injury, necessitating surgery, after which all his mobility and swiftness was gone forever

Allan had brains too. Both our parents must have been so proud of him. I learned later that Father was often very hard on him and Allan suffered from Father's attempts to impose discipline, which, although probably well-intended, left Allan emotionally (and sometimes literally) somewhat bruised. Our Father did have a very bad temper and mother and Allan would have seen the worst of it as Jill and I really saw little of Father when we were younger. That said, Allan himself had a bad temper, as does Jill. My own temper is there too, deep down. All three of us, when angry, have the habit of grinding our teeth and almost growling—a characteristic inherited I believe from our grandfather, mother's father, 'Pom Pom' Webb.

How my brother developed an interest and an aptitude for medical science is a complete mystery (no one else since the dawn of time had ever been a doctor in our family). Fact is, he did though, and went on to study medicine at Bristol University, qualifying as a doctor and going on to specialise in Obstetrics and Gynaecology. His professional life has always been littered with

161

success as qualification after qualification piled up around his name. Alas, his private and family life has not proceeded so smoothly. In truth, does anyone's?

While Allan was a medical student he met and fairly rapidly married a nurse also working at The Bristol Royal Infirmary. Her name was Jean Coward. She was a cheerful and engaging girl, the daughter of Frank and Pat Coward. Frank was a businessman of some standing in the Bristol area. He was the founder and owner of a large retail business dealing principally in batteries and with its main premises prominently situated on Stokes Croft. Frank Coward was a pillar of the community type of man. He was a magistrate, a Rotarian and an all round good egg. He had the bushiest eyebrows that ever sprouted and he was a really very genuine person from every point of view. Frank was a wealthy man and had a house in Stoke Bishop, one of Bristol's most desired addresses. His wife Pat was a harmless soul, empty headed and well intentioned. However, she was a fearsome social snob and to a large extent set the family agenda. Not that Frank was what we would call today pussy-whipped—he was far too astute and intelligent to allow that to happen. It's just that life was easier if he appeased Pat in her day-to-day absurdities and prejudices. So, the apple cart of orderly middle class life must have been shaken for all concerned when daughter Jean turned up pregnant by her medical student boyfriend Allan Dutton.

Thus it was that my brother was rapidly married and set up in his own home very shortly before his son Barry Dutton was born. The Cowards (especially Mrs.) were happy enough to have a prospective doctor as a son-in-law but the rest of the Dutton family was decidedly from across the other side of the tracks. This divide that was never really breached was a wonderful little microcosm of the English class system in operation. Of course, with our Father being such a tainted individual, it was easy for The Cowards to see the wreckage that Billy created as the antithesis of the order and stability they valued.

Of course Mrs Coward's snobbery raised all our mother's hackles and there was never any love lost between those two. Jean Coward herself was a friendly and forthright sort of girl. She had a distinctive and infectious laugh. She was mercifully free of her mother's snobbery and had inherited common sense and a sort of 'get on with it' attitude, principally from her father. Later in life she became an accomplished artist making and selling a variety of objets of the knick-knackery variety. She was a disastrous cook though and would cheerfully massacre most events in the kitchen. In addition to Barry, she and Allan were to produce three more children... Anne, Jackie and Robbie.

Allan and Jean were married for the best part of thirty years before it all came completely off the rails. All of my brother's story is a fascinating and interesting one as a matter of fact. Perhaps it is really for him, not me, to ever tell it, should he choose. One thing I'll say about my brother though without fear of contradiction is that he is probably the most generous person I have ever known, frequently to his own detriment. Also, he has always had the very highest of standards in his professional life.

Back there though in 1955 he was a young doctor in one of his first posts at Sheffield City Hospital. He was living in a flat which was really the entire ground floor section of a very large old house called Norwood Grange. The residence was only a very short walk from the hospital. His son Barry was by then about six and daughter Anne was three. It was to this house and into this circumstance that I descended in the summer of 1955.

That time I spent with my brother yielded four memorable experiences. First, he and Jean owned what was called a radiogram. This large piece of furniture, about the size of a sideboard, played records as well as being a booming out radio. The records it played were chiefly '78's'. These were brittle and breakable 12-inch monsters upon which most recorded songs, music and voices of the day resided. My first record ever purchased then was by Eddie Calvert (the Man with the Golden Trumpet) and was called 'Cherry Pink and Apple Blossom White'. I bought it in Sheffield and played it and played it to distraction. Secondly, and thrillingly, I saw (nearly, will explain) my brother doing actual surgery. Thirdly, my brother took me to Bramhall Lane to see a day's play in the 'Roses' Cricket match between Yorkshire and Lancashire. On this day I saw the great Johnny Wardle bowling for Yorkshire. Also, there was the experience of the Yorkshire cricket crowd. So very, very different from the polite rippling applauses of the County Ground in Bristol! Here in Sheffield the crowd buzzed and yelled at the players. Everywhere was movement and noise amongst the watchers. Quite a shock believe me, so in contrast to the genteel manners of we southerners! Finally, and by no means least important... I contrived to nearly accidentally kill my own brother!

(ii)

During that visit with my brother in Sheffield I think he thought he would expose his soft-centred kid brother to a little blood and guts reality. Thus it was that one day he had me wearing a white coat and accompanying him around the City of Sheffield Hospital's Pathology Museum. Here were displayed in jars and pickled in formaldehyde dozens of infants' body parts. Now, if you're the kind of person who enjoys looking at pickled human foetuses in their various stages of development, peering out at you from inside bell jars, every day just before you sit down to a full English breakfast, then this would be the place for you! My dear brother was clearly enjoying my discomfort as he pointed out the interesting features in each exhibit. Now and again he'd throw in a helpful remark such as, 'Oh yes, that reminds me, I must get some vinegar to go with our fish and chip supper tonight!' A real jester, my brother!

A day or two later my cavalier sibling continued to press my education by inviting me to 'come and see me do some surgery'. Before I knew it I was in a green surgical gown, all scrubbed up and inside an operating theatre. My brother, assisted by another doctor and a couple of nurses, was about to do a caesarean section on a patient in urgent need of such a procedure. 'By the way,' he said casually waving the scalpel in his right hand in my direction, 'this is my younger brother David who has come to see what I do for a living.' Without any further ado they wheeled in a huge belly protruding from between the folds of white sheeting. Allan and his little gang began to hover over this mound and commenced going about the business of releasing the pressing little life inside.

A huge belly protruding from between the folds of white sheeting

Frankly, that was enough for me! I was suddenly overwhelmed by a wave of nausea as the first rivulets of blood began to dribble from the incision. The floor under my feet began wobbling and my senses began abandoning me as oblivion engulfed me. Next thing, I'm coming round in an anteroom where I must have been dragged. So, I never did actually get to see big Bruv really in action. Will just have to take his word (and the word of just about everyone else) that he is very good at what he does!

Now it may look as though nearly killing my brother a day or two later was a calculated act of revenge on my part. Not so, really. Allan was not the least dismayed at my wimpish reaction inside the operating theatre and, perhaps still harbouring the hope that I might follow him into eventually taking the Hippocratic Oath, the persistent fellow got the bright idea of teaching me how to do injections. 'There's really not much to it,' he said brightly, 'just a little practice and some confidence.' He than produced the family fruit bowl and soon had me plunging away at the apples and oranges like Don Quixote with a hypodermic. 'Of course,' he added suavely, 'actually taking blood can be a little more tricky, but it's basically the same idea.' Well, as if I didn't know all about *that*, remembering the squads of medics who were always assembled to assist in trying to extract my blood on so many occasions during my sickly childhood!

Anyway, by now big Bruv really had the bit between his teeth. 'Come on, you can take some blood from me,' he smiled. So, nothing daunted, I made a really good start, located a big fat vein and slid the needle accurately into place. (Interesting in these more sensitive days that all givers of injections are trained to say just prior to the needle being pushed into flesh or vein 'just a sharp scratch David'... how much less provocative and suggestive than the language of yesteryear 'just a little prick David!'... I beg your pardon, what did you call me?)

So, back to the near assassination of my dear brother. At the critical moment of my taking his blood his attention must have been momentarily diverted. Unfortunately this moment coincided with me mixing up that when giving injections you *pushed* the plunger of the hypodermic and when taking blood you *pulled* the plunger of the hypodermic. So, not an awfully good idea then to be pushing air into his vein! By the time he realised what was going on there was every chance I had done enough to create an embolism, which at that very second was on its way to send him off to Paradise! He went as white as a ghost, even whiter than ghosts taking part in the championships of 'who can be the whitest ghost in the history of the world' competition. The poor fellow literally swooned before my eyes, more, it transpired, from sheer terror than anything else.

Mercifully, what air had gone into him wasn't enough to have done much damage although it was a scary few moments. As he slowly recovered and realised he was looking at me and not at St. Peter, my brother discharged a volley of abuse in my direction, some of it, it must be said, a little stronger than 'that was a very silly thing to do David, please don't do it again'.

Perhaps a few things were learned on both sides through this experience. I sensed that from that day forward I would have a squeamish nature concerning all things medical, and this has indeed turned out to be the case. Certainly my brother would now know for certain what most others could have told him, namely that he had a brother who was a daft as a brush. Possibly, just possibly, he himself may have learned that confidence is one thing and that over-confidence is another creature altogether.

(iii)

When my Mother first floated the idea that she might go to Southern Rhodesia for a year it didn't go down at all well with selfish little me. It must have been very hard for her to put up with all my emotional blackmail and yet push ahead with a plan which must to her have represented a rare and special opportunity to escape the somewhat bleak realities of her impoverished struggles. It would be an adventure and a change of circumstance at the very least. Her problem was to prevent her youngest offspring bleating too much and setting as many roadblocks as possible to prevent the enterprise. She succeeded in overcoming all these obstacles of course with a mixture of promises, assurances and smooth accommodations. Thus did she pacify me and got me to accept going to be a temporary boarder at Q.E.H.—Mr. Gillett, long having succumbed to mother's charm offensive, falling in with her scheme. Mother really was a good fixer, it must be said!

The way things turned out it was a real watershed in my (very) slow maturing and in the process of emotionally detaching from my mother. That umbilical cord had always still been firmly in place from day one and it now seemed that the natural order of things was causing it to loosen at last. In short, I'd always been a real mummy's boy and now circumstances were dictating that, however reluctantly, the time had arrived to start standing on my own two feet!

So, bless her, with her sulking son sidelined for a while, mother set sail from Southampton on the *S.S. Windsor Castle*, with her friend Betty Block in the Spring of 1955 bound for South Africa and thence on to what was then still the colonial territory of Southern Rhodesia.

This was the very fag end of the era when journeys were made to far-off places by sea in leisurely style on steamships. The age of the jet airliner and the total revolution it heralded in mass transportation was already gathering itself on the world's runways. What a grand adventure it must have been for mother! She had been pretty well shackled by misfortune and responsibilities for most of her life to this point. She had never really been anywhere or done very much, with one notable exception. In the 1930's she and father had had an (unlikely!) holiday in Germany with some wealthy friends of father's who possessed a car and the enterprise to undertake a motoring holiday abroad in the days when the risks of breakdowns and misfortunes generally must have lurked around every bend in the road. Be that as it may, it was a rare 'hol' for my ill-suited parents.

Visiting Germany in the 1930's was to find oneself in a country of rare ferment. By the time our intrepid motorists turned up to drink their morning coffee in the cafe situated on the plaza in the lea of the awesome, towering and overpowering Cologne Cathedral, political power in Germany had passed into the hands of bigoted and dangerous lunatics. Not that mother and father would have really completely appreciated the implications of what was going on around them as The Rhine flowed by and they sipped their coffee on that spring morning in 1936. Quite by coincidence, Hitler was visiting Cologne that very day and addressing a Nazi rally at a nearby stadium. His speech was being relayed through loudspeakers throughout the town. I recall my mother telling me later that, although she and father did not understand a word of German, they were transfixed by the weird fanatical screeching of the voice that bounced around the square where they sat and the looks of adoration and concentration on the faces of the German people around them as they stopped whatever they were doing to listen attentively. For many years after mother would recount this occasion. It was, after all, something of note for her to be so very close to history in the making, even though she never recognised it at the time.

Apart then from this pre-war trip to Germany she had done little, certainly no major wing-spreading of the sort she was now undertaking as the *S.S. Windsor Castle* steamed into Cape Town.

Betty Block's sister Joan had emigrated with her husband and young family to Southern Rhodesia some years earlier. The husband (whose name I don't recall) had a good job in engineering. For white people Southern Rhodesia in those days was a land of milk and flowing honey. The vast majority of whites had a great lifestyle, inhabiting large lawned houses and near mansions with numerous servants and just about plenty of everything. In addition, Southern Rhodesia was blessed with an equitable climate and a varied and beautiful landscape. In fairness, for the best part of a hundred years, the whites had built up the country in an orderly and fruitful way. By the mid-1950's the country was still a prospering and prosperous little nugget in Britain's rapidly shrinking Empire. The problem was the whole thing was built on the sinking sands of white supremacy over a hugely obvious and subservient black majority. So it couldn't last and within another twenty turbulent years or so the whole cosy set-up had crashed down around the whites and the new country of Zimbabwe had been born out of the power of African nationalism and the shifting tides of world order. The fact that the subsequent misgovernment of Zimbabwe and its total impoverishment and near collapse under its present regime is an irony not perhaps lost on everyone.

So, when my mum was there she had the best of the last of it (from a white person's perspective at any rate!). Mother told me stories on her return of her embarrassment at having to have a servant for just about everything and how uncomfortable this made her feel. She lived with Betty Block's sister Joan and her husband in their grand house and participated (and as far I know, enjoyed) the social life of wealthy white folks. She certainly enjoyed all that dressing up in long dresses for dinner malarkey. Such a contrast, it was, from toiling up Grayle Road in Henbury in Bristol after a long day on her feet doing ladies' hair, and on arrival. slithering out the freshly made tripe from its newspaper wrapping, peeling a few spuds, popping them into a pan with a couple of onions and boiling them up to feed the kids. Finally, the eventual and welcome slump into the armchair for a cup of tea and a fag. Interesting thing, although quite a heavy smoker, mother never inhaled. She just puffed the smoke in and shortly after puffed it out. You couldn't persuade her that the whole pastime was therefore totally pointless! Even if the smoke never went down into her lungs, it sure enough would circulate around the back of her throat and larynx for most of the day. Since it was a very nasty cancer of the oesophagus which eventually saw her off, there simply must have been a connection. All smokers play ducks and drakes with their health whichever way they deal with the filthy stuff. Trouble is, as Shakespeare says, 'The deaf have no ears.' People are stupid... aren't we?

Mother obtained a job too, working in an office in downtown Salisbury (Harare). She also had the one (as far as I know) sexually satisfying relationship of her life with a married ship's captain. So, the little tinker certainly packed a lot into her year's safari. She found time too to write me long interesting letters on those special blue airmail letterforms.

Had it not been for me (and to some extent for my recently and prematurely married sister) I think Mother may have stayed in Rhodesia and made a completely new life. (Mind you, that wouldn't have been all that sensible really with the trap door already groaning underneath the whites out there at that time.) So, she did come back. I was getting towards the exit at Q.E.H. while we resumed the tenancy of our prefab on the Henleaze Road. Mother got another (pitifully paid) hairdressing job and our attention turned increasingly towards my utterly daft and self-willed sister Jill who, a year or so earlier, had barged off helter-skelter into a marriage that virtually had 'early exit' even stamped on the wedding invitations!

(iv)

Having had a good look at nursing as a career and not liking the whole idea in close up, my sister Jill had returned to Bristol and got a job at Boots, the Chemists in central Bristol, employed as a sales assistant. It was with a friend from work that she visited one day Winsley Chest Hospital near Bradford-On-Avon, this friend having a relative in that hospital convalescing from tuberculosis.

Tuberculosis was one of the real curses of that age. Britain's lovely damp climate gave the virus which caused the disease perfect conditions to make whoopee over several decades of the twentieth century. Countless thousands of lives and lungs were ruined until medical science eventually (hurray!) came up with a curing vaccine. In the 1950's and 1960's mass immunisation programmes were mounted and delivered throughout the country and as a result almost the entire population was immunised against T.B (a very similar and parallel situation happened with polio, that other horror disease of the age). All credit here to our frequently maligned National Health Service. The protection of whole populations against disease through mass immunisation was really first seen in Britain in the immediate post Second World War years.

Nevertheless, prior to its eradication through immunisation, T.B. was rampant—so much so that there were sufficient numbers of sufferers to fill whole hospitals. Just like the Winsley Chest Hospital into which my naive and impressionable seventeen-year-old-sister wandered with a friend one Sunday in 1954.

The rest is briefly told. In the hospital she met a young man, himself recovering from a serious bout of T.B. His name was Mick Jones and he had an amusing line in chat, enough to fascinate young Jill for certain. He was somewhat older than her and had been in The Royal Navy for five years or so before being invalided out. Mick must have seemed a worldly and wise figure to my insecure and emotionally floundering Sis. The fact that he had a very uncertain future did not deter our Jill one jot and before you could say 'splice the mainbrace' she was declaring herself deeply in love and much more keen to splice herself than any mainbrace. Within weeks she was waving an engagement ring proudly under our mother's nose. Mother once again demonstrated that phlegm and coolness under fire that had been forged in the furnace of the Percy Harding School of Tyranny. Instead of freaking out and giving her headstrong daughter the bollocking she was expecting (and some would say should have received!), Mother closely examined her daughter's bejewelled finger and, after a considered pause, said, 'Congratulations dear, I hope you will be very happy!'

The Percy Harding School of Tyranny

However, neither Mother's haughty disapproval or reasoned pleas could deter our girl and her sickly matelot beau. They had set their course and compass and weren't going anywhere except up the aisle. Even Billy Dutton was utilised to bring some pressure to bear on his errant daughter. This was not perhaps the most brilliant of ideas, as Billy was about as well qualified to give advice on relationships as the Hunchback of Notre Dame to give beauty tips. Even big brother Allan weighed into the fray with letters and phone calls attempting to dissuade our determined Sis and her sailor boy from their hasty voyage into matrimony. All to no avail.

To be fair, Mick Jones turned out to be an extremely amusing and engaging fellow. He had a friendly manner, always had a funny line or two (or three or four!). He was smallish in stature, had prematurely receding fair hair and a pleasant face, the principal feature of which was a prominent hooked nose.

His mother Ethel Violet seemed at first glance and meeting to be a right Gorgon. She had a rasping deep masculine voice, an abrupt and domineering manner and an overwhelming 'what I say, goes' way about her. This alone put most people's backs up within seconds. 'Eth' as she was universally called (to her face at any rate!) was overwhelming really and she controlled and dominated most situations. She swore and smoked a lot with a very unique way of flicking her ash from her cigarette with her little finger (usually onto the floor!). It has to be said that we came generally in the end to accept and, indeed like, the old blunderbuss. She really had a heart of gold underneath all the noisy bluster.

Mick's father Len (always called 'Pop' by one and all) was also a really fascinating person. It seemed on first impression his personality was totally obliterated by his steamroller wife, but this was deceptive. For a start he was a brilliantly talented wood carver. The shed at the bottom of his garden not only provided a refuge from Eth, it was also where Pop would produce the most perfect and delicate wood carvings of every kind. Working often on commissions and through reputation and recommendations, his work adorns many churches, buildings and private homes to this day and into the future. A proud legacy for a little man from Devon. Nothing in fact to be prouder of than the woodcarving he was entrusted to do on The Speaker's Chair in the Canadian Parliament in Ottawa.

Pop was completely gentle and unassuming. He had a Devon accent as thick as clotted cream, completing most sentences with the characteristic 'ma dear'. His pleasures were simple. He passionately followed the fortunes of Exeter City Football Club all his life. He enjoyed his garden and his kids Peter, Barbara and Mick.

I visited Pop and Eth towards the end of their lives in the little bungalow they ended up in at Claverham. By then, Eth had mellowed from a dragon into a pussycat and I was much touched by the tenderness she showed towards her, by now, almost bed-ridden husband. Not exactly 'Derby and Joan', but they really were an interesting couple of characters in their own right. For some reason, I often think about them today.

In any event, Mick and Jill were married at Yatton Parish Church in 1954. Their wedding turned out to be quite a bash. That day is still quite vivid in my mind....

(v)

My sister's wedding day was a real gathering of the Clans. All the Webbs were there, including our lovely grandmother 'Nanny' Webb, with their spouses (minus Auntie Dorrie in Australia). At this point all were still living. Jill's wedding must have been pretty much the last occasion they were all together as it wasn't too long before they started fading away (Uncle Sonny's wife Ada being the first as I recall). Naturally most of Mick's family were there too, a good many of them having travelled up from Devon, including Pop's mother. She was a very ancient little lady indeed.

Although young, Jill had already made a number of good friends and several were there including Sally Ford, her very oldest friend. Steve and Selman, the old antagonists from 121 Stoke Lane, were there. Brenda Bamfield, another friend who later committed suicide because her husband Paddy was such an abuser, was there too. Brother Allan, looking extremely smart in a dark blue pinstriped suit, was there to give the bride away. All the photography was in the hands of our Uncle Allan who was a real professional. It was so nice to see him happy and snapping away, temporarily released from the demands of poor Auntie Daisy, his mentally ill spouse.

A notable absentee was the bride's father, Billy Dutton, who was unable to attend (!). He did send a telegram which turned the whole jolly atmosphere somewhat icy when read out aloud by the Best Man to all the guests at the Reception: 'Good Night Sweet Repose, Keep Your Nightie Over Your Toes!' Father, *really*!

Elsewhere Mother and Ethel Violet were trying to outdo each other in the battle of the fur coats. Both had got wind of the fact before the wedding that the other was going to be wearing a fur coat. Now, in those days a fur coat was the ultimate fashion and status symbol. Ironic, really, how times have changed. (Even saying 'fur coat' these days has to be done in a whisper, let alone actually *wearing* one!)

Our mother really did look good, it must be said. Looking much younger than her 49 years, her actual age at that time. Her fur coat was black and she had a small feathered matching black hat. It must be admitted though that it was Eth who carried off the best fur coat award. Hers was a light grey and somehow more fluffy and furry than Kitty's. It looked more expensive and that was the real point! Sorry Mum, you were still tons better looking than crinkly old Eth even though you were about the same age!

The Reception was held in Eth's little house and it was more of a sausage rolls and cups of tea affair apart from a few bottles of Rich Ruby sherry. I recall at one point standing next to my Uncle Sonny and him saying to someone, 'Not much beer about, shall we go down the pub?'

Eth and Pop had a large parrot named 'Uckle'. It was a mangy looking thing that, taking its lead from Eth's frequent use of expletives, had an extensive vocabulary of swear words. Normally it lived in the small living room but in order to make space and avoid embarrassment its cage had been covered with a shroud and placed in the corner of the house's only small bathroom, out of the way. The theory was that when the parrot was covered over it never said anything. Unfortunately no one had explained to Uckle himself that 'in theory' he was supposed to keep his beak shut when covered over and placed in the corner of the bathroom. Thus, great commotion and excitement ensued when dear Nanny Webb let out a piercing scream from within the bathroom, eventually stumbling out through the door with the voluminous knickers, worn by most old ladies in those days, still around her ankles. Apparently, she had sat on the lavatory and just settled contentedly into her purpose at the very moment Uckle decided to break all the rules. He screeched out from under his shroud: 'What the bloody hell do you think you're doing!' At which point, as a dazed Nanny explained later as she recovered slowly from the shock, 'I shot straight up in the air.' A sympathetic and somewhat incredulous group of listeners attended to the swooning ancient, all contemplating her suspended in mid-air 'twixt lavatory bowl and ceiling, clothing awry and hair standing on end! Hold that thought!

Of course, my sister's wedding was an important event, but for me though it was overshadowed by that day being the Third Round of the F.A. Cup. Bristol City were playing away to Southend United and I and all the Webb males were on impatient tenterhooks throughout the day. City lost 2-0 as it happens. Had they won, it really would have given us something to celebrate...

(vi)

Shortly after Jill and Mick were married they obtained a flat in Clevedon. Why Clevedon is a bit of a mystery, as, at face value, it didn't seem to offer much opportunity to the young couple trying to get established. Situated on the Bristol Channel, Clevedon was something of an old fashioned sort of place even in those days. It was a town built largely with sturdy stone three-story Victorian and Edwardian houses and inhabited by a population of sturdy and not so sturdy genteel elderly folk. Most of

Clevedon Pier

Clevedon's population would have been born at the back end of the nineteenth century. Nothing wrong with that, of course; indeed, there was a blend of elegance and refinement which permeated the whole place. This was evident from its rocky little beach and foreshore, its meandering promenade following the contours of the bay and finally in the several levels of fine houses rising to the top of Dial Hill which, at about three hundred feet, commanded the entire little town below. At one end of the bay was a large artificial boating pool and at the other end a small but elegant pier with distinctive hooped metal arches every twenty yards or so across the central little boardwalk leading out to the end of the pier. Here a small rectangular pavilion housed a few seats and amusement machines. These machines would have been of the more refined 'roll a penny' or 'look through the telescope' sort, not the kind of vulgar and gaudy machines you would find on the pier at Weston-Super-Mare, Clevedon's brash resort neighbour situated a few miles down the coast. Weston was always full of day-trippers from Bristol and even more horrible further away places like... Birmingham, the very mention of which would have made most of the inhabitants of a place like Clevedon faint within seconds! Clevedon was a nice place, full of nice harmless people all living... nicely. Clevedon was entirely symbolised somehow by its elegant little Victorian pier serving no purpose whatsoever except as a bracing tottering walk to its extremity for the ageing locals.

So, quite how my sister and new hubby pitched up there in a large flat, situated on the first floor of a house on the corner of Gardens Road, is a mystery to me. It was here that I lived with the newly weds for a few months during late 1955 and early 1956 before Mother returned from Southern Rhodesia. I was still at Q.E.H. at that time and would travel the twenty miles each day by bus into Bristol, returning each evening to Clevedon.

The flat we lived in was owned by three ancient spinster sisters, the Misses Farmer. These ladies occupied another part of the house and, although completely harmless, they were always flitting around twittering about something or other. They resembled stick insects. Through some idiosyncratic plumbing arrangement of that house we all had to share a very large bathroom and toilet. The ladies were obsessively fussy about everything being kept clean and tidy. This was not too much of a problem for Jill and Mick (she in her desire not to upset the ladies and Mick with all his orderly naval background). However, for me, thoughtless and uncaring as I must have been, such practices as dribbling onto the floor around the toilet bowl after peeing and not cleaning the bath after use, were standard procedures. Poor sister Jill. She was always getting nagged by the ancient sisters about 'please tell your brother this or that'. The poor girl practically had to come along behind me with a cloth or a dustpan and brush, just to keep the old girls smiling.

We had absolutely no money whatsoever and it was a real hand-to-mouth existence. The reality and realisation of an impoverished married life was staring my sister in the face and must have hit her like a train. To be fair, she didn't really show it much and seemed cheerful enough and content to battle away. Can't have been much fun for Mick either with seemingly very few prospects. Still, they were both at that time, just about, still on love's magic carpet. Whilst I was there we did have a few good times, although these days it would all seem a little tame and innocent. On Saturday nights I would be sent out to fetch a couple of bottles of beer for Mick and some crisps and (wait for it, yum, yum!) three pickled eggs! Then we would write out all the letters of the alphabet on small pieces of paper and place them in order in a circle on the table. We'd put an upturned glass in the centre and all place our forefingers on the top of the glass. The object of course was to have a séance and communicate with loved ones who had passed over. We were all completely nuts, that goes without saying, but it was good fun when the glass started to move around spelling out messages in answer to the question (which was usually posed by my giggling sister): 'Are you with us?' Well, one thing for sure, eventually that glass always started whizzing around the table with all kinds of predictions and prophecies from our deceased forbears. There can only have been two possibilities. Either we really were in communication with the beyond or one of us was shoving the glass around. So, frankly, which one of us was shoving the glass? The other two always maintained it was me! Well I can say categorically that it wasn't. I naturally wouldn't think it was my sister, mainly because she so *wanted* to believe all this tosh. So, Mick, who could it have been...?

Jill was quickly having to learn all sorts of domestic skills that had hitherto, to her, been part of a completely foreign country. Skills like ironing and cooking. The cooking wasn't so much of a problem as there usually wasn't really very much around to cook! 'En passant,' I may say that my Sis is these days a truly excellent cook! Today of course the trouble is there is far too much food around. The world is full of 'fatties' waddling embarrassingly around. Had people of such a size that is commonplace today turned up on the streets of Clevedon back in the 1950's, there would have been a major 'alert' and they would all have been recaptured and returned to the Circus.

Anyway, my Sis's ironing skills were fully tested on one occasion. She was asked to iron my cricket whites (trousers) before a game. We were always expected to be well turned-out if we were representing the school. Fair enough. Jill ironed my stuff, folded it up in my bag and off I went. It was a home game for Q.E.H., I recall, at Eastfield. In the changing room we began to put on our cricket gear. Too late! Unthinkingly, I had my cricket trousers on before I noticed that my dippy sister had ironed them with creases up the sides and not the front! Thus I looked rather more like Jolly Jack Tar than W.G. Grace. By now of course my merciless team mates were all rocking with mirth. I can even now get embarrassed just thinking about it! She meant well, nevertheless.

Mick too was a mischievous fellow. Knowing how much I was in awe of Q.E.H.'s Headmaster E.B.P. Gillett, Mick would stage a pretend telephone conversation when ringing the school to explain that I was not able to attend through illness (a deceit, of course, but I really did get fed up with that forty mile round trip bus journey each day). Now, Mick was only kidding but I was daft enough to think he was for real. So, the conversation would go thus: 'Hello there, is that Mr. Gullet?' (at which point I would be reduced to extreme silent agitation as I stood alongside my playful brother-in-law)... 'Oh, hello there Mr Gullet, I'm ringing up about our Dido—he won't be in today as he's not feeling very well.' After he put the phone down I would worry for hours if he had *really* been speaking in such a manner to the great man! Silly me.

It was a time of considerable teenage angst for me during those months at Clevedon. I desperately wanted a girlfriend and didn't really know how to go about it. Spots and acne were something of a worry too at this time. I would be forever squeezing pimples and blackheads in front of the mirror and wondering if, in spite of my hitherto confidence in the matter, that I might after all be really *ugly*!

There were two girls I really fancied at this time. One was a regular commuter on the bus to Bristol each day. She attended school in Long Ashton as she got off the bus there. She had a ponytail and was called 'Trish'. She always sat amidst all her own pals and never gave me as much as a glance folks, even though I used to put extra Brylcream on my hair and arrange it so that I would arrive at the bus stop at the same time as her each morning. So that got nowhere. Then there was the girl who always used to be sitting on the rocks rising from the beach alongside The Walton Hotel by the pier. Every day she would be there on her own, reading a book. I took to going down there too and placing myself a little distance away from her and well, just staring in her direction! Didn't have the guts, you see, to make my move! So, she slipped away too and I was left with that longing and lusting which crowds around in your head and inside your trousers when you reach a certain time of your life!

On another occasion a Fair came to Clevedon and set up on the open space alongside the boating lake. I must have been having a prowl around in the lonely sort of way I was getting used to when I invested sixpence on a stall where you bought a name on a ticket and a light flashed up and down dozens of names on a spinning device at the centre of the stall. The process started quickly and gradually slowed down. Quite simply, if the light stopped on the name corresponding with the name on your ticket, you won a prize. You then could take your prize or pay another sixpence and if the light stopped on the same name again, you could win one of the prizes from the top shelf, these being the prizes really worth having of course. So, in any event, I did invest a further sixpence and, indeed, the same name came up again! Without hesitation I chose a large boxed 'Pressure Cooker' from the top shelf and ran, yes ran, all the way back along the Promenade and up to Gardens Road to present my Sis with, what was considered to be in those days, something of a luxury item. It wasn't long before Mick and Jill were poring through the book of instructions working out how to use the thing. Well, they certainly didn't get it right as on the very first experimental attempt to boil potatoes the entire lid of the damn thing blew straight off and put a large dent in the kitchen ceiling! For the remainder of the time they lived in that flat Jill and Mick lived in fear of The Misses Farmer noticing that their pristine premises were now in danger of a roof collapse!

Not too long after, Mother got back from Southern Rhodesia and Jill and Mick moved up to a flat in Bristol. They were still poverty stricken and Mick was looking for work. In addition, their first born, Susan, arrived in July 1956 at Bristol Maternity Hospital. (Jill and Mick must have been doing some other things to keep themselves occupied during those boring Clevedon days!) The first time I ever got what would today be called 'bladdered' was on the night Susan was born and I ended up with Mick in 'The Eastfield Inn' on Henleaze Road. He was so happy and wanting to wet the baby's head with pint after pint of 'Georges' Bristol Bitter'. Nothing wrong with that. However he expected me to drink pint for pint with him. Now this was ridiculous. Mick had quaffed his way around the world from Tokyo to Timbukto with his Navy mates and could still pickle himself without batting an eyelid. Up until that point my own exposure to alcohol had been a couple of glasses of sherry at Christmas time. Therefore, which of the two of us came nearest to expiring from alcoholic poisoning would you guess? I recovered, but every July 25th since then, I have had no difficulty, thanks to my mad matelot ex brother-in-law, recalling the date of my niece's birthday. It was the day that alcohol and I first really got it on, and one way or another, I have gone through the rest of life handcuffed, mercifully fairly loosely, to this lunatic!

My sister Jill's wedding to Mick Jones, Yatton Parish Church, Somerset, November 1954. L to R: Auntie Daisy (on one of her better days although still looking very stressed), Steve, Me (in school uniform, note the scarf), Auntie Margie (concealing cigarette in right hand), Auntie Ada (note the fox fur!), Uncle Sonny, Mick Jones, Jill, Brother Allan, Nanny Webb, Mother (note the fur coat and very stylish shoes, 'Pretty Kitty!), Brenda Bamfield (a couple of years before she took her own life), Auntie Edie (Mother's cousin), Rose Selman (our helper at 121 Stoke Lane) and Sally Ford (close friend of Jill's).

Me heading for the church with Auntie Ada '....a large, domineering lady ...
jolly and kindly but kept Uncle Sonny on a short lead ...' and Auntie Margie,
'... all the Webbs had a marvellous sense of humour but Margie's was, perhaps,
the wittiest and funniest of them all.'

Chapter Eight

A Lot Goin' On

THERE WAS A LOT packed into the period between leaving school and starting Teachers' Training College. These were the years 1957 to 1960, taking me neatly from age 17 to 20.

During most of this time I was living in the prefab with Mother and working as an Unqualified Teacher at the Crescent School. However I spent long periods in Weymouth during the summers working on the beach and living with my father (although he died on November 4th 1958, I returned to work in Weymouth after that for several more summers). Also, on my 'curriculum vitae' during this time, were spells as a temporary postman and as a shift worker in a bakery. Phew! Tires me out just writing it all down.

If you throw in too another encounter with my old pal 'streptococcus' which plonked me back in hospital for a few months and also the huge impact on my life of discovering Elvis, Jerry Lee Lewis and Roy Orbison and their pals, oh, and not forgetting losing my virginity, then you may deduce these were eventful years!

These were eventful years

After the luxuries of Southern Rhodesia it must have been a shuddering contrast for Mother to have to, again, mount the familiar treadmill of long working hours for a sparse wage. The fact that she did this without too much complaint speaks volumes for her character and her stamina.

Our connection to the Hardings was still in place through Mother's kinship and friendship with Auntie Olive. It had long been assumed that 'Teaching' was a career for me to aim at and, frankly, way, way back in the days when I was a little fella carrying Miss Elliot's bag across the playground at Stoke Bishop Primary school, the notion had lodged in my mind that 'teaching is a job I could do'. So, the cliché, 'I *always* wanted to do

179

it' happens to be true in my case. After all, realistically, what else could I have done? Certainly nothing requiring any practical or technical skills as both such aptitudes come out as a great big zero on this boy's job potential profile! The old adage about 'those who can, *do*, those who can't, *teach*' really fits me pretty well! Put another way, a job requiring good communication skills, backed up by some knowledge and generous dollops of bullshit, was tailor-made for someone just like little old me! So, teaching it was going to be.

The problem was that it was not easy to gain a place at Teacher's Training College. This was partly to do with limited capacity and partly because many places at such Colleges were held open at that time for men who were doing compulsory National Service in the Forces. It certainly didn't help my cause either that I only had the barest minimum of entry requirements (5 G.C.E.s at 'O' level). In reality, you needed one or two passes at G.C.E. 'A' level (hence the short-sightedness of quitting the Sixth Form early at Q.E.H., or so it seemed).

So, when Mother sniffed out that The Crescent School might have a position for an Unqualified Teacher, it all seemed to fall neatly into place. As aforementioned, I was needing to earn some money to assist the family budget and taking a position as an Unqualified Teacher would not only provide valuable experience, it may also provide a shortcut to a place at college and possibly a way around the complication of not possessing any 'A' levels. As it happens, this in fact turned out to be the exact case, as will be seen....

(ii)

Thus it was, somewhat bizarrely, that I returned to the school at which I had been such an unhappy bunny as a pupil, now in the role of a teacher! The Crescent School was still presided over by Oscar Dahl as Headmaster and was owned by my uncle Percy Harding. Oscar had calmed down a little and the cane on his wall was a little less active. This may have been due to a combination of factors, not least his ever swelling corpulence and the consequently increasing health issues. Also, I suspect, the slowing down of his libido and that constant urge to gaze at little boys with their trousers down around their ankles.

Be that as it may, the old rascal interviewed me and offered me a job, initially to help out, at the princely wage of £1.10 shillings a week! (Yep, you read that correctly, £1.10 shillings a week!) Admittedly, the average wage in those days was probably around only £10 to £12 pounds per week... but

£1.10 shillings really was a joke. However the die was cast, I had burned my boats by leaving Q.E.H. and, as explained, this job held out the prospect of a shortcut to Teachers' Training College. I still had my paper-round each morning paying 12 shillings a week which it was obvious I would have to keep. How many schoolteachers in Bristol would you say were doing a paper round every morning before striding into a classroom to do their stuff in front of the blackboard? Not too many.

To begin with it just made me chuckle at the situation. That was until one morning as I pushed *The Daily Express* through the letterbox of a house in Henleaze Gardens, the window opened and there was a pupil named Christopher Walling from the Crescent School! 'Morning Sir,' he said to me brightly, standing alongside his astonished looking mother. 'My mum wouldn't believe that Mr Dutton was our paper boy!' So, that caused some embarrassment that soon blew over, partly because Christopher Walling was a good little footballer and I had started up a school football team of which Christopher was a key member.

One little innovation I had been able to promote at the school was a certain amount of Physical Education to improve a dry and dusty curriculum. Hitherto, Physical Education had been restricted to a few little games throwing beanbags around in the tiny recreational space at the rear of the school. I started to take classes across to the triangular little park just opposite 10 Eaton Crescent. This park was just large enough to organise some team games for both boys and girls. This was when it first occurred to me that it might not be a bad idea to take up Physical Education as my principal teaching subject if ever I could obtain a place at College and get qualified. The idea turned out to be a disaster when I did eventually go to Teachers' College, but this is a story yet to be told...

Meanwhile, back at the Crescent School, I knew enough about traditional subjects like English, History and Geography to carry it off in front of a class full of youngsters...just! Remember, these 'children' were only a very few years younger than me. I made mistakes for sure but I discovered, even at that early stage, that it was always better in the classroom situation to admit openly if you didn't know something. Kids will always accept this I found. Anyway, one thing for sure was that the good foundation I had in General Knowledge (all that reading of the daily papers... thanks Dad!) nearly always put me ahead of the kids. I learned quickly too some of the very basic rules of becoming a successful classroom practitioner (some of them, the hard way!). Rule one, don't be too familiar or over friendly in order to court popularity. Rule two, always try to be prepared and have some idea of where you wanted to go in a particular lesson. Rule three, don't talk too much and always have some activity for the kids to do, be it writing, drawing, reading or a controlled discussion. I also learned that I could read aloud very well and, with the right book or poem or piece of prose there was no difficulty in keeping a class in the palm of my hand. In short, I was *good at it*! So, it wasn't long before I was making an impact there (he says modestly!).

Unbelievably, the two ancient retainers, who had both been bath chair candidates when I had been a pupil at the school some years earlier, were *still* on the teaching staff! Bill Meredith must have been about 90 and was completely ga-ga. God knows how he even reached a classroom, let alone got through a lesson. (I seem to remember I was assigned to help him up and down the stairs!) Also, Karl (Kreaky) Kreling, that lovely old Polish gentleman, was still performing. Most of the time Karl would be patting his clothes to release clouds of chalk dust everywhere and mumbling away to himself in Polish as the thin edge of dementia began to take hold. In the Staff Room he would sometimes forget that he already had a cigarette in his mouth and commence to light another one. This was OK, except on the occasions when he tried to place the second one in his mouth at the same time as the first. As a consequence of the ensuing singeing and momentary panic, he had a moustache the colour of an over-ripe banana and a series of little burn marks on both forefingers and thumbs. Nice old guy—I liked him a lot, as did the pupils.

Also on that staff at the time of this, my teaching debut, was June Wadham and a little mouse of a lady called Mrs. Davenport. These two were well contrasted. June Wadham was about thirty, big busted, bespectacled and a loud machine gun voice that pretty well shut everyone else up. June was the nearest I came to making a friend on that staff. I used to tell her things too 'in confidence'. From this miscalculation I learned another one of life's hard lessons—ever tempted to tell people things 'in confidence'? Well, 99 times out of 100, *don't*! Mrs Davenport was intensely proud of being the only properly trained teacher on the staff and who had been to Training College. She never let anyone else forget this when she wasn't quietly complaining about 'all the mess you men make'. So that was the staff as I remember. Jack Oxland was still there too, although he kept himself pretty much to himself. A real odd-ball, although whether he and Oscar were still playmates is not known.

Anyway, everything pretty well shuddered to a halt one bright spring morning when Oscar keeled over in his bedroom and died right there and then from a massive stroke. We had to keep all the kids in their classrooms as the ambulance men manoeuvred his great bulk down the stairs on a stretcher. Can't say I shed too many tears. He didn't have many, correction, any, redeeming features as far as I could see. I suppose that's a little uncharitable on my part as he did, after all, give me a really good leg up into my teaching career.

The future of the school was in some doubt with Oscar's sudden demise. Pressure was on Percy Harding to speedily appoint a new Headmaster. (Note, in those days of female subjugation, the appointment of a Head*mistress* was not even contemplated!) Of course Percy rushed the job in order that appearances should be rapidly maintained. Knowing nothing about education he was likely to appoint just about anyone who sounded right for the position. So it was that the new Headmaster, Mr. Harmer-Smith F.R.G.S., joined the school. He turned out to be an unmitigated disaster and managed to do what Oscar Dahl, notwithstanding his pervy ways, had been unable to do in the twenty or so years of the school's existence... totally collapse the confidence of parents, pupils and staff alike and lead the school into oblivion. Not quite, though, before one aspiring young man had secured a firmer hold on the teaching ladder by gaining a Training College place... take a bow 'H'!

(iii)

Our prefab (163 Henleaze Rd) was one of a collection of approximately forty to fifty others, arranged in two equal ranks with just a couple of them situated on their own at the very rear of the development. We lived in one of these set-apart prefabs, slightly isolated and at odds with the two evenly arranged and spaced front rows. These prefabricated dwellings built in their thousands as temporary accommodations to serve the country's chronic post-war housing shortage had, by the mid-fifties, acquired a much more settled and permanent status. This is certainly true of those in Henleaze Road, Bristol. The little gardens around each dwelling were overwhelmingly cared for; hanging baskets of plants and flowers were common features, paths were swept and gates painted, signs of careful maintenance were all around. Indeed, everything was 'neat, tidy and Bristol fashion', one might say.

Occupying the other of the two set-back prefabs, and our near neighbours for the duration of the time we lived there, was The Gilmour Family. Mr. Gilmour was a large thickset friendly man who worked for the Bristol Council in some kind of administrative post. He had either once lived in The Far East or spent time out there in the Forces as, at some time in his life, he had suffered from a bout of smallpox. As a result his face had been quite badly pockmarked. He was a decent man and arranged for mother's rent to be paid while she was away in Africa and, as I recall, he kept our little bit of garden tidy and generally maintained an eye on the place. Mrs. Gilmour was a somewhat reserved lady who kept well in the background. Her main concern in life was their son Paul who was much spoilt and fussed over. Paul was about twelve or thirteen and they were always keeping him off school because he had a cold or a tummy upset. In truth, Mother used to flirt a bit with Mr. Gilmour and, looking back, this may have been one of the reasons why Mrs. Gilmour was always just that little bit stand-offish. Anyway, they were our neighbours and we lived peaceably enough alongside them for quite a few years.

During this time, as ever, Mother was doing her hairdressing and struggling along from week to week. She'd get up each morning at around 6.30 a.m. and insist I ate the plate of porridge she placed in front of me before I set off to collect my bag from the paper shop. Then, I would always be entreated to 'wrap up warm, David, Jack Frost is out there this morning'. By the time I returned from delivering the papers she herself would be almost ready to leave for work but not before I had been told to 'comb your hair for goodness sake David' and 'surely you're going to give those shoes a clean?' Bless her!

Saturdays we had a bit of a different routine. Mother only worked until lunchtime on a Saturday and she would arrive home with the perennial bags full of shopping at around midday. As often as not I would be playing cricket for The Old Boys' Cricket Team in the afternoon (after leaving Q.E.H. I played cricket for the Old Boys for a few seasons). So, prior to my setting off, Mother would make a wonderful fry-up. (Perfect food for an athlete!) Included on the fat-drenched plate of bacon, eggs, tomatoes, fried bread and mushrooms she placed before me was always my all-time favourite... 'pig's kidneys'!

Over these few years, when opportunity occurred, I supplemented my very meagre earnings as a teacher with other employments. These jobs were in addition to the more or less ever-present paper round. Christmas always meant being taken on as a temporary postman. I was assigned to the large Sorting Office situated near the Railway Arches at Zetland Road. This was a few miles from where we lived, certainly a bus ride. The way it worked was that temporary workers, who were hired just for the Christmas rush, were attached to a permanent postman whose post 'round' they would take over whilst the permanent incumbent of the job would sort out the post and pack up the (extremely heavy!) post bags which must be lugged around to deliver the (mainly) Christmas cards. Those bags were crippling, trust me! One of the postmen to whom I was attached was a jovial fellow called Bill Hamilton. Along with all his regular mates in the Sorting Office he found the occasions when the temporaries were drafted in to be a time of great amusement. This was when all the novices undertook the tasks that came second nature to the regulars. Thus it was that one morning, as I was about to stagger out towards the starting point of my 'round' with the Christmas cards overflowing from my two bags, old postman Bill proffered a raised thumb toward my nose. 'Have a little sniff of this mate, it'll 'elp you on yer way.' Stupid as ever I sniffed up what turned out to be a heap of snuff. My ensuing coughing and spluttering and general confusion was much enjoyed by most of Bill's pals and all the other permanent employees of The General Post Office who happened to be standing around! I suppose this sort of thing made their Christmas every year.

The money was always very welcome

In those days there was a delivery of the post actually on Christmas Day itself. This was a problem to me as there were no buses. Nothing for it but to walk. There and back, approximately eight miles, with two hours' work delivering the post in between. Ideal way to spend your Christmas Day! You'd think that a lot of folks wouldn't have bothered to turn up. They'd thought of that one though... you had to collect your pay at the conclusion of your round on Christmas Day! Can't blame them I suppose. The money was always very welcome.

At another time I obtained a job on the night shift at Parker's Bakery situated on Kingsdown Parade. This really was a high pressure eight hours. The loaves of bread would come tumbling down a chute, as far as I could tell straight from the ovens where they had been baked. Anyway, they were red hot and the job was to collect half a dozen loaves as they tumbled haphazardly towards you, turn them upright, get hold of the six together, arrange them in a block, then, gripping from either end, stack them neatly onto a wooden pallet. Of course the loaves were much too hot to handle directly so you wore a large pair of gloves made from a sort of sacking. It was frantic work to keep on top of the ever-cascading manna from above. It was also extremely boring, tough, relentless work, stretching almost continuously over an eight hour shift. Many of my fellow workers I recall were Hungarians who had come to Britain as refugees after what was known as The Hungarian Uprising of 1956. This was the event when the people of Hungary (as it turned out about thirty years too early) had risen under the leadership of their Prime Minister Imre Nagy to establish a more democratic government and to throw off the Soviet style communist system which had been pressed on them by the Russians after World War II. This rebellion was ruthlessly crushed by the Russian military might—with the Western Powers standing impotent and frozen on one side, a striking example of the *realpolitik* of the times! The upshot for little me was, whenever I screamed out in that Bakery in the middle of a shift such things as 'Bugger me, that one was really scolding, burnt me thumb off nearly!' or 'Sod me, I'm so bored and stressed I could shoot me Granny for something to do!'... all such exclamations would be met with a shrug of the shoulders and a look of complete incomprehension by my newly arrived and non-English speaking workmates! Having said that, I'm sure they would have got the general idea. Body language is body language when all is said and done!

Emerging from that Bakery into the early morning Bristol sunshine with near blistered hands and a pounding head was an immense relief. I'd pop into a little newsagents on Jamaica Row and buy my favourite daily newspaper of that time, *The News Chronicle* (long since 'passed away'). Then, I'd sit upstairs on the number 142 bus and quickly dive into the sports' page all the way back to our little prefab in Henleaze. Life was a little topsy-turvy for a while back then!

(iv)

Without any doubt my prized possession was my little auto-change red-lidded Dansette record player. I'd bought it on the 'never-never' from the Electrical Goods shop situated in the row of shops on the opposite side of Henleaze Road. This little machine definitely heralded in a large, new dimension to my life. It played records at all three speeds (78 r.p.m., 45 r.p.m. and 33⅓ r.p.m.). This was the time when 78's were still the most common records but the 45's were just starting to appear. Whatever the size, my little machine dispensed its magic! I loved everything about it—the 'clunk' when it dropped a heavy '78' down onto the turntable contrasting with the smoother 'click' sound as it released a '45' from the tiny stack of others held by a spindle and waiting their own turn to drop.

Then, the magical way the playing arm moved exactly onto the first groove of the record and returned to its rest when it had finished. I even loved the very smell of my baby Dansette which was a new and slightly lacquery smell when you bent down to sniff it. What joy! Wish I still possessed it. These iconic little mechanical pioneers would sell for thousands of pounds, probably, these days!

'The Hit Parade' (forerunner of 'The Charts') was published weekly in *The Record Mirror* and I would study the movements of records up and down each week just as avidly as The Football League Tables, and you can't really get more avid than that now, can you?

The first few records I acquired were 78's, mostly Bill Haley and The Comets. Then, along came Elvis! So much has been said and written about his impact and the socio-economic, historical and simply sexual explanations of his emergence and his effect on so much and so many, especially upon we young people of that generation. I prefer the simple notion of 'cometh the hour, cometh the man'. John Lennon's assertion that 'before Elvis, there was nothing' may be over egging the pudding somewhat but it does have validity in my view.

In short, I bought into the whole Elvis thing totally. I went on to almost wear out my Dansette with every record he made over this period. There was no time for books, other forms of music (although traditional jazz did get a nod), any interest in any kind of hobbies, be they practical or mentally stimulating. No, just Elvis and a little later Roy Orbison, Jerry Lee Lewis and Buddy Holly. What an uncultured and uncultivated fellow I was becoming!

Not even this new obsession, though, could dim the ever-pressing question of the opposite sex. Especially, one may say, as the whole rock and roll thing, the entire bag of tricks, was about sex anyway. So it was never going to just go away or shunt contentedly into some other emotional siding.

Thus, the often-asked question, sometimes by one's friends, but more frequently by oneself to oneself, was, 'Have you done it yet?' The answer was an increasingly loud 'NO!' Here was I, by now in my late teenage years. This had to be sorted out.

Most weekends I would switch off the Dansette, splash on the 'Old Spice', put on that blue flecked Harris Tweed jacket that I *had* eventually bought from Hector Powe's Gents' Outfitters on Park Street and, usually, with my old pal from Q.E.H., Robin Thomas, head for central Bristol for a trawl around the coffee bars and, increasingly as we became bolder, the pubs. By the end of my teen years Robin and I would make regular weekend appearances in 'The Mauretania' at the bottom of Park Street, 'The Hatchet' in Denmark Street or 'The Bunch of Grapes' on The Centre. Sometimes even 'The Rummer' which was off Baldwin Street.

Our favourite place though was a combined coffee bar and restaurant, halfway down Park Street, called 'The Bali'. Here we would spend ages with a growing circle of regulars of about our own age. Occasionally we would spend some money on a coffee or even the excellent spaghetti bolognese they served for two shillings and sixpence. (That bolognese in the 'Bali' ruined me for ever on the question of bolognese; it was the yardstick by which all other bolognese has since been measured. It had a thick, very crispy, deep cheese topping and a combination of ingredients and flavours beyond any comparisons I have ever come across since.) 'The Bali' was owned by a Swiss man named Claude who was extremely smartly dressed. His clothes were immaculately cut, he wore dark glasses and had the smooth manner of a confident and wealthy man. He owned a very expensive car into which he would frequently invite us for a ride... Once the penny dropped that he was much more interested in the boys than the girls, we grew to accept him and he sort of joined our little social circle for a while—very much at arm's length though, as this was still the age when 'Queers' were treated largely with suspicion and hostility.

Nevertheless, all this chatting, drinking, laughing, sitting about, smoking, walking around between coffee bars and pubs, listening to Elvis and the gang; was edging me inexorably towards actually 'Doin' it' with a girl. It is simply told in the end.

The deed was fairly quickly done

She was a girl named June and, with her friend Beryl, was a frequent visitor to 'The Bali'. She was a pleasant, friendly, Bristolian girl, in her early twenties. She wore a charm bracelet and her fair hair was well lacquered. She was, what my mother would have called, 'a bit common'. To make a short story even shorter, she came back with me to the prefab one evening and the deed was fairly quickly done, once we got to the bedroom. I was hopeless of course, fumbling and uncertain. June, bless her, was more assured. She was certainly disappointed too, that's for sure! I don't recall her saying much except, eventually, 'What time's your Mum getting home genius?' So, there it was. All that fuss about just that. Perhaps I should have stopped right there. Life wouldn't have been half as interesting though!

(v)

With all this going on you wouldn't have thought it possible to include a trip around several European countries now, would you? Wrong! It happened like this. Colin Townsend had been one of the coffee bar gang during my last year at Q.E.H. He was a couple of years above me at school and therefore somewhat older. He was a large framed fellow with tousled hair, a somewhat gaping mouth, an extroverted and confident manner and a generally sunny disposition. Also, he had very large hands with stubby fingers and an unusual accomplishment in that he played the accordion brilliantly. This talent was to feature prominently from time to time throughout our forthcoming trip.

It turned out that his father worked for British Railways and was entitled to free rail travel throughout Europe for himself and close members of his family. Colin was anxious to take advantage of this excellent perk but not so keen to travel around on his own. So, generously, he offered to share the benefits from his free ticket by halving with me the cost of the other tickets that would need to be purchased. In short, a unique opportunity for me to share the adventure he had planned around several European countries.

Mother was apprehensive but eventually agreed to my going. Even with the cheap travel, the whole thing would be on a shoestring. So it was, in the early summer of 1957, Colin and I met at Temple Meads Station for our adventure. Colin had a suitcase and his accordion; me with just a suitcase (don't think rucksacks were much used for such journeys in those days, if at all).

Nothing daunted, we headed straight for Rome! The idea was to travel as far as possible during the nights so as not to have to pay for overnight accommodation. It all worked pretty well at first and our main concern was ensuring always to collect a stamp on our passports as we crossed the border from one country to another (mainly for bragging purposes back in jolly old Bristol!). The trains were usually steam and seemed to run very well to time. Now being more used to British Railways, this was something of note. Europe was just getting back onto its feet and the remains of World War II were still evident here and there. Nevertheless, there was confidence and bustle and signs of prosperity even then so relatively shortly after the war.

The overnight train we took from Milan to Rome was just about as crowded as crowded can be. We ended up propped on our suitcases on the floor of the corridor and found ourselves sharing our tiny space with a young Italian guy who just wanted to chat away in near perfect English. This was my first exposure to that phenomenon of the just about anybody foreign person who *always* seems to be able to speak English to some degree compared to lazy English people (us!) who cannot converse in any language except our own. It's a national embarrassment, really, and a situation which, in spite of the zillions of pounds having been invested in our schools in the teaching of foreign languages, seems to be no better nowadays than when Townsend and I were talking to our new found Italian pal on that train.

Be that as it may, I recall this fellow telling us about Italian girls and how girls in Italy specialised in the dispensing of various sexual pleasures depending on the region of Italy they came from and that the girls from Bologna (where our train had recently passed through, which is probably what prompted the conversation!) were especially gifted in one particular aspect. I've often recalled this conversation whenever the subject of Italy has arisen. As to the veracity of its content, I suppose one just has to take that fellow's word for it...

The early morning daylight gradually revealed the arid and vine-strewn landscape that was whizzing past the carriage windows. Arriving at Rome's main station, the architecturally impressive Statsioni Termini is forever branded into my memory box.

(vi)

Just being in Rome was a great enough cultural shock! The people, the vehicles, the sounds and the sights bombarded one's senses from all new directions. Townsend had somehow arranged our immediate accommodation within walking distance of the main Railway Station. It was in a flat belonging to and also lived in by a fat and kindly Italian lady who soon had us facing our first bowls of spaghetti and had indicated the two single beds in a tiny room not much larger than a broom cupboard. I've never been as tired or sort of disorientated in my life and slept like a log for certain.

I wish I could say that the next few days were spent discovering the joys of 'The Eternal City'. Alas no! Talk about pearls before swine! We really were a couple of Philistines. The Colosseum got a nod but not for us The Sistine Chapel, The Vatican, The Fountains of Trevi or all the other surrounding wonders. Perhaps it was to do with the lack of money, but I must say there was a wall of ignorance around us both too. We did a lot of sitting around drinking coffee and smoking and Townsend was a great one for striking up conversations with assorted folks. It has always been one of my regrets that the blinkers of youth spoilt this opportunity. I've long intended to put this right but so far to no avail.

After a couple of days we moved on to a small village outside Rome called Castel Gandolpho. Colin had heard that we might get a cheap room there for a few days and this indeed was the case. A much greater surprise turned out to be that it was in Castel Gandolpho that the Pope (Pius XII at that time) had a magnificent Summer Palace. This marvellous building overlooked the typical small red stone houses of the village that stood in its lea. From our room we opened the simple wooden shutters in the morning to the sight of the Palace in our foreground and the hills of Rome beyond. So perhaps, after all, and inadvertently, we did salvage some of Rome's glory!

After an early conversation with a few locals in the Village Square, it so happened that the next day, a Sunday, there was a football match planned between Castel Gandolpho and a neighbouring village. Townsend, who was useless at football, was quick to volunteer 'my mate Harry, he's a really good player'. In those days the word 'Englishman' was synonymous with 'good footballer', as is 'Brazilian' these days!

Thus it was that the next day I found myself pulling on the green shirt of Castel Gandolpho and lining up at Right Back for the kick off! It has always been one of my subsequent claims to fame that I played for The Holy Father's XI! The pitch was rock hard mud and hopelessly uneven. I think the result was a draw. I know I took a bad tumble and injured my thumb. This turned out to be painful and, in return for some of our rapidly disappearing lira, the local Doc. x-rayed my hand and bandaged it the following day.

That Sunday evening we downed plenty of wine with the locals in the Taverna and Townsend played his accordion. I'm not sure what it signified but the Italians were singing 'The Internazionale' (the international communist anthem). How strange was that in the very heartland of Catholicism! Townsend soon mastered the tune on his accordion and shortly everybody was belting it out! The wine flowed along with the camaraderie. It was all young fun, good-natured and innocent. What did we know really? What does Wordsworth say about 'splendour in the grass'?

Next, Townsend announced we were leaving for, wait for it, Hamburg! Just about as far away as you could go from Rome before sliding off into Scandinavia! So then, the very long journey North, with little money and living on more or less bread alone and fresh air.

Eventually emerging from the Railway Station in Hamburg, we encountered an exhibition of photographs displayed on the forecourt of the station. These striking images showed Hamburg after having been totally devastated and destroyed by Allied bombs a dozen or so years before. One had to bear these photos in mind when walking around, as the speed with which the City had been rebuilt was truly amazing. There were some bombed sites of course but really not very many. It was little short of miraculous how the place had been restored.

A banknote dropped to the floor

We had just enough money left to book into a Youth Hostel for a couple of nights but we were very hungry. We stood in a small queue in a food shop intending to buy some 'pumpernickel'—a highly compressed block of black bread, bland to the taste but reputed to be very filling. There was a well-dressed and middle-aged German lady in front of us in the queue. As she opened her purse and started fiddling for her money, a banknote dropped to the floor. She had not noticed it fluttering down but I had! In one of those defining moments life sometimes delivers I placed my shoe over the money. No one else, it seemed, had noticed. I was eventually able to pick it up and secrete it in my pocket. I didn't even tell Townsend about it until we were some distance away from the shop. 'How much is it?' he urgently inquired. 'I'm not really sure,' I replied, which was true. Imagine our joy when from my pocket I pulled a banknote to the value of one hundred marks! Whoopee! It turned out to be not enough to be able to say you would never have to ever go to work again in your life, but it was quite enough for two hungry English lads to have quite a junket in Hamburg for a couple of days!

We did too, spending the first two hours at least after the good luck event in a restaurant scoffing down as much bratwurst and sauerkraut as we could shovel in—all washed down with a few steins of best lager naturally!

Nothing daunted, we had a good prowl around Hamburg's famous 'Reeperbahn'. There were the girls all hanging about in their scanties and in the windows too (well, behind glass mostly, to be accurate). They didn't have anything like this back in Bristol, that was for sure! We did discuss having a dabble ourselves but funked it. To be frank, that sort of thing has never appealed greatly to me when it actually comes to it. Probably too full of myself to allow for any chance of failure. Perhaps, not sure.

So, it was home again, home again jiggety jog shortly thereafter. All quite an experience for a sixteen-year-old. More bricks in my wall without a doubt.

(vii)

Jazz music did invade my little rock and roll heaven around this time, although its intrusion was, in fairness, not really a great bother. I never really got into jazz music to anything like the degree of my devotion to Elvis and the Gang.

'Beefy' Philips, yet another pal from Q.E.H., lived not far away in the posher part of Henleaze in a proper semi-detached house in a pleasant little tree lined cul-de-sac. True, our prefab was actually *in* Henleaze, but according to the iron laws of the class system, we were really interlopers as we were still, however you glossed it over, *council house dwellers*!

Unusually for a Q.E.H. boy of this generation, Beefy Philips had an almost impeccable middle class background. He was quite small in stature so God knows why we called him 'Beefy', but we did. The point about him was he thought himself a cut above the rest of us in the matter of musical appreciation. Thus, jazz music was his great enthusiasm and he considered it to be music for more acquired tastes. Rock and roll music was vulgar, Beefy would have thought, and more for the masses. Interesting really how subtly notions of class pervaded our existence, even when it came to recreational preferences. It was really the old 'rugger' for the 'toffs' and football for the 'oicks' syndrome dressed up in different garments. Ah well.

The point is that my pal Beefy not only preached the virtues and superiority of jazz music at me but he had the audacity to bring his records around to my place and expect to play them on my Dansette! I'm not sure how Elvis, Roy, Jerry Lee and Buddy felt about being elbowed out the way by Louis Armstrong and Co. (and even worse The Modern Jazz Quartet!) but I was pretty annoyed, trust me! Good old Beefy, he was a genial fellow though and best of all he wanted me to go with him to a weekly Jazz Club at The Worrall Rooms near the top of Blackboy (tut, tut Bristol!) Hill in Clifton. During the tiny amount of time my sister Jill had had to be free and enjoy her youth, The Worrall Rooms had been one of her haunts a year or so before, I know.

The very favourite venue for the young people of Bristol during those years was 'The Glen'. This was a building set in a deep quarry just opposite the Maternity Hospital at the top of Blackboy Hill. For some reason our Mother put us off ever going to 'The Glen'. Probably she thought it was rough and full of threats. Certainly by the end of the 1950's, 'The Glen' had become the mecca for Teddy Boys and the like. Out of rock and roll had come the teenager and the attitudes and tastes of the new young. In a curious offshoot, many of Britain's teenagers had adopted, as a uniform, a style of clothing not dissimilar to the Edwardian era of fifty years previously (hence Teddy Boys): an exaggeratedly long jacket over tight thinly cut trousers (drainpipes), a ruffled shirt with a tiny shoestring tie, large shoes with thick crepe soles (brothel creepers) and a pair of bright orange, blue or yellow socks peeping out in the gap between shoe and trouser bottoms; hair combed forward to a peak at the front and swept back into two equal tapering folds at the rear making the D.A. (duck's ass). Not to mention a set of long sideburns stretching down as far as the jowls. So, thus attired, off you strutted to a place like 'The Glen' for a weekend night out. But this was a working class thing, you see. Not for the products of schools like Q.E.H. who lived in districts like Henleaze. Oh dear no, dressing this way was the badge of class it was unthinkable one could consider wearing. It would have given my mother the very apex of discomfort she always declared so loudly when her 'two much' became 'three much'... 'If you ever appeared dressed like that my son you'd give me *the screaming ab dabs*!'

So, it was 'The Worrall Rooms' and the 'Jazz Club' then, with my middle-class pal Beefy. that were much more acceptable. Turned out to be good fun too!

(viii)

The Worrall Rooms were not spacious, in fact quite cramped, especially when hundreds of people packed in there to dance and listen to The Avon Cities Jazz Band. When everything was in full swing it was downright uncomfortable with all those sweating bodies trying excitedly to express themselves on the dance floor more or less all at the same time. Add in the fact that at least half the participants would have cigarettes creating large palls of smoke, hovering and drifting over the proceedings (fire regulations...forget them!) and it wasn't the most comfortable of environments! Not that we gave a jot. We were there for the music and the girls and the whole experience. The Avon Cities Jazz Band and their leader Ray Bush had a certain local celebrity at that time.

They were loud. Good, but loud! Their music reverberated the whole Worrall Rooms as they belted out their repertoire of 'trad jazz' numbers. A typical number would nearly always feature solo instrument players in turn driven along by a rhythm section of drums and bass. So, perhaps the trumpet, clarinet and trombone weaving their way in turn around the central melody before all the instruments joined in a swinging ensemble playing to bring the number to its climax. Trust me the place was really jumping, literally it seemed at times when the floorboards of the small wooden stage vibrated under the stomping feet and weight of the musicians. When the Band was belting out 'Tiger Rag' or 'When The Saints Go Marching In' and suchlike, there was an intoxicating atmosphere in that place. (En passant, there was no alcohol as I recall, we were all 'dry'. How unlike the alcohol-fuelled unpleasantness of many of the bars and clubs of today!) We loved these occasions at The Worrall Rooms. Me and my pal Beefy Philips didn't stand around gawping either. We plucked up our courage and asked girls to dance or sometimes

We plucked up our courage and asked a girl to dance

'split' two who were dancing together. Then we 'jived'. This was the dance of the times. Forget the waltz and the quick step, they had no place here. Jiving it was! It was a tough dance on the girls, I always thought. Spinning like bobbins, they were pushed and pulled in every direction whilst the boys, it seemed, only had to twirl their arms and wiggle their backsides occasionally. The girls seemed to do all the work. Perhaps, in these days of equality, it is no surprise that jiving has gone completely out of fashion. What self-respecting female nowadays would participate in such a male dominated strut about? Not many!

Be that as it may, I became a pretty good jiver and when I reached College a year or two later this was to be as important as any number of academic or sporting accomplishments... As a matter of fact I was never any good at any other kind of dancing. No timing or grace about me whatsoever. Mother always said I was born with two left feet. Jiving, though—eight out of ten!

After most of these sessions at the Worrall Rooms, Beefy and I would walk home together back to Henleaze where we both lived. I remember several cold frosty late nights walking with my pal Beefy Philips across The Downs—that large area of open grasslands in the north west of the City, the lungs of Bristol and the pride of Bristolians! We would be still steaming from our dance floor exertions. There used to be a seat just under The Water Tower on The Downs and we would sometimes pause there to gather ourselves together before striding off across the grass towards The White Tree, keeping just to the right of a landmark cluster of trees known as The Seven Sisters. On reaching The White Tree it was turn right through North View, left onto the long Henleaze Road and thence home. This whole journey was about three miles and there were never many people about. Ideal exercise for a couple of young fellas after a night's boppin'! One thing though, whatever time I got home, my mum's bedroom light was on and a little tired strangulated voice would call out, 'Dido, is that you?'

That bumpy lane had a few more bumps yet. It just started with feeling generally unwell. Then a couple of days off work (by now I was working as an unqualified teacher at The Crescent School). This was shortly followed by my pee becoming the colour of a Cardinal's Cassock.

Within hours this had all escalated into a ghastly reprise of the health disasters of early childhood. Our faithful old Irish physician Dr. Coulter drove up from Westbury in his cranking car. Now ten or so years older than when he had first packed me off for my extended stays as a guest of the, then, newly created National Health Service, the kindly old boy was at my bedside in my little tin prefab bedroom. Still with his trademark blocked and snorting nose, heavy overcoat and homburg hat askew on his head, he felt my fevered brow. He then gazed at the sample of my red urine that mother had thoughtfully preserved in an old coffee jar. 'Mmmm,' he said, 'I tink, I'll tek dis away wiv me and I'll give you a ring tomorra.' With that he threaded his way back to his car through the little maze of pathways from our prefab to the main road.

By now I had a temperature that was threatening to pop the mercury through the top of its tube. I had a burning fever yet couldn't stop shivering, not a comfortable combination, trust me. Poor Mother was now lumbered with all my ghastly health stuff yet again. We spent a horrible night. She lay down beside me on my bed and cuddled me and calmed me. It was all she could do. Another calamity had befallen us. I was eighteen years old. It wasn't long before I was back in The Bristol Royal Infirmary, this time on Budd Ward. After a rapid visit from the booming voiced Professor Bruce Perry it was speedily ascertained that my old pal the streptococcus bug had done for me yet again. This time I had developed Acute Nephritis (sometimes known as Bright's Disease). With this charming little fellow, the kidneys swell (hence the blood in the urine) and unless proper treatment is rapidly prescribed there is a distinct possibility of an early meeting with The Grim Reaper. So it wasn't long before they'd pumped me full of penicillin (let's hear it for Sir Alexander Fleming folks!). Then there were numerous needles for blood tests (which I never exactly fell in love with but, now older and a little wiser, learned to tolerate). Included in the fun was another bout of deliberate aspirin poisoning (mercifully short this time) and a diet about as appetising as the contents of a flooded ash tray. All this and the ubiquitous bed rest for the next couple of months.

So, there it was, sort of back to square one. Not that a couple of months in Budd Ward was completely devoid of interest, nor even a little naughty pleasure, it has to be said...

(ix)

Budd Ward at Bristol Royal Infirmary is on the top floor of a four-storey building. Like the three Wards on the floors stacked identically beneath it, there was a glass-fronted balcony housing about six patient beds. Since the hospital itself was already built in an elevated position, the view from the fourth floor balcony of Budd Ward was splendid. Had it been a hotel and not a hospital one would have had to pay a lot more for this Penthouse Suite! So, if one absolutely had to be in hospital it was quite a good position to find oneself. By virtue of, I know not what, it was in one of these balcony beds with its panoramic views across central and southern Bristol that was to be my home for a some ten weeks. Can't grumble about that!

There had been a good view from The Children's Ward (Ward 20) where I had spent several months of my earlier childhood, but the view from Budd Ward was even better. On the horizon one could see out to Knowle and around to Dundry Church Tower looking one way, then across to the hills above Bath looking another. In the middle distance were Temple Meads Station and the Feeder Canal and industrial parts of Bristol. In the foreground was what is now Broadmead and the main city centre shopping zone. At the time of my occupancy Broadmead was being recreated and rebuilt after its bashing by the Luftwaffe in the war. In fact, right below my eyrie position swarms of workmen were clearing what used to be called 'Magpie Park'. Here, it was said, had been one the City's main burial places during the Great Plagues of the 17th Century and earlier. It was on this site that John Lewis's flagship department store of the whole burgeoning new shopping area was to be built. I believe an awful lot of human remains had to be shifted and reburied. Nice work for someone! Some twenty-five years' later I took my eldest daughter Jane (aged about 12) to Lewis's to buy her first ever bra. So, I guess the area is famous historically for more than one reason!

My fellow patients on that balcony were an interesting bunch. In the next bed was an odd lad called Rowland. He had a complaint similar to mine. Come to think of it so did the other inhabitants of that balcony. I guess it was a sort of kidney corner as far as the medics were concerned. Anyway, Rowland was a slightly built young man of about sixteen. He had one of those permanently thin red sinusy noses at which he was constantly dabbing all day long with the same handkerchief he retained up the sleeve of his dressing gown. Hospitals, it seems, in those days hadn't *really* discovered bugs and infections! Anyway, old Rowland wasn't the sharpest scalpel in the operating theatre and he thought it a great jape to do things like put his thermometer into his tea just before having his temperature taken or dropping a couple of grapes into his urine bottle to freak the nurse who had to empty it. The nursing gals were on to him however and came to treat him as a sort of ward pet. They humoured and patronised him and treated him generally as the village idiots of old would have been treated. Just about right really!

There was an Irish cleaning lady called Hannah who sloshed around the balcony every day with her mop and bucket wearing a green apron and cap.

Rowland would try to wind her up too and was slightly more successful with her than with the wised up nurses... 'Yer, 'annah, you missed a bit under me locker, wos wrong wivee?', teased our Bristolian halfwit. Such remarks would enrage Hannah: 'Be Jeysus, ya daft litel bugga, you'll be betta off doin' it yerself then!'

Wise old Hannah knew a thing or two about horse racing though. 'Wud ya like a tip boys?' she'd say daily from behind her flailing mop, 'Botany Bay in de tree-tirty at Kempton, that'll win ya a few quid lads now, tek me word fur it.' I always used to check Hannah's tips the next day. She had more winners than losers without a doubt. As a matter of fact, all my life subsequently, on the extremely rare occasions I've had a successful bet on *anything*, I've intoned to myself, with an Irish twang, Hannah's little homily, 'I backed a winna!' Strange how some small things follow you through life!

(x)

Also perched on my balcony with me was a stoutish man called Mr. Smith. He was some kind of farm worker and came from Tetbury in Gloucestershire. He looked quite smart in his own green dressing gown, not a standard hospital issue three quarter length piece of towelling like the rest of us. A softly spoken man in his thirties, he had a round face and a full head of black hair. I used to feel quite sorry for him as he never had any visitors whilst on Budd Ward. There always was a surplus of visitors around my bed, as I had by now made many friends through school, football and work, not to mention visiting relatives. When I asked Mr. Smith about this it turned out he lived with his elderly mother, had no family and... 'the journey's too long for me mother down from Tetbury on the bus.' Some of my overspill of visitors would end up talking to him and my softhearted mother would often leave him a few loose cigarettes on his locker before she left the hospital. Amazingly, yes, we could smoke away quite happily on Budd Ward! The other interesting thing about Mr. Smith was that he knew a lot about birds. Up on that balcony was an ideal place for a 'twitcher'. He would be forever pointing out the sparrows, wrens, tits and blackbirds that would perch on the balcony rail or on prominent jutting walls or roofs. Mr. Smith could identify them all. Not that it interested me too much, for I was far too engrossed in my own stuff. In fact my deaf ear was usually in place when his soft Gloucestershire burr might say, 'Dozens of small birds down there around the church spire, think those magpies must scare 'em to gather up there.' (Prominent in our foreground was a church called St. James Priory. Legend has it that every tenth stone brought from Normandy to build the castle was set aside to build the Priory and now that the castle has long gone these stones are like an echo from 800 years ago.) I wish now I'd listened a little more to Mr. Smith—he might have opened my interest in the natural world a lot earlier. As it was, the raising of the shutters on my eyes to Nature was put on hold for many years. Regrettably!

In another bed on that balcony was a Mr. Carter. He was a middle-aged man and was clearly very ill. Unlike the rest of us he remained permanently in bed and the screens were often around him as the nurses tended to his needs. Sometimes I would stand at his bedside and try to talk to him but he could only whisper his responses which didn't make a lot of sense anyway. I recall holding his hand on one occasion when he pushed it towards me from underneath the sheet. Things were really nose-diving for poor Mr. Carter and there were considerable comings and goings of white coats to his bedside both day and night. Finally, it was finally, as those screens stayed around his bed all the time and the news filtered out that Mr. C was no more. It wasn't my first

in life there is death

encounter with death as very shortly before this time both my father and my Nanny Webb had died within a few weeks of each other. Mr. Carter's demise, especially being so close, drawn out and under my very nose as it were, reinforced a message I had already begun to understand. In life there is death.

It wasn't all doom and gloom though up there on Budd Ward. Once I started to feel like a normal person again it came increasingly to my attention that inside those starchy uniforms, underneath those little caps, beneath those severe hairstyles and within the black stockings and flat shoes were a number of good-looking females! It wasn't long before 'that' chemistry was bubbling up nicely. In particular it was starting to fizz a little with one of the night nurses called Vivienne (not a name you come across too much these days but quite a popular name for girls back then). Anyway, somehow Viv would find more and more time to spend standing and chatting (whispering actually) to me at my bedside, especially during the quiet dead of night. Wasn't too long before she'd perch on the edge of the bed and not a whole lot longer before holding hands and snatched kisses became the order of the night. Trouble with snatched kisses is they always sort of want to last a little longer.

Now, Viv was a pretty enough girl but she did have rather prominent front teeth. She was aware of this herself (she'd kissed the boys before!) and before the actual meeting of mouths she would try to push her lips forward so as to lessen the risk of those forward 'nashers' bashing into the recipient's own front teeth. Sadly, this well thought-out technique wasn't always a winner and there was just no kissing Viv without the very unsexy and uncomfortable 'clunk' of tooth enamel colliding. Also, it took a little moment for her to get lined up before going into forward gear in order to attempt a successful docking. This was all well and good until one night Viv and I had successfully locked on when a very slight cough from the balcony doorway revealed the presence of a visiting Night Sister on her checking 'Round'! Well, a hugely embarrassed and terrified Viv shot into the air and retreated back into the main body of the ward to await her fate. Happily, it didn't turn out too badly for her. After all, snogging with the patients in the middle of the night was a sackable offence by any standard. It turned out that the Sister involved was a compassionate soul and Viv got a warning and moved onto another Ward. We even had a few dates after I left hospital. We would meet under the Clock on St. Augustine's Parade on The Centre (commencing point for countless Bristolian romances down the years!). One thing though, often people look more attractive to the opposite sex wearing a uniform than in their ordinary clothes (in 'mufti' as nurses used to refer to it). At the time Viv and I had a few dates the fashion was for girls to wear very big 'hooped' skirts. It was like walking around with a miniature roundabout! Not very practical either for going through doors or squeezing past other people as you got off or on a bus. An utterly daft fashion as a matter of fact and one which, mercifully, didn't last too long. Anyway, Viv and I never reached our secret hospital heights of passion out in the big wide world and things cooled off fairly rapidly. Must confess though that ever since then, girls with protruding teeth have never really done it for me. Have to be honest!

(xi)

A number of visitors always flooded in and ebbed around my bed at visiting times. In addition to my blessed Mother and other relatives there were several others from the developing quarters of my life. Among them were the pals from my peer group at Q.E.H. such as Robin Thomas, Barry Coombs and Beefy Philips. By this time I'd started playing football regularly for an unlikely named team, 'Cardiff City Juniors' (more anon!) and had made a number of pals from amongst my Saturday afternoon playmates—in particular a very tall fellow called John Gregory ('Greg') who was our goalkeeper, and 'Robbo' Robinson, a large limbed and cheerful lad who lived in Filton. Then there was Trevor Ball and his lovely blonde girlfriend Judy (Trevor and I were to become lifelong friends long after the last ball had been kicked and the last goal had been scored). Finally, by no means least indeed, was John 'Nig' Southern. Nig was our captain and one of the nicest, most genuine blokes I've ever known. He was 'Bristol, through and through' and worked as a fireman on British Railways. We were still (just) in the age of steam, remember. Nig would come in to see me regularly on his way to or from work. He'd be wearing a short black workman's waistcoat over a grey shirt, dark serge trousers and a pair of steel capped boots. He'd be holding a small peeked cap in one hand and carrying a tin used for his sandwiches in the other. He would stand a little awkwardly at my bedside looking rather uncomfortable amongst the furniture, fittings and medical paraphernalia of a busy hospital ward. 'I brought you a few sweets, 'Ar, and a couple of "Buck Jones" comics' (Nig was really keen on The Wild West and collected books and comics on the subject. He also belonged to a 'Square Dancing Club', to which he used to invite me 'when yer better, 'Ar'). Nig had a sweet friendly way about him and a soft distinctive chuckle: 'We, missed you Saturday 'Ar, they 'ad a reely nippy winger, gave us all sorts of trouble, you'd uv sorted him out though, 'eed uv taken one look at your face and tripped over laffin!' Nig would have a little guffaw at his own joke and eventually shuffle off to the shunting yards at Temple Meads for his shift on the footplate. I loved that guy. He visited me almost every day. Nig was unfailingly nice; I think being 'unfailingly nice' goes an awful long way in this world and he was such a person. He was a brilliant left back too, one of the best I ever played with, sincerely!

Steve visited me one day on a visit to Bristol. We didn't see quite so much of him during these years as he was working in London. We were to see even less before too long as his blossoming academic career took him further and further away. Steve really was a top man in his field. By now he was becoming a noted statistician and over the following years of his career the noted edged inexorably towards eminent. He built up an impressive C.V. Name the famous University and Steve has done his numbers in many of them: Harvard (Massachusetts), Johns Hopkins (Maryland), McGill (Montreal), MacMaster (Ontario), Stanford (California), Nottingham (only really *just* counts in such an august list!), and latterly at Simon Frazer University in British Columbia. Wow!

Anyway, back there on Budd Ward in 1959, my wandering 'sort of' brother was not much impressed with me lying in bed 'blowing smoke professionally down your nostrils Nuthead' (his favourite name for me). Nor was he too pleased at my resistance to the fact that the hospital powers-that-be wanted to send me for two weeks to a Convalescent Home in Bournemouth for a topping off of my treatment and to assist my recovery in a controlled and restful environment. Being sent to such a place seemed about as attractive to me as a fortnight in a cemetery! I was anxious to get back out there amongst the mates, the footballs and the girls (not to mention Elvis, Jerry Lee et al!). Consequently, I was digging my heels in like mad against any such a proposal. This uncooperative stance was worrying my mother even further. Steve, of course, dismayed at my obstinacy and general posturing ingratitude and short sightedness, was siding with Mother. They were both ganging up on me. Eventually, I buckled under the pressure and agreed to join the living dead (as I saw it) in the haven of peace(!) in Bournemouth. They meant well—Mother and Steve, and probably I was behaving like a selfish brat. However, in truth, once I pitched up at the Convalescent Home, having travelled down from Bristol in a hospital transport with a couple of septuagenarians and their walking sticks, I'd made up my mind. All my worst fears were confirmed. As soon as I could escape I'd be off!

(xii)

On arrival at the Convalescent Home in Bournemouth (which actually turned out to be a large rambling old house on the outskirts of that rather overrated seaside town (lousy beaches!)) we were sent to rest in a cavernous upstairs' bedroom. Naturally we were exhausted after the 75-mile(!) drive down from Bristol. Perhaps that's not fair. The 'old 'uns' were probably really ready for a couple of hours' kip. Certainly the old fellow who had travelled down with me and who was now my bedroom companion, was soon into his nightshirt and off into the land of 'z'. Meanwhile I was wide-awake and alert and ready to wrestle gorillas if necessary to get out of there! I had been addicted for some time to World War II escape adventures and I had no trouble at all in slipping into the role of Flight Lieutenant Harry Dutton of Bomber Command, shot down during a raid over Berlin and ending up at Stalag Luft 9. Being situated conveniently only 75 miles from the Swiss Border, once through the secret tunnel and beyond the perimeter fence, supplied with false documents and disguised as a farm worker, there should be little problem in my making a 'Home Run'! Dream on MacDutton! The reality was a little more straightforward...

I repacked my recently unpacked case, crept unnoticed down the hallway and down the stairs and was soon crunching down the gravel drive towards the gate. One astonishing thing that occurred as I was almost outside was that a sports car turned into the drive and pulled up beside me. Crikey! This was it, back inside and into solitary confinement probably. In one of life's curious watershed moments the moustached fellow in the car wound down his window and said cheerily, 'Had enough already old boy!' He rewound his window, had a little chuckle and went his way. I have long cogitated on this encounter. The best explanation is that my brazen body language led him to believe I was a tradesman or just a visitor. What he could never know of course is how thorough had been my training for how to act if you ever found yourself behind enemy lines! I continued to indulge myself in such fantasy as I found my way to the railway station and worked at being inconspicuous on the platform as the mid-afternoon train to Bristol steamed into sight. A helpful lady in the railway compartment in which I found myself travelling agreed to go to the nearest Post Office when she alighted at the deliciously named Blandford Forum and sent a telegram to the powers that were in the Convalescent Home back in Bournemouth. I recall the wording of that telegram exactly: 'REGRET INCONVENIENCE. WELL. ON WAY HOME. DUTTON.'

My surprised but unflappable and tolerant Mother was not exactly happy when I breezed back into our little prefab. 'Well, that's good then,' drawing hard on a cigarette, 'just about upset everyone good and proper this time... dear dear me'—then breaking into one of her favourite little ditties when · stressed: 'There ought to be a society for the preee...vention of cru..el..ty to poor unfortunate *mothers*...' The word '*mothers*' would be sung through gritted teeth and in an extended and exaggerated manner, as in 'M...O...T...H...E...R...S!!'. Bless her! Needless to say there would be food on the table and a warm drink in my hand within minutes. Spoilt? Who, me?!

Within a week or so I was back at my teaching job at The Crescent School. My relationship by now with Mr. Philip Harmer-Smith had really gone south and was hanging by a thin thread. This was a situation I shared with most others as the school was nose-diving towards oblivion. This was almost exclusively because of its hapless new Headmaster.

Philip Harmer-Smith was a phoney through and through. His qualification was almost certainly bogus... F.R.G.S.—Fellow of the Royal Geographical Society! This was a meaningless title, probably purchased or perhaps merely honorary. It had no academic credibility or standing whatsoever. Remember, in those days, people's qualifications were rarely verified and there was inevitable and probable widespread abuse. Anyway, Mr Harmer-Smith had pulled the wool over my Uncle Percy Harding's eyes with ease. Strange thing with Percy Harding, he was as cunning as a family of foxes winning a gold medal at the cunning foxes' Olympic Games when it came to any sort of business deal. In contrast, anything to do with appointing an appropriate person to an educational post and he was completely clueless. He was probably bamboozled by Mr. Harmer-Smith's double-barrelled name as much as anything. A double-barrelled name automatically signalling upper class and quality in the jolly old English class game. Then, if that was not enough, a qualification that had *four* letters in it! Old Percy would have been well impressed.

Anyway, he had appointed the guy in haste and ignorance and by the time I returned to work there after my Bristol Royal Infirmary and Bournemouth frolics all the pigeons were not only coming home to roost but plastering their droppings over everything and everyone.

he was a dud   Now, had Mr. Harmer-Smith had the personality and social skills to carry off the situation, then he might have got away with it and the school may have survived for much longer. Unfortunately, he was hopeless. He didn't understand or relate to children. He was quickly sussed by the teaching staff who realised he was a dud virtually after the first introductions and Staff Meeting.   Finally, all-important in a Private School in which parents coughed up hard gained earnings for the privilege of their children attending the school, he showed no leadership skills to such parents. Mr. Harmer-Smith was unconvincing, with a false charm and an embarrassing manner which soon switched them off. It wasn't long before existing pupils began to leave the school and no new ones arrived. A disastrous state of affairs. One thing Percy Harding did understand, quicker than a coin dropping into a slot, was when he was losing money. So, after I left the school in the spring of 1960, my place at Teachers' Training College in Birmingham safely secured for the forthcoming September, The Crescent School staggered on for only another couple of years.

At the time I left I was hardly speaking to Mr. Harmer-Smith. On top of everything else he was of the Plymouth Brethren and never missed an opportunity to paddle that little religious canoe. This stuck in the craw of most folks even before his other weaknesses surfaced. The girl pupils especially were always uncomfortable with Mr. Harmer-Smith as anytime he spoke to females he rarely took his eyes off their bosoms. He had a very dowdy wife who was quite a nice person actually but as plain as plain could be. She had prematurely grey hair gathered tightly in a bun, was bespectacled and wore no make-up of any description. Mrs. Harmer-Smith wore long skirts, flat shoes and woollen stockings. Her jumpers and cardigans were always stretched and loose fitting. She was controlled by her husband, spent much time in the kitchen either cooking or ironing and seemed to take the brunt of looking after her own two children who were kept very much in the background.

Mr Harmer-Smith himself was extremely opinionated too and I remember one row I had with him at the lunch table (if it was your duty-day you sat with him and his wife at their lunch table in his study). Mrs. Harmer-Smith was largely silent on these occasions and was constantly bobbing up to fetch and carry the dishes from the kitchen. Towards the end of my time there the loquacious Mr. Harmer-Smith regarded me as a dangerous radical. Our row was about The Suez Crisis which had occurred in 1956 and was one of the last convulsions of Imperialism. In it, a weakened Britain, behind the back of The United States and allied with France and in a secret deal with the Israelis, had invaded Egypt. The reason for this invasion was that The Egyptians had taken over the running of the Suez Canal. Although the Canal was within Egypt and most would say rightfully belonged to them, it was held to be necessary for Britain and France to invade Egypt to re-establish their own control over the canal. In short, to impose a solution on foreigners just as had always been the case throughout the previous times of European nations imposing their will on the rest of the world. Well, the lesson of Suez was that there was now a different world order and countries could no longer act unilaterally. The limits of Britain's erstwhile power had been exposed for all to see once she and her allies withdrew with their tails between their legs. The end of European Imperialism. Some may say only the start of American... another story perhaps.

Back at Mr. Harmer-Smith's lunch table. He had asserted that Britain had been fully justified in invading Egypt and it was all a Russian plot to take over the world and that Russians had been seen walking around Cairo with snow on their boots. Well, I just finally couldn't stomach such nonsense (can't say the same about Mrs. Harmer-Smith's cheese and onion pie though, which was always delicious!), and I told him boldly that he was talking rubbish in my view. From that point we didn't really speak much, relations between us having become very frosty.

One thing which turned out well for me during the stewardship of Mr. Harmer-Smith was that at Easter 1959 he had arranged a visit to Germany for about twenty pupils and I had agreed to go along. We might have guessed when we got there that it was going to be somewhere where the pupils would undergo some religious indoctrination (not much mention of *this* though in all the pre-publicity to parents, it being billed as a week's holiday in Rhineland). Typical Mr. HS, up to his smoke and mirrors again!

Well, would you believe it, this trip proved hugely enjoyable for me in spite of, rather than because of, our devious leader. Indeed, it was at Klostermuhle on the banks of The River Lahn shortly before the point at which that river joined the mighty Rhine, that I had as much fun as I'd ever really had before...

(xiii)

Klostermuhle on the River Lahn turned out to be a holiday centre for young people run by Evangelical Christians. It consisted of several newly constructed large wooden huts. At least two of these huts were dormitories, another was a used as a kitchen and dining room and there was one hut even larger than the others, which was used primarily for what were euphemistically called 'Meetings' but turned out in fact to be used as an Evangelical Church. The site itself was close to an old Monastery and within a few hundred yards of The River Lahn.

How Mr. Harmer-Smith had discovered such a place is unknown but almost certainly through his own religious network in which he was deeply involved there in Bristol. Klostermuhle was run by two Americans, a man called Tom and his wife Sheena. They were both very American. Tom was a man in his thirties. He was very tall and sported a hairstyle that was new and unusual to me. It was short and spiky and cropped at the same level over his whole head. This was my first look at the crew-cut! This hairstyle was shortly to spread rapidly among young males everywhere and was soon competing with the more greasy 'forward peaks', 'ducks' behinds' and 'Toni Curtis' styles. This was in Britain anyway. The hairstyles of the young of other European countries always seemed more conventional and did not follow the extremes of the styles sported on the bonces of the British young. The crew-cut was soon everywhere though and was as American as apple pie. It was as much a badge of being young and American as jeans and tennis shoes. It was fresh, clean cut and, importantly, since it was a style only suited for a very full head of hair, it was *only* for the young—or in the case of Tom, the head of Klostermuhle, the youngish!

It turned out Tom and his wife were from Iowa. They were both nice people who had a pleasant and relaxed attitude with all the young people who visited Klostermuhle. They were both always very casually dressed, usually in shorts and 'T' shirts. Tom was very athletic and he was soon introducing us to volleyball. This was a game that was virtually unknown in England at that time. I recall some fiercely competitive matches between England and Germany. Since there were mostly German youngsters there, Tom would become an honorary Englishman for the purposes of these volley ball matches and with his age, height and experience he evened up the odds considerably. I became quite accomplished at volleyball and during the early years of my subsequent teaching career I promoted and encouraged what was then largely a neglected and unknown activity in English schools.

So, Klostermuhle was great for the sport and very good too for making friends with young Germans. I had soon palled up with a German boy called Gerhard Stephan. He was there with a group of others from his church in Ludwigshafen-Am-Rhein. Gerhard was about my age and spoke almost perfect English(!). He had a great sense of humour and, like me, a healthy dislike and suspicion towards all the Meetings we were obliged to attend each day, one each morning and one each evening as I recall.

You see, likeable as old Tom and wife Sheena may have been, they definitely had an agenda of their own. Once a Meeting got underway it was easy to spot the zealots underneath Tom's crew-cut and behind Sheena's softly strummed guitar! *evangelical shindigs* These Meetings were nothing more than evangelical shindigs during which the youngsters present were gradually indoctrinated into the paths of righteousness. Or, at least, this was the clear objective of the organisers,

Once the daily morning Meeting concluded I usually joined up with Gerhard and his pals and we escaped from Klostermuhle and walked half a mile or so down the river to a point where the river was quite shallow and bending. Here, we would spread our towels and loll about in the warm spring sunshine and dangle our feet in the river shallows. There were about eight or ten of us in this little gang, including a pretty, fair-haired, German girl called Jutta Pfitzner who was aged about seventeen. Readers of these words may by now have noticed that by this time of my life my interest in the opposite sex was, shall I say, healthy! In short, Jutta and I were soon having a bit of a pet and a snog on the warm river bank. This whole little group became really bonded during our time at Klostermuhle and when the time came to leave arrangements had been made to correspond—yes, write *letters* to each other, how quaint does this now seem in a world of emails, mobile phones and all the rest of the modern paraphernalia of instant communication!

Indeed, for the following six months or so I kept up a correspondence with both Gerhard and Jutta. The letters between Jutta and I became quite steamy at times and during the Autumn of 1959 the invitation came from Gerhard for me to visit with him and his family in Germany for that approaching Christmas. Thus it was that once again, with very little money but the prospect of Christmas in a foreign country, being reunited with my jolly new German pal Gerhard and perhaps some smooches with my sweet

Jutta under the mistletoe, that I set off by train and ferry for Germany a few days before Christmas 1959.

Going back to Klostermuhle in the previous Spring; it seems strange that I didn't spend much time looking after and doing things (apart from volleyball) with the pupils we had taken there from The Crescent School. I cannot recall doing any of the supervising or other duties you would expect me to have undertaken as a teacher accompanying the school party.

The reason for this I think is that by this time, the very fag-end of my employment at the school, relationships between me and Mr. Harmer-Smith had become so poisonous and rancorous that he considered me such a disruptive influence that he was happier when I was out of his sight. This must have been it. At the time we went to Klostermuhle he already didn't like me very much. Once there, he sensed my dislike as to how the whole enterprise had been misrepresented to the parents and my consequent cynical and subversive attitude. Then it was end game and better we more or less ignored each other. So that was that.

Back in Ludwigshafen-Am-Rhein on December 24th, it was a different scene. By now, in the bosom of Gerhard and his large and loving family, 'Mutti', 'Fatti', sister Isobella and brothers Karl-Heinz and Franz, the presents were coming out from under the tree for the family members and even one or two for their young English visitor. In German tradition the presents were distributed on Christmas Eve and not on Christmas day itself.

The Stephans were a loving and close family. Like most people in that town, Herr Stephan was employed in the giant Chemical Works of B.A.S.F. (Badische Anilin-Und Soda- Fabrique). There was absolutely no doubt that the town was dominated by a Chemical Works! A sort of sulphurous smelling foggy blanket was permanently draped over everything. There must have been legions of folks in that town with chest problems. Probably in time the town was cleaned up somewhat, but at that time it was dreadful.

On New Year's Eve in every window of every house there was set a burning candle. This was done as a token of solidarity with their kinfolk in East Germany. Remember, after the war Germany was divided into Communist East Germany, which became part of Stalin's Empire after Russia conquered and claimed the whole of Eastern Europe when Germany fell in 1945. West Germany was created as a separate State with a democratic government set up in Bonn and was rapidly rebuilt after the war helped by American money (The Marshall Plan), the zeal and energy of the Germans themselves and the happy embracing of a capitalist system. Between these two German States was what Churchill named the Iron-Curtain in his iconic speech at Fulton, Missouri in 1945. This became the very frontier of The

Cold War which held as the 'realpolitik' of international relations for the next forty years.

That was the situation that existed on the evening of December 31st 1959 when the citizens of Ludwigshafen-Am-Rhein lit their candles for their friends and families in the 'other' Germany on the other side of the 'Iron-Curtain'. That night, as the fifties decade died, with my pal Gerhard, I walked at midnight through the smelly streets of Ludwigshafen. With the candles glowing in the claggy darkness we walked towards the home of my, by then, sort of German girl friend Jutta.

Gerhard, who was a great jester, had been rehearsing me all day in the use of a suitably amorous German phrase to say to Jutta when we met at the very moment when the sixties decade tiptoed into view. He assured me that in holding out my arms towards her and proclaiming loudly 'Jutta, du bist mein spullappen!' that our love would henceforth be sealed. Thus it was, that at the stroke of midnight we knocked on the door of family Pfitzner who lived a short walk from the Stephans. A radiant Jutta answered the door, wearing, as I recall, a somewhat daring yellow dress. Taking my cue from my almost smirking pal I blurted out: 'Jutta, du bist mein spullappen!' Instead of falling into my arms as I had hoped, the yummy fraulein dissolved into giggles. She knew a thing or two about the tricky ways of her friend Gerhard and, picking up quickly on his little joke, she said to me with her blue eyes twinkling and, naturally, in perfect English, 'David, do you really want to call your girlfriend a dishcloth!'

(xiv)

Crossing the stormy Channel, when returning from Germany after spending Christmas with Gerhard and his family, introduced me to seasickness for the first time. I spent much of that little voyage vomiting back the greasy fry-up I'd greedily scoffed as soon as I had boarded the ferry at Boulogne. Taught me a lesson though and I've always subsequently watched it on ferries and suchlike as the dreaded 'voms' can suddenly make you feel as ghastly as ghastly can be. There's no escape either until you're ashore and those waves stop, gently and insistently, rocking and slopping your entrails around inside you.

The origins of how I came to be a regular player with Cardiff City Juniors have dimmed somewhat into the memory mist. I think a pal of mine at Q.E.H., called Roger Gould, knew somebody who knew somebody and recommended me. Roger Gould was a really engaging fellow with wavy fair hair and a permanent grin. He was a dayboy at Q.E.H. and he lived in Fishponds just the other side of Eastville Park. We became quite friendly at one time and I would go across to his house and we would take a tennis ball out and play football in the road outside. This was called Thingwell Road to my recall although there won't be many traces of Roger or his family around there now. As a matter of fact Roger in later life became one of the stalwarts of the Q.E.H. Old Boys' set-up. He was a very nice fellow. It must have been football which drew us together as Roger was an 'A' Former so I wouldn't have seen that much of him around the school. I recall he was a Bristol City fan which was odd as he lived only a couple of stones' throw from The Bristol Rovers' ground at Eastville. Something a bit dodgy about that!

Anyway, it was through Roger I think I went to meet Reg Preece the manager of Cardiff City Juniors. At first It seemed really promising, joining a team in Bristol run by Cardiff City Football Club as a nursery team from which they may recruit young players into the professional game. A stepping-stone for impressionable youth! Of course the whole thing was a preposterous sham invented in the strange tiny mind of Reg Preece who turned out to be a real fantasist. There was no connection whatsoever with Cardiff City Football Club except inside Reg's balding bonce.

Nevertheless, I came to really like Reg. He was a real character, as Bristolian as any Bristolian in the history of Bristol. He lived with his long suffering wife and teenage son John in a council house at Stapleton. I think he may have had a daughter too living with them. When I first went there, his son John was in the little alleyway at the side of the house repairing a motorbike. John Preece impressed me. First, he had a spiky blond Toni Curtis forward peak hairstyle. Then he was wearing tight jeans and a brightly coloured T-shirt. This seemed the height of teenage modernity to me. Most impressive of all, perhaps, standing alongside him, was his very pretty dark haired girlfriend, Cheryl. She was chewing gum, dressed like John in tight jeans and T-shirt and had very black make up on her eyelids and eyebrows. The kitchen door was open and just inside, standing on the draining board of the kitchen sink, John had his record player plugged in and he and his girlfriend were listening to the music flooding their little alleyway whilst John messed with his piston rings. The record being played was unforgettable. Out blared the first few exciting and shuffling beat bars of 'Bye, Bye Love' by the The Everly Brothers! It was the first time I had heard this record as it was just released, as they used to say. The whole cameo— John, the girlfriend, the motorbike, and the Everly Brothers—all fused together instantly to make a lifelong, frozen picture in my mind. Somehow all making the then and there of that time significant.

Bye, Bye Love.
Bye, Bye Happiness,
Hello sweet caress,
I think I'm a gonna die

Nowadays, that song is a standard, familiar, old, tired rock 'n roll song tucked safely away in a karaoke machine waiting for an old timer to give it an outing. Then, vibrating around Reg Preece's Council House and garden in Stapleton, Bristol, on a warm September evening... *electric*!!

'Jew wanna see ar Dad?' said John, moving aside so I could squeeze past him. 'Dad!' he shouted into the interior of his little house, 'there's a kid yer, wants yew.' 'Hello, Mr Preece, I came about joining your football team...' My first impression of Reg didn't alter from the moment I set eyes on him throughout the whole time I knew him. He was in his forties, prematurely balding, only about five feet two tall. He had a slight potbelly and a round puffy face. The broken blood vessels on his cheeks suggested he might enjoy a drink or three. His trousers were baggy and ill-fitted and, strangest of all, his trouser bottoms were tucked inside a pair of short wellington boots which appeared to be at least one size too big for him. Reg, then, not your average looking manager of a football club! Frankly he never looked any different whatsoever. During our matches he would patrol the touchline dressed exactly the same but also carrying a white enamel bucket and a dripping yellow sponge. On these occasions he would be shouting such tactically astute remarks as, 'Kick the little twat Harry, let 'im know yer up 'is behind!'

His trousers were baggy and ill-fitted

Dear Reg. We played our home games at Oldbury Court. From the changing rooms we walked through a wooded area, thence down to and across a little brook. Then up the other side to emerge virtually straight out onto our own pitch. We were a successful team. We played in The Bristol Church of England League and, judging by the expletives frequently whizzing around the pitch during a match, it would have been perfectly understandable if God had withdrawn his sponsorship altogether!

Included among my team mates were Nig Southern, our captain and my frequent hospital visitor whilst I had languished in The Bristol Royal Infirmary with my kidneys on fire, 'Robbo' Robinson, our large centre half from Filton and 'Greg' the goalie; all loose limbed tall and elastic, as all good goalies should be. Then there was John Preece himself, the manager's son. John was picked only *because* he was the manager's son as he wasn't very good at all. The rest of us were always covering his mistakes. John was completely uncoordinated which was a bit of a handicap for a footballer. I never ever played with a player who had so many 'air kicks' as John. He was forever missing the ball and tumbling over. It was awful when he went into a tackle because you knew exactly what was about to happen... John was going to be about five seconds late in his lunge and his opponent would be lucky ever to walk again.

Then there was Freddie Watts our left half. Freddie always brought his girlfriend, Sal, to watch the games. Those two really had the teenage hots badly for one another and they would be unconcernedly pawing and stroking each other even during our walk from the changing rooms to our playing pitch. Just before the whistle blew to start the game Freddie would disentangle himself from Sal as they stood almost fused together up against a tree at the edge of the small wooded area alongside the pitch. At half-times Freddie would disappear with Sal out of sight and rather deeper into the little wood and remain there until just before the ref blew the whistle for the start of the second half. At which point Freddie and Sal would emerge, panting slightly, from their glady nook and with a knowing little smile between them. 'Blige Ref,' Freddie would say, 'ain't I got time fur a little smoke for we starts again!'

Later, in the showers after the game, someone would tease Freddie about his half-time disappearing act. To which he would respond, 'Just knockin' a round off', wos smatter wiv that, makes I play better!'

Also in our little team of Christians were the Clarke Brothers, Ron and Bill. The two brothers were a genuine pair of honest grafters who turned many a game around in our favour. Bill Clarke was as good a goal scorer as I ever played with. Left footed, strong and determined with a shot like a cannonball, Bill was destined for better things. Later he went on to play as a semi-professional for Trowbridge Town. At centre forward we had a comedy act called Shaun Mulligan. Shaun was born in Bristol, but as his name indicates, his parentage was Irish. When they coined the phrase 'fighting Irish' they clearly had Shaun in mind. It was fisticuffs every game with Shaun, often with players on his own side! Once something had lit his fuse he wasn't going to be happy until someone's lip was split or he had handed out what he called his 'Dublin Kiss' (banging someone in the face with his forehead... nutting them, in common parlance). Shaun was a 100% Teddy Boy—sideburns, drainpipe trousers, a jacket down to the knees, crepe-soled shoes and shoe-string tie. Also of course, he was a 100% idiot!

Somewhat surprising really that we gelled as quite a good team and topped the League pretty well throughout my time. Must have had God on our side after all! Mustn't forget my pal Trevor Ball who also played for us and who became a life-long friend with whom I was to share an adventure or two in several places, including Weymouth, the Dorset town that was to figure prominently throughout my latter teens. I'll come to that. First though, the hot summer of 1959!

(xv)

One consequence of the illnesses of my childhood and teens is that I never learned to swim properly. In fact, I rarely went to the swimming baths as Mother was convinced it was not good for me and 'just the sort of place you get germs'. She was almost certainly correct but most people seemed to survive all right. The upshot was that by the time I arrived at Q.E.H. at age twelve I'd not got any confidence or skill in the water at all. Whilst most of my contemporaries frolicked around like porpoises I remained feebly anchored to the side of the swimming baths making a little splash here and there and forever fearful of 'going under'.

Frequently in Assemblies at Q.E.H., swimming badges, cups and certificates were handed out to successful boys who took the long walk up to shake the limp hand of E.B.P. Gillett. The rest of us applauded and the recipients smiled their watery and embarrassed smiles as they retook their places on one of the long benches we sat on in The Dining Room where our Assemblies were held. On such occasions I would have stabs of envy. Such feelings would only increase as each year passed and I became older and the swimming prizewinners seemed younger and younger. This was especially true of the 'four lengths' certificate which was awarded to virtually a hundred percent of boys within their first two years at the school. Not this boy though, and that state of affairs increasingly rankled!

Things did improve slowly and, by the time I did my boarding spell at the school, I was a fairly regular attender at Jacob's Wells Swimming Baths where I would go with a couple of pals, usually Ram Cockram and 'Coline' (rhymes with 'towline') Thorne. You may recall Coline had been the chief maker of mud pats during the 'Left-Overs' rugby games at Eastfield. Being generally scruffy and unwashed this was a task for which he was eminently suited. Coline was a very small, almost tiny, boy who was completely unsuited to the rugby field and was generally trodden on in life wherever he went and whatever he did. However, he was a really accomplished swimmer and this is how he made his mark at Q.E.H., being frequently found in the winners' enclosure whenever there were swimming galas and suchlike. Coline's other claim to Q.E.H. fame was that he was one of the favourites for 'the dimmest boy ever at Q.E.H' award. Poor fellow left Q.E.H. with hardly a G.C.E. subject to his name and disappeared somewhere into this big wide world forever. Whether or not he ever overcame the shame and stigma of leaving school without much in the way of paper qualification is unknown. He was an amusing, if sometimes irritating person and, like myself, something of a clown. I like to think he went on to make his fame and fortune somehow somewhere. His contribution to my life is that, along with Ram Cockram, he taught me to swim! Thanks Coline!

Now I never ever mastered all that correct breathing stuff and could never manage the crawl (which, after all, is the stroke the whole world seems to be able to do, except me that is). However, after Coline and Ram had finished with me I could do the breast stroke sufficiently well to gain some forward momentum, albeit painfully slowly, and, just as important, I acquired the confidence to go under the water and even jump in from the side. I could sort of do a very elementary dive too although I didn't try too often as it frequently turned into a painful belly-flop and left large red painful weals across the chest. Not good. That's just about where my water proficiency has remained all my life with a few detours here and there—like the time in the summer of 1959 when I got the courage to jump off the high diving board at Henleaze Lake!

Henleaze Lake was very deep indeed. It was a sort of geographical freak really as Bristol is about as well known for its lakes as it is for its volcanoes. But there it was, tucked away between the bottom of Henleaze Road and the start of Southmead Road. Long ago the locals had commandeered it as a private swimming club and there was something of the exclusive about it. This was Henleaze after all. Didn't want those 'oiks' who lived only a mile or two down the road in Southmead to get any ideas at all above their station—that wouldn't do.

The summer of 1959 was glorious. It was wall-to-wall sunshine every day seemingly guaranteed. How natural then that the young folks of Henleaze at that time should congregate daily at Henleaze Lake. How natural that they should become known as 'The Henleaze Lake Crowd'. How natural that their fun in the sun at the side of the lake during the day should ripple outwards to some fun in various homes, usually when parents were absent, at other times! Yep, a real teen scene filling those warm days of '59!

It was through my pal Barry 'Pancho' Coombs that I obtained my membership card to this exclusive little crowd of youngsters. Not that I was ever entirely accepted into the core of the group as it was well known that I lived in a prefab. The prefab was *in* Henleaze, it's true, but when all was said and done it *was* a prefab. My membership was considerably strengthened however by being an ex-Q.E.H. boy and was even more reinforced by being a friend of Barry Coombs.

Barry and I had become quite friendly at Q.E.H. He was a likeable and popular figure at school being very good at sports (especially rugby and swimming). Everyone liked Barry then and, indeed, even now half a century later the same thing applies! Just about everyone it seems in Bristol knows and likes the fellow, no exaggeration! Barry spent his working life in the travel business in Bristol and in the course of his job made zillions of contacts. Many times Barry's name has come up and someone has chimed in: 'Oh, we know Barry Coombs, he booked a holiday for us... nice fellow.'

Barry was a good-looking boy with a very full head of black hair brushed into a 'forward peak' style. Never ever was a peak more forward than Barry's! It flopped down neatly, almost symmetrically, right in the middle of his forehead. He was a brainy guy too. He initially went to Bristol University to study Geography but dropped out after a year or so as it didn't seem to suit him. Barry wasn't too keen on the study requirements, one reason being that there was so much more of interest going on around that time. More specifically, like the rest of us, it was the female geography that commanded most of his attention.

Thus it was that Barry was a leading player amongst The Henleaze Lake Crowd. Also cruising around the lake that summer was Roger Dufell. The girls were really crazy about Roger. He was fair-haired, tall and drop dead handsome. He was known as 'Lord Dufell'. Then there was 'Podge' Nash. He was a big built, strong, athletic fellow with a confident manner and always had a big following amongst the girls. There were others, now forgotten, who made up 'The Crowd'.

Among the girls was Christina Tandy, a slender and obliging flower and Eve Dennis, who was somewhat shy and all the more appealing for that. Then, 'Toni' Matthews. Toni was a pretty elfin-like girl with dark hair which she wore short and which was parted down the middle, allowing two short quarter-moon-shaped pieces to drop down perfectly on either side to frame her face. One of the popular films around this time was 'Roman Holiday' which launched the career of Audrey Hepburn and I suspect that Toni Matthews may have seen the film and been influenced by it. After the Henleaze Lake days drifted into history, Toni became a Dental Nurse and later went to live in the United States where she married a doctor and last I heard was a doting grandmother with shoals of grandchildren in the Seattle area.

There were other girls too. By day we slopped around the lakeside and in the evening might meet up again to do some snogging and 'spinning' Elvis 'discs' on the old Dansette. Notice, no drugs and hardly any booze (a few beers perhaps). All fairly tame by the standards of today. How appropriate that Jerry Keller's record 'Here Comes Summer' should have been a hit record of the time and it fixed that summer so firmly into the memory.

> Here comes summer
> Almost June the sun is bright
> Here comes summer
> Gonna see her every night
> It's the greatest
> Lot's more time to hold her tight
> Oh, let the sun shine bright
> On my happy summer home!

Henleaze Lake was dominated by an extremely high diving board. It was a green painted, metal structure with about three stages and then the very top board itself. Not even those in the gang who were good swimmers and divers ever actually dived from that high board and by no means everyone had the bottle to even jump from it. It had been noted that I largely avoided actually swimming in the lake. It was too embarrassing to reveal my general incompetence in the water. Things were teetering on the edge of humiliation as the teasing grew more frequent and persistent. Nothing for it to restore my rapidly fading image than an act of bravado sufficient to jerk my popularity barometer back up several notches. 'OK, I admit I'm not a very good swimmer, but I'm not scared to jump off the top board!' God, I must have been desperate to make such a public boast! 'OK, let's see you do it then...'

I can remember that slow climb up four sets of metal rungs to the top of that diving stage as if it were yesterday. In later life I have had similar terrified feelings; in a hospital when heading towards the theatre for an operation or walking into a room to face an interview panel for a job. Absolute dread! Thank goodness we don't have to experience these things too often in life.

In the event, I got to the top and didn't think about it. I didn't look down even. No hesitation, jumped straight off. It's better to do things that way, I've found, at life's crucial junctions and moments. Just screw yourself up and get on with it. Some things, however unpleasant or uncomfortable just have to be done, don't they?

One thing though, that's the one and very only time I ever jumped from a high diving board. Scared myself to death!

Pictures of 'Prefabs' like the one we lived in at 163 Henleaze Road, "…were small rectangular units, all prefabricated walls made of artificial materials (no brick or concrete) which were assembled 'on site'…" They were only intended to last ten years but some are still lived in some sixty years later, as seen in the more recent picture, on the right.

Chapter Nine

Weymouth

MY FATHER lived in Weymouth for the last few years of his life. During those later summers from 1956 to 1962 I spent most of my long summer holidays in Weymouth, staying at first with my father and his new wife Olwen. After father died in November 1958 I continued to live and work there during those later summers, until the real world poked in its nose and I began my teaching career 'proper' in Birmingham in 1963.

The years in Weymouth were a kaleidoscope of experience. I'd first visited the town in the early 1950's as a breathless (and usually silent!) companion to my Uncle Percy Harding as he whizzed there and back from Bristol in his sleek black Jaguar car when he made his flying visits to attend to his business interests.

Approaching Weymouth by road never failed to excite. First passing into Dorset itself with its characteristically rolling landscape, then through the old town of Dorchester and onto the long straight road pinging due south towards the chalk uplands which had to be climbed before first sight of the blue waters of Weymouth Bay. Weymouth really is a little geographical jewel. It is enclosed by its guardian chalk hills, its generous and broadly sweeping bay curving eastwards towards Lulworth Cove and westwards, more sharply, out to Portland Bill. Slightly further on from Portland lies the phenomenon of Chesil Beach, several

Dorset coast showing Weymouth beach on the right, Portland Harbour centre 'enclosure', Portland Bill promontory to the bottom and the long Chesil Beach on the left.

miles of pure mounded shingle, dramatically sculptured by the ocean, cutting off and enclosing a long lagoon on its landward side. On its Weymouth side, Portland offers a natural deep-water harbour which has long been utilised as a naval base.

The town of Weymouth had grown up originally around its own little

fishing harbour and it had expanded rapidly as the town developed as a holiday resort, especially towards the end of the nineteenth century. Indeed Weymouth's popularity had started to grow long before this when back at the end of the eighteenth century the town was a regular watering hole for King George III and his entourage. The town has always milked its association with its royal connection and this has always bolstered its self-esteem. Indeed, the principal architectural feature of the town, in fact its very anchor by which all 'Weymouthonians' fix their position, is 'The King's Statue' built towards the western end of the Promenade.

Weymouth's Landmark Statue. George III

'Meet you by the King's Statue' or 'Get off the bus just by The King's Statue,' or, 'We'll cross the road to the main part of the beach by The Statue.' Second, but only just, as the major fixing point in

Weymouth, is The Jubilee Clock, constructed at a point roughly in the middle of the Promenade to mark Queen Victoria's Golden Jubilee in 1897. This distinctive, rather ornate clock tower is very Victorian with its little lantern-shaped roof plonked on its top. The Victorians so loved their lantern and triangular roofs. These can still be seen in their thousands throughout Britain in the parks, atop pavilions and bandstands. The Jubilee Clock, then, is another Weymouth landmark. The town always plays up to its association with the novelist Thomas

The Jubilee Clock

Hardy. The great writer of tragic and sweeping stories set his tales in Dorset or Wessex as Hardy named the whole area. This was the setting for all his novels. Weymouth was named 'Budmouth' by Hardy, charmingly I think.

By the beginning of the twentieth century the railway had arrived at Weymouth and this increased the number of visitors dramatically. It was very much the fashion to take holidays by the seaside. With its shallow waters and safe bathing Weymouth was the perfect place to take children. From the 1920's onwards Weymouth was firmly established as a popular holiday resort. To meet the needs of its visitors the town was soon one of hotels and boarding houses, shops and cafes. Along with these came the Amusement Arcades, Fun Fairs and all the rest of the 'Honky Tonk' of a popular Seaside Resort. Weymouth's economy firmly wrapped itself around these realities and the town expanded greatly throughout the years between the wars and immediately after the end of World War II. During the months of May until September, (The Season), the population of the town would double at least. In addition to those who came and actually stayed in Weymouth for a week or more for their holidays, a new sort of creature was born—the 'day tripper'! The motor cars, coaches (charabancs as they were once known!) and the railway had put Weymouth in reach of people living much further away who could still get to the town early enough in a day to make a visit worthwhile. By lunchtime they had arrived in their hordes disgorging from their means of transport, filling the narrow streets and flooding towards the magnetic Promenade and beach.

So, Weymouth became brash and popular. In some ways it still hankered after its more refined and genteel past. This was evidenced by the clear distinction between the popular end of town where the beach was sand and only a short walk from the railway station and the coach park. Then there was the posh end—the other side of The Pier Bandstand, where the beach was pebbled and there were bathing huts and large stone setback houses. Here were no Arcades or 'Kiss Me Quick' hats or naughty postcards on sale. Refreshments were still largely served from neat little kiosks and there were no fish and chip cafes within sight!

Weymouth could flex its self-esteem muscles too by being the ferry-port for boats to and from The Channel Islands. A familiar sight and sound of Weymouth were the trains cranking and snorting their way right down through the old harbour to tip out their travellers onto the quayside and thence aboard the large funnelled ferryboats. These giants, on departure, let out their own hooting siren screeches that echoed around the bay a couple of times each day.

Weymouth also had a professional football team playing at that time in The Southern League. I was to become friendly with many of its players who, like me, found summer employment on the beach.

Now, as aforementioned, by the mid-fifties the post war boom in the popularity of speedway racing was over. Somehow, they forgot to tell a consortium of Weymouth businessmen who, at that time, got the notion that Weymouth would be the ideal place for a new Stadium for greyhound racing and speedway. Not only was this a considerable miscalculation in itself, as speedway racing had come and gone by then, but it was a monumental blunder to build this new 'Wessex Stadium' on the very fringes of the town some three miles from its centre. It was doomed from the start!

However, they set out with high hopes and good intentions and these gentlemen installed, as the General Manager of this enterprise, my itinerant Father, one Bill Dutton! Latterly Father had been the manager of speedway teams in several other towns, all of which were now, one way or another, on the skids, which is a pretty appropriate way for a speedway team to go!

This then, was where my father's meanderings had taken him by 1955. On arrival in Weymouth he had already made one attempt to set up a new domestic situation in the bungalow with young Sheila. This had disintegrated when the pregnant girl fled home to her mum. Then Father lived for a while in what used to be called 'digs', probably a cheap guesthouse; there were plenty of them in Weymouth, after all. Although working hard in his new job managing the fledgling Weymouth Scorchers' Speedway team and running the dog racing on two evenings a week, Bill took to taking his meals in one of the many cafes situated on the Weymouth seafront. His favourite was a cafe known as 'The Dorothy' owned and run by a genial Lancastrian named Wilfred Cockcroft. Now, Wilfred had a daughter, Olwen, who was temporarily residing with her father. She had with her two children, Barry and Lynne. Olwen was getting back on her feet after a turbulent number of years with an abusive husband. To assist her father out in the busy cafe she would frequently help out as a waitress. Olwen was an attractive softly spoken lady with a calm disposition and a measured and common sense manner.

Billy Dutton rides again

One of the regular customers always seemed to sit on one of Olwen's tables in the restaurant. He not only enjoyed his fish and chips but also liked to chat and crack jokes and generally spread his charm with his infectious laugh. This was a man somewhat older than herself, although not too much older... Yep! Billy Dutton rides again!

(ii)

It wasn't long before the amorous William had guided the attractive divorcee into The Registry Office for the tying of his latest knot. Even Olwen was surprised at how swiftly the courtship with Father advanced. Not perhaps as surprised though as the two American sailors wandering through Weymouth town one Friday morning. They were visiting Weymouth (Portland to be exact) on a courtesy visit aboard their ship, the *U.S.S. Constellation* and during a few hours of shore leave, they were doing a little exploring. As they strolled past the Weymouth Registry Office they were assailed by a middle-aged man in a state of some agitation. Turned out that in his haste to get spliced, Father had turned up with his bride at the Registry Office forgetting that they would need a couple of witnesses to the marriage ceremony. Panic momentarily took over until Father got the bright idea of asking a couple of passers by if they would do the honours... and so enter two of Uncle Sam's Floating Finest to the timely rescue! Apparently, Father gave his new transatlantic pals both five pounds each for their time and trouble! Later, the whole wedding party adjourned for an hour or so of merry making into a nearby hostelry. Then, Father obtained a taxi into which everyone piled and headed out towards the naval base at Portland Harbour, dropping Father and the latest Mrs. Dutton off at the semi-detached house they had rented on Portland Road.

It was to this house that I went during that first summer I spent with my Father in 1956. Later, he and Olwen moved to a house at 84, Spa Road, Weymouth. This was a road off Dorchester Road, the main artery leading into Weymouth from the north. However, from the back windows of the house on Portland Road where they first lived together there was a view of a couple of miles right across the Portland Harbour to numerous grey warships anchored there and silhouetted against the towering cranes and twinkling lights on the quayside of the naval base. During that summer the Suez Crisis erupted and the warships seemed to be coming and going with some frequency; circumstances doubtless not unconnected.

There was a crisis of another type altogether on one occasion in that house when Olwen got food poisoning. It transpired that she had eaten some pineapples taken from an open tin in the larder. Many homes did not have fridges in those days. It was a time when Britain was on the cusp of acquiring those labour saving and electrical domestic devices and appliances that were by this date completely commonplace in places abroad such as the United States and Canada. By the mid-1950's fridges, washing machines, steam irons, tumble driers and suchlike were appearing rapidly in British homes, but nevertheless it was still a time when it was by no means unusual for such acquisitions not to be found in every home. Witness Father and Olwen's rented house on Portland Road in Weymouth and their reliance on the old-fashioned larder to keep food rather than possessing a fridge. Olwen was very ill indeed on that night and there was a considerable panic for a while as we waited for an ambulance and Olwen's screaming with her pain filled the house. She spent a few days in hospital after her stomach had been pumped and she was gently eased back to normality. Taught me yet another lesson, though. I've always been very cautious about eating food from tins which were opened earlier or, indeed, any food which strikes me as a bit suspicious for one reason or another. It's never been difficult to recall that horrible night in Weymouth should doubts occur about whether to scoff something or not. That's certainly true, although, by general agreement, I've always been considered a very greedy fellow. This is a characteristic of which I'm not especially proud, but 'if the cap fits, wear it' as the saying goes...

(iii)

At that time my father was not without a certain celebrity in the town of Weymouth. He was, after all, the manager of the town's new sports' stadium and, only comparatively recently, had been the manager of the England Speedway Team. So, the old rascal had a bit of influence and knew a lot of people. In the event, he had a word in someone's ear and, hey presto, the next thing is I was given a job hiring out the deckchairs on Weymouth Beach. Now such jobs were highly coveted and were the preserve of retired ex-council employees, professional footballers needing work during the summer months and students working in their vacations. The families of such students usually had enough local clout and influence to pull some strings in favour of their offspring (e.g. Dad had been The Lord Mayor, Mum was a Councillor or Uncle Bill was Chairman of The Local Chamber of Commerce... that sort of malarkey!). The result was that summer jobs on the beach were highly prized and virtually a closed shop. My Dad swung it for me though. I was to work on that beach for the following seven summer holidays (except in '59, the year of my exploding kidneys).

I was given the job of hiring out the deckchairs

Thus it was that, one warm morning in mid July 1956, I was instructed to report to Mr. Gallagher, the Beach Manager, at the green-painted wooden hut serving as The Beach Office situated on the Promenade opposite the King's Statue. 'Paddy' Gallagher sat behind a wooden counter and first thing I noticed was that he remained seated throughout that first meeting. I subsequently discovered the reason why. Paddy indeed rarely stood up; it was because he was not a well man. A very frail, thin, soft-spoken man in his sixties, he wore a trilby hat, always slightly tilted back, which never left his head. His distinctive Irish accent had been smoothed out somewhat by the previous forty years he had lived in England. Sporting a neatly trimmed, thin moustache of the matinee idol type so popular in those days, Paddy had a half-smoked cigarette between his nicotine-stained fingers from which drooped a quarter inch of un-flicked ash. Most distinctive of all and perhaps not so surprising, is that he appeared breathless and at every half dozen intakes of breath he would interrupt his own speech with a pause and the clear search for a deep sucking of air into his lungs. At that time I wouldn't have known any names for medical conditions but it is fairly obvious to me now that Paddy was suffering from emphysema or a heart condition, probably both. Paddy turned out to be a lovely man with a wry sense of humour and a great deal of warmth. I liked him instantly. 'Hello Davy, ask yer Dad if he's a few tips fur me if I tek meself up to de dog races at de Stadium on Satday, ha, ha!' 'I will Mr Gallagher, I will,' I replied as jokily as I could, being a bit nervous and not knowing what to expect at that stage. 'Don't bodder wid the Mr. Gallagher, Davy, just call me Paddy. Now de best ting fur you to learn de job is to spend de day wiv young Rod here, he'll teach ya all der is to know.' At this point he indicated a tall bloke standing at one end of the counter who was clearly about to set off for the day's work. 'Rod' turned out to be Rod Finnimore, a second year student at the London School of Economics. Rod was a local boy and from amongst the elite little student band who had cornered the beach jobs each summer when down from University. Rod rapidly put me into the picture.

The deckchairs on the beach were hired out from nine different stacks placed at regular intervals and stretching from one extreme end of the beach to the other. Starting at No.1 stack at the western end, where the Pavilion Theatre now stands (although when I started in 1956 the Pavilion Theatre had yet to be built) through to the other extreme end, on the pebbles, where No.9 stack was situated near Greenhill Gardens. The largest and the busiest stacks were Nos. 4, 5 and 6. They were in the middle of the beach and at points where the most people flooded down from the Promenade. This was the area between the King's Statue and the Jubilee Clock.

On a hot Sunday in the summer you could hardly put a pin between the thousands sitting 'cheek by jowl' on the beach and engaging in those most British of summer pursuits—manufacturing some fun from sand and salt water, mugs and jugs of tea, donkey rides and swing boats, chips and burgers, Punch and Judy, candy floss and toffee apples, air-beds and kites, seashells and seaweed, funny hats and windmills, 'naughty this' and 'saucy thats'. Indeed, the whole tacky bag of tricks!

It wasn't long before one put on the knowing persona of the 'I've seen it all before' deckchair man. One soon adopted the requisite style, put on the dark shades, and effortlessly bronzed the body as the summer days rolled along. We were there of course to help the jollity along for the hordes of peasants as we younger deckchair men somewhat arrogantly labelled all the holidaymakers. What a great job it was! I wish it had lasted a lifetime! We got paid for it too!

Stacks numbers seven, eight and nine were much smaller and quieter than the others. It was at these stacks that our more elderly colleagues were to be found. Men like 'Sandy' Carr who was in his seventies and had served all through the First World War. Sandy had come through it all completely unscathed apart from 'lost the top of me little finger, look, caught it on a piece of barbed wire and it went septic on me, otherwise, came out without a scratch'. An immensely modest man was Sandy, never really seeming to realise the enormity of his achievement indeed or of his luck!

Then there was Bill Moore. Bill was definitely the most ancient of deckchair men, possibly in human history. He was somewhere in his mid-eighties and was an ex-naval officer. A charmer with twinkling blue eyes and a fund of stories about his navy days. He was gentle and kindly and although somewhat stooped he had a real dignity about him. Since Bill was always permanently assigned to No. 9, the quietest stack of all, serving the most select section of the beach, many of Bill's customers hiring their deckchairs were regulars. Bill would know them all and refer to them by name: 'Morning Mr. Hargreaves, looks like we could get a shower later on.' Bill knew the local weather better than most forecasters and he would point the stem of his briar pipe towards the sky by way of emphasis. A marvellous old salt of a man!

We younger ones, students and footballers, were always assigned to the busier stacks. Busiest of all was stack No.5, right on the beach and opposite the King's Statue. There were usually three or four of us working on that stack, especially on Sundays when the absolute maximum numbers would arrive in the town. Most of them at some point would head for the beach.

Among the footballers I worked with at different times were Willy Ormond who, in his earlier career, had played for Glasgow Celtic and Scotland, Ron Fogg and Alan Wright and Ken Bryan who all had played in the Football League. Among the university students I got to know, apart from Rod Finnimore, was Phil Daubeney. He too was at the London School of Economics. I used to have good discussions with Phil and it was he who led me to some understanding of how a capitalist economy actually works. This was a subject to which I had never frankly given much thought before! Then there was Bill Boggis who was at Bristol University. Bill used to live at Yeovil and make the forty-mile journey to Weymouth each day by train. Quite a commute in those days.

There was a large powerful man too called Mr. Sambell. We knew him just as 'Sam'. He wasn't the highest deckchair in the intellectual stack and he was not entrusted with looking after or collecting any money or any form-filling aspects of the job. Sam was therefore permanently on 'stacking' on No.5, which was hard labour really but for which Sam was much better suited. During his midday break Sam would rush to the pub and down three or four pints of scrumpy. Now scrumpy is a form of cider, strong and widely popular throughout the West of England. By the time Sam returned to the stack for his afternoon shift, he was 'well pissed' each day. His mood would not be improved either with the heat of the afternoon sun nor if he were working alongside students, all of whom Sam resented and was always complaining about their being stuck up and spoilt. He was possibly correct on both counts as a matter of fact! However, we students had been warned about Sam and not to take much notice of him as most of it was just hot air.

He wasn't the highest deckchair in the intellectual stack

On this particular day I found myself working alongside Sam upon his drunken return to work in the afternoon. My presence was the proverbial red rag to the bull and Sam started a tirade against student softies: 'Just like you Dutton, I'd like to knock yer block off!' Not, a problem, I thought to myself, Sam's only hot air. 'Why don't you try it then?' I teased. This was an incredibly unwise thing to say to a very large man when he was full of scrumpy and hatred, in roughly equal proportions, and all in the heat of the day! I have to say that the next quarter of an hour of my life is a total blank! I was told later that Sam landed one on the point of my chin with a velocity and force entirely consistent with one of Rocky Marciano's best efforts.

Served me right I suppose. There was quite a brouhaha about it at the time and Sam was suspended from work for a day or two. I recovered with a bit of a bruised ego and the never forgotten lesson that if someone is threatening to do something, they are by no means always bluffing! This was to stand me in good stead in later years, especially dealing on one occasion in my teaching career with a self-harming disturbed female pupil and on another occasion with a lad threatening to jump down a stairwell. Guess I eventually owed 'Cider Sam' some thanks after all!

(iv)

Working on No.4 stack was an especially noisy and lively experience. No.4 was situated very close to Weymouth's Punch and Judy Show. There was an absolute rhythm to it each day. A show every two hours. Half an hour before the start of a show the children would start arriving and spreading themselves, increasingly expectantly, on the sand in front of the red and white painted ten feet high and three foot by four foot booth. It had a square space at its top which was the 'theatre' where the puppets played out the familiar and traditional battles between good and evil. The trials and tribulations between the naughty and hook nosed Mr. Punch and his incredibly long suffering and frequently abused wife, Judy. Then there were their babies who were tossed around and battered, willy-nilly, by Mr. Punch. Also, Mr. Crow, another of Punch's victims, and the policeman, forever seeking to impose some restraint on the crazy, stick-wielding, wooden star of the show. Throw in the crocodile, the sausages and Mr. Punch's amazing plate-spinning skills and there were all the ingredients for a half hour show. It was a show to thrill the watching little ones and in which they could participate with shouts and screams throughout. It was a little theatrical masterpiece every day, trust me!

Now, working on No.4 stack, we had The Punch and Judy Show about six times a day and became very familiar with its story lines! The man whose hands were inside the puppets was Frank Edmunds. He was a truly brilliant practitioner of this very special and historic theatrical art form. Frank did the Punch and Judy on Weymouth Beach for his entire working life and I believe his father had done it for years before him. We rarely actually saw Frank himself. He kept well out of the way being a somewhat modest and retiring sort of person but it was his nephew Sid who was the front man. Sid would wander amongst the seated children before each show shaking the coins around in the long handled, oblong box with the thin slot running across its top for dropping in the money. 'Come on now children, any more pennies for Mr. Punch, come on now, make Mr. Punch happy...' Sid was a man in his thirties with a head of thick curly hair. He was tanned a dark beetle-nut brown by his years in the sun and was never seen without his very thick black-lensed sunglasses. There was something of the gypsy about Sid. Whilst the show was on he would stand just to one side to keep his eye on proceedings and occasionally would step forward to snuff any over exuberance by the children. This rarely occurred as these were the days when youngsters were somehow more innocent, generally nicer and more controlled in their behaviour. It's so sad to think that today amongst a large group of young children watching a Punch and Judy Show there would be the distinct possibility that a few little nutters might throw objects, shout things or do something horrible so as to demonstrate the sheer nihilism of our age. You'd be taking a chance putting on a Punch and Judy Show before today's kids. Punch and Judy eh? A barometer of the rate our society is crumbling—there's a thought!

After a show, Sid would often wander across to the deckchair stack and have a cup of tea and a chat. There was also a kiosk nearby run by a stout lady who dispensed candyfloss and toffee apples by the ton into the upraised hands thrusting their threepenny bits and sixpenny pieces towards her as she stood at her little counter. This lady would send Sid across to the stack where we were working with a tin tray on which she placed several thick white cups swilling with sweet tea. She gave the tea to us for free and she would give us a cheery wave in between thrusting her hand back down into that spinning metal drum, from which appeared the sticky pink cotton wool called candyfloss. Yuk!

Ships of many foreign navies visited Portland and their sailors were soon wandering by on the Promenade. It was never very long before you'd see the same bunch of sailors pass by again but this time with two or three girls in tow! Same the whole world over!

I always thought it was the French sailors who cut the most impressive dash. With the little red pom-pom set in the centre of their round sailor hats and their bum hugging, seemingly tailored, uniforms. There were also the whiffs from Gauloises and Gitanes cigarettes whose aroma seemed to follow them about as they strolled by, and not least, their Gallic mannerisms with face, body language and speech. A fascinating total package!

There were always lots of young French people too in Weymouth during those summer months, sent by their parents to stay with English families and attend courses at English Language Schools which operated throughout June, July and August. Their presence in considerable numbers gave Weymouth something of a cosmopolitan atmosphere.

On one occasion I became friendly with a group of sailors from a French ship and we teamed up for the duration of their stay. Soon a number of the French youngsters spending their summer in Weymouth attached themselves to our little crew. I greatly enjoyed mixing with them and practising my atrocious French. This, for me, was another beginning in my life, although I did not recognise it as such at

...having visited France on umpteen occasions

the time. For many years now I have been a keen 'Francophile', having visited France on umpteen occasions, enjoyed and admired most things French and certainly, not least, walked the length and breadth of that great country using its marvellous network of long distance footpaths, 'Les Grands Randonee'. The origins of this obsession are right back there in Weymouth in the 1950's with my French sailors and English Language School youngsters. Being me, I even had a French girlfriend for a month or two one summer. Her name was Chantal Ouvrey and after she went back to France we corresponded for almost a couple of years. And, no, she was a really good Catholic girl from an impeccably middle class French family so there was 'rien hanky panky absolument'! The number of times I wrote her address on an envelope has remained imprinted in my mind over an almost entire lifetime... 'Mademoiselle Chantal Ouvrey, 21 Rue Franklin, Saint-Germaine-En-Laye, Paris.'

I have often thought about turning up at that address over fifty years later, just to see what may happen. Just for 'the craic' as our Irish friends might say! Wouldn't I be surprised if an ancient Chantal opened the door? Not that I'd recognise her of course, or her me. Getting older really 'sucks'!

(v)

During the summers I spent at Weymouth and during the times I was not working on the beach hiring out the deckchairs, if one can really call this work, I would probably have been found hanging around in one of three favourite places. There was a great deal of hanging around done by most younger folks in Weymouth in the summer months. After all the evenings were long and warm and the thronging numbers of holiday makers in the cafes, amusement arcades, shops and pubs combined into an ever lively churning and interesting scene.

The big attraction was the American jukebox

Most evenings I would catch the bus into Weymouth from the bus stop at the bottom of Spa Road. More than likely I would head for the large amusement arcade situated almost directly opposite the Jubilee Clock. The big attraction for me there was not the number of slot machines, nor the mechanical grabbing arms robotically hovering over carpets of fairly worthless prizes. Nor the bingo or the numerous other noisy and brightly lit games or attractions. Certainly not the hot-dogs, burgers or chips, although all these splendours were available within the confines of this single Temple of Fun. No, for me and the little gang of my contemporaries, the big attraction was the chrome edged, six-foot high, American jukebox situated right slap bang in the centre of the arcade!

As a matter of fact, slot machines and suchlike have never appealed to me in the slightest. Not that gambling as such has not featured quite prominently at times in my life. In my twenties and thirties, gambling seriously threatened the good foundations I had built up by then, both domestically and professionally. Roulette, blackjack and the occasional lump onto a good thing on the racecourse were my preferred methods of being parted from my money. Just pulling a handle at the side of a slot machine never did it for me at all. Anyway, what finally choked off any prospect of gambling ever really taking control of me was a 'Saul on the road to Damascus' moment in my life. It occurred like this. One early Saturday morning, when I was in my early thirties, I emerged from the 'The Rainbow Casino' on The Hagley Road in Birmingham. At that time I was earning a modest teacher's salary and had acquired the first really, really, serious responsibilities in my life of a wife and child. Thus it was that, on that early Saturday morning, I sat on a bench at the junction of Hagley Road and Portland Road and considered the immediate implications of having just lost the whole of a month's salary on the roulette table! A stranger walked by and paused, 'Do you know anywhere open round here mate, where I can get some cigarettes?' he asked me. 'Sorry, got no idea,' I mumbled in reply, caught up as I was at that moment in the bubble of my own misery. 'You been in there, have you?' he said, nodding towards the bright lights of the Casino beyond the wall behind my bench, 'Mmm. money's hard enough to come by without giving it away mate'. With that he continued on his way.

Now all that next day I wrestled between the desire to go back to the Casino that very evening to try to get my money back and the nagging thought that such a move may be disastrous. 'Money's hard enough to come by without giving it away,' said my conscience, the words of my Hagley Road stranger tugging insistently all day at my mind. Mercifully, my conscience won that battle and the gambling has never again been a serious issue in my life. I've always had the little beast firmly locked up and under control. Having said that, a few bob here and there, now and again, on this and that, has always been subsequently a fairly harmless feature in my life. As Shakespeare says, 'there shall still be "cakes and ale"'! Have to live a little, don't we!

Back to my American jukebox in The Amusement Arcade in Weymouth in the 1950's. We'd stand in front of that jukebox for hours, drop your sixpenny piece into the slot, select the song you wanted and press the button. Then watch the mechanical selector slide its way along in front of the discs stacked side by side vertically along the entire width of the machine. The selector would 'click' to a halt at the chosen disc ('records' were now much smaller, played at 45 r.p.m. and were referred to more frequently as 'discs'). Then the selector would tilt its little claw towards the chosen disc, grasp it in its pincers, pluck it out from its rank, draw it forward, twist it and lay it down onto the spinning turntable. Then the needle arm would rise from its rest position, swing across and drop precisely onto the edge of the disc and within seconds the first bars of the latest hits from Elvis, Jerry Lee Lewis, Roy Orbison, The Everlys, Pat Boone, Little Richard, Fats Domino, Buddy Holly, The Coasters, The Dream Weavers, Gene Vincent and now forgotten others, filled the air and mixed into the hubbub of the rest of the Arcade. We watched and we listened, watched and we listened, if not until the cows came home then up until ten minutes before the last bus to 'The Uplands' left at 'The Statue' at about eleven o'clock! Then there would be a mad dash so as not to miss that bus. It was a long walk if you did miss it! Trust me, I did that walk a few times!

Dead smack opposite the Weymouth Railway Station was 'Dave's Café'. This was another of our haunts. Dave had a jukebox too which was always an attraction. The cafe wasn't exactly 'Egon Ronay' (although, Egon Ronay, whoever he was, was probably still himself a pimply youth at this time!). Dave's Café was rather greasier than the greasiest spoon. Here, the burgers floated on the sausages which floated on the bacon which floated on the eggs which floated on a surf of fat which then spread in little waves from the middle towards the edge of your plate. That's why most folks usually stuck to coffees and the occasional pieces of toast! We locals did anyway, leaving Dave's other specialities of the house to the unsuspecting holidaymakers!

The point about Dave's Café is that it was a great hanging around sort of place and Dave himself was extremely tolerant towards us, allowing us to sit for hours without contributing much towards his profit margins. Here the Weymouth kids would gather. This was the time when girls' skirts were still flared but not quite to the exaggerated levels of a year or two before. It was the fashion for girls to wear a headscarf tied beneath the chin. The local accent was distinctive. It was nothing like as broad as the 'stereotypical' West Country farmers' hard 'r' growl, as in 'Arr, let's get they cows in furr milkin' then, m'deerrr'. The Dorset accent is gentler altogether, not as sing-song as the Devon accent either. It is unmistakeably West Country though and has one or two very distinctive little vocal twists. These include adding 'going on' to describe people's movements, as in 'Right then, I'm going on now, time to catch the bus', or, 'When I saw them they were going on to his mother's for tea.'

It was in Dave's Café that I met the one proper girlfriend of my Weymouth years. She was called Anne Radmore and she used to come into Dave's just like the rest of us in order to hang around, drink coffee, listen (and watch!) the jukebox and no doubt suss out the boys. Boys like me!

Anne was a pretty, slim and cheerful girl of about sixteen when we met. She lived at 10 Court Rd, Redlands (funny how I can always remember my girlfriend's addresses from long ago). We had a sort of on and off friendship which spread itself across about three summers. We stayed in touch long after the Weymouth days. Anne eventually had a failed relationship in her twenties and was left as what would be known today as a single mum. After my first marriage went down the tubes, Anne came to stay with me for a couple of weekends in Birmingham. This must have been in the very early 1970's, so we did remain in touch for many years. There was just the slight flicker of a possibility at that time that we might actually reactivate our teenage romance and set up together, but it didn't work out. Back in the Weymouth days of the 1950's we were really keen on each other and there was much talk of love and the future but it all eventually dribbled away into the sand.

The other great hanging out place in Weymouth at this time was Fortes Cafe. This had to be the largest cafe and restaurant in Weymouth. It was situated across the road from the Statue and the Promenade. It was in a prominent position stretching along two sides of a corner. This was another landmark in Weymouth and was known locally as 'Fortes Corner'. The young people who frequented Fortes Restaurant considered themselves just a little superior to those found in the Amusement Arcade or Dave's Cafe. The Fortes Crowd were usually the offspring from Weymouth's yachting and boating set, plus the sixth form boys and girls from Weymouth Grammar School and the sixth form girls from the Convent School. Here too, in Fortes, would congregate all the foreign students from the several foreign language schools in the town. Fortes was so large and impersonal that one could hang around as long as one wished, making one coffee stretch across several hours if needs be. One or two of the older boys from the Fortes scene rode around on scooters. These little motorbikes were just really becoming popular at this time and within the reach of youngsters from more affluent families.

We might actually reactivate our teenage romance

Scooters were shortly to become an extremely desirable fashion accessory for young males and within a few years were within the financial reach of every young man who had a job and the desire and inclination to possess one. These were the embryonic days of the next identifiable surge of youth culture to replace the fast fading Teddy Boys. The Teddy Boys were to metamorphose within a few years into 'Rockers' and 'Bikers' and the lads on their scooters scuttling around Fortes Corner in Weymouth with their classy babes hanging on to their waists, were the forerunners of 'The Mods'. Looking back, all the clues were there even though as far as we were concerned it was just the now that was important and the future was stretching away for ever...

I guess the sudden rapid demise and death of my dear Dad, which only took about four months from start to finish, brought my summer pleasure train to a halt and gave me a jolt of reality of the sort I'd never experienced before...

(vi)

During the summers of '56, '57 and '58 I spent quite a lot of time in the company of my father. One could say that I got to know him a lot better during these times than hitherto. I had never spent any long periods with him in my much younger days as he was simply never around. Then, of course, he and Mother had divorced in 1948 so after that he had become an even more shadowy figure in my life.

As we have seen, my Father's life had meandered on its own chaotic course for several years before he arrived at Weymouth in the mid 1950's. During the following few years, which were to be his last, he found a degree of domestic tranquility with his new wife Olwen. He and Olwen even produced a child together, Peter Dutton, who was born in January 1958 and who was destined never to know his father. Father made his exit in November of that year.

'Domestic tranquility' is a trifle misleading as Father, the leopard never being able to change his spots, did frequently make Olwen's life a misery with his, by now, trademark bouts of jealousy and bad temper. Overall though, and with some large pinches of salt, Father and Olwen had a few good years together. Father was truly working hard trying to rescue the whole Wessex Stadium debacle. It is to his credit really that the speedway racing and the greyhound racing kept going at all, sailing, as these two sports were, against the changing tides of public taste and the initial madness of building The Wessex Stadium at such a distant and inconvenient location.

However, this was Father's cross to carry and, in fairness, he carried it fairly valiantly until the catastrophic collapse of his health in the Autumn of 1958.

As far as I was concerned, these were the best years I had with my Dad. Many times I would assist him at the stadium, especially when there was an event taking place—selling programmes, watering the dog track and the speedway track, collecting litter, even occasionally working a turnstile. All such things were on my dogsbody's list! Best of all though I enjoyed accompanying Father as he drove through the thronging narrow streets of the town in a car with a loudspeaker attached to its roof. Our purpose was to publicise whatever event was to be held that evening at the stadium. Dad and I would share spouting the blurb into the microphone: 'Greyhound Racing, Greyhound Racing, tonight at The Wessex Stadium, Radipole Lane,' our voices would blare out, often distorted by some crackling static which caused many a holidaymaker to put their fingers into their ears or gesture angrily towards our loudly talking vehicle! This was not really the desired effect! But we ploughed on, literally when Father was on the mike! He had to master using the microphone at the same time as nosing the car through the throng of people spilling from the pavements onto the streets. Frequently, it seemed folks were in distinct danger of disappearing under our wheels and bonnet! So, Father's spiel would sometimes come out like this: 'Greyhound Racing, Greyhound Racing this evening at The Wessex Stadium Radipole Lane, buses for the Stadium leave... ooops, sorry missus... from Edward Street near The Statue... that was very rude sir, no need for that... come along this evening for all the excitement of.... careful mate, why don't you use a crossing... Greyhound Racing, tonight at The Wessex Stadium, first race 7.30... and the same to you missus!' It would go on something like this, mostly good natured I have to say. It seems you could always get away with almost anything with holiday makers, temporarily anaesthetised as most of them seemed to be with a little sunshine and salt briny!

Once or twice, after a Meeting, Father took me to Pullinger's Restaurant which was upstairs on the Pier Bandstand. This was one of his favourite places. The restaurant's curved windows looked out across Weymouth Bay and it was here I ate my very first ever prawn cocktail which impressed me no end. It was clear that Father was a regular in this restaurant as I recall he would banter with all the staff, especially the waitresses! They all seemed to like Billy!

Just going to a restaurant at all was a real event for me anyway. In truth, before Father took me to Pullingers there had only really been one previous occasion I had ever been to a posh restaurant. This was as far back as my twelfth birthday when Mother took me and Jill to 'The Happy Pig' restaurant in Bristol. This was by way of being one of a tiny handful of posh restaurants in Bristol at that time and it was situated at the bottom of Stokes Croft opposite the Registry Office and set back from a bend in the road which led down to Broadmead. I recall this restaurant had a neon lighted large smiling pig attached to the wall above the entrance. Going there was a real event for me, Mother and Jill. God knows how our impoverished Mother afforded to take us, but she did!

It seems strange that eating habits in Britain have revolutionised over the last half a century. Increasing prosperity and mass immigration has led to the arrival of countless thousands of restaurants bringing their own specialities that have changed the habits and tastes of a nation. Back in the innocent days of 'The Happy Pig', the nearest Indian Restaurant to Bristol was probably in Bombay and the nearest Chinese one was in Peking (well almost!). Not to mention either, the importing of all the American fast food franchise restaurants—McDonalds, Burger King, Kentucky Fried Chicken and the rest. Never before in the history of human munching has a nation's stomach gone from so little to so much in such a short time!

Father and I got on well together. I'd always loved him of course—he was my Dad. However, getting to know him as a three dimensional person, spending time with him, laughing with him and enjoying the warmth of his personality bonded us in a way that had not happened before. Dad is always in my head whenever I want him there nowadays and it is that time in Weymouth that has made this possible.

Mind you, he gave Olwen a torrid time sometimes. She would confide in me whenever Father was accusing her of some ridiculous thing or other. On one occasion she was in tears because Father had accused her of hanging out the washing in a certain arrangement so as to send a message to workmen who were doing some repairs on the roof of a nearby dwelling! Another time, I was happily listening to the jukebox in The Arcade with my pals when I caught a glimpse of a figure looking suspiciously like my father suddenly ducking down behind an adjacent slot machine. I walked up to the machine and there he was crouched beside it! It turned out the poor tortured fellow had been spying on me as he thought I might be having an affair with Olwen and I'd taken her out with me for the day! Can hardly believe it, can you? What's that about truth being stranger than fiction!

Leaving such blips aside (!) there were many evenings with Father at home when there was laughter and enjoyment. In that very last summer he adored his new baby son Peter. Father had named Peter 'Pud, Pud' and he would joyfully toss him in the air and do all the 'Goo, goo's' and 'Ga, ga's' as enthusiastically as any young Dad. Remember, Father was now turning 53 years old. He was so happy that his baby was already smiling...

In his younger days Father had been a keen amateur boxer. He loved to watch the boxing on the television. At this time the B.B.C. would broadcast the whole of the Amateur Boxing Championships. With a mountainous pile of Spam sandwiches we would settle down in front of the small 14-inch screen of his black and white television in that little front room at 84 Spa Road. Since, by then, Father had already done two or three commentaries for the B.B.C. himself on major speedway events like the World Championships from Wembley, he not only enjoyed the flying fists of the fighters but the wise words of the young commentator, one Harry Carpenter by name. Harry Carpenter went on, for the next fifty years, to be the main B.B.C. Boxing Correspondent.

In early September of that year it was time for me to return to Bristol and my teaching job at The Crescent School. Father and Olwen hugged me farewell and I set off for the bus stop. He himself had been off work for a couple of days with a pain in his back. This was a little worrying because virtually everything that went on at the stadium required his presence and attention. Not that any of this was my concern and I was soon back in Bristol juggling with all the early term's issues in Oscar Dahl's unhealthy little seat of learning.

Therefore, it was with genuine surprise when I returned from work one evening about six weeks later to be informed by my Mother that Father was 'very ill and you and Jill must go down to see him'. Still not really grasping the gravity of the situation, Jill and I freed ourselves from our commitments and took the train to Weymouth. Once there we went straight to The Weymouth and District Hospital. Seeing my Dad there in his hospital bed was, to coin a phrase, the meaning of which, on this occasion, was totally accurate, 'the shock of my life'. He had been struck down in a few short weeks by a grotesque, ghastly and merciless monster. 'What is it?' my Sis and I asked the Ward Sister who withdrew us to an anteroom. 'Your Dad has a blood disease called multiple myeloma. I'm afraid he's not going to get better'. We stood at the bottom of his bed, his unfocused eyes staring straight ahead. He didn't know us. Oh Dad, dear Dad.

'We all loved Bill.'

His funeral at Canford Cemetery in Bristol was one of the biggest they had had for quite a while. All the speedway folk came from far and wide. I stood in the pale November sunshine beside Don Weeks, the little hunchbacked wizard mechanic who had been a good friend of Dad's when

Dad was Manager at Exeter Speedway. 'Oh, so you're his son, are you?' he said. 'We all loved Bill.'

(vii)

I returned next time to Weymouth in the summer of 1960. The former beach manager, dear Paddy Gallagher, had finally smoked himself to death and had been replaced by a Scotsman named Bill Stranaghan. Bill was as opposite in nature to the laid back and friendly Paddy as any opposite could be. He was an abrupt and unsmiling fellow who ran a tight ship and brooked no nonsense. If you arrived late for work you were told about it and if your moneybox didn't balance at the end of the day there would be a full-scale inquiry until it was sorted out to his satisfaction. No one really liked him very much. When the job had been on Paddy's watch and it was raining, we idle fellows would soon have the deckchair stack tied down and be inside with a pack of cards. Indeed Paddy himself would be at the heart of the dealing and shuffling! We treated the Public with contempt, it must be said. Well, by the time I started the job again in 1960, Bill Stranaghan had swept the stable clean and a new order was in place. It didn't really bother me much but during any spells of prolonged rain there was much discontent amongst our unofficial deckchair-men's union that we were instructed by Bill Stranaghan to remain at our stacks till the rain eased. On these occasions we sheltered under the tarpaulins with raindrops dripping down and the yellow sand turning soggy and brown before our eyes.

On arriving in Weymouth that year it was necessary to find some accommodation. Olwen had left the town with her infant Peter and her little girl Lynne and sought refuge again with her father. He had quit Weymouth himself a year or so before and was running a hotel in Malvern. I think, at this stage, Olwen's older son Barry was attending boarding school and was more under the care of his own father, Olwen's former husband. The fact is, I lost touch with her for dozens of years after this until I was in my forties and, by then, teaching in Bury, Lancashire. Then, knowing that Olwen may have landed up back in her hometown of Burnley, very close to Bury, I traced Peter through the Burnley education system, following the reasonable guess that Peter would have gone to school in Burnley. This indeed turned out to be the case. To make a long story short, I met my brother Peter again, now a man in his thirties, married and living in Stockport, about five miles away from where I was living myself. What's that about a small world?

Fact was though that there were no home comforts for me to fall into when I arrived in Weymouth back in 1960. I had persuaded one of my footballing pals from Cardiff City Juniors to come with me for the summer. Trevor Ball was in roughly the same position as me insofar as he was waiting to start College in London the forthcoming September (Bata Technical College). Trevor was an athletic, blond-haired fellow with 'Buddy Holly' glasses. He had done his education the hard way, attending at first a dreaded Secondary Modern School, then managing eventually, through good results and hard work, to obtain a place in the Sixth Form at Fairfield Grammar School in Bristol. As a matter of fact, hard work and endeavour turned out to be Trevor's middle names and after Weymouth, he became an extremely successful businessman, at quite a young age, dealing in property and finance. Back there in Weymouth though, we were just mates looking for somewhere to live. The pressure was on, though, as our jobs on the beach were commencing that very next day. Not sure how it transpired but we found ourselves knocking on the door of a large old three-storey house situated on the main Dorchester Road about a mile from 'The Front'.

The door was opened by a large-framed, middle-aged man, shabbily dressed, unshaven, wearing slippers and a buttoned-up black jacket, all of which struck me immediately as somewhat odd. This man turned out to be a person we only ever came to know as 'Roberts'. He was in fact a lodger himself in the house but was lodging actually with the owner. This lady rarely moved from her chair situated in the gloom of the interior of a living room at the end of a small corridor. You could just make her out sitting there when the external door to her quarters was opened. So, Roberts would open this door and speak to the lady from the doorway. As we peered past him we could see the large seated figure within. 'These two have come about the room,' Roberts gloomily droned. 'Go and show them it, Roberts,' said the voice from within, clearly dictatorial in tone. 'It's five pounds a week, one week in advance, yours if you want it.' We discovered later that the reason this lady rarely stood up or showed herself was because she was wearing one of those heavy surgical boots, just like my Auntie Sis from Tankard's Close all those years before. Henceforth we always dealt with Roberts, who would take our rent when we knocked at the door each week and pass it on to the lady who we thereafter, and somewhat unkindly, always referred to as 'The Boot'!

> *It's five pounds a week, one week in advance, yours if you want it*

The room 'The Boot' had let to us suited our purpose just fine with a bed, a dressing table and a large wardrobe. Now the bed was a double which these days would have made me squeamish. The thought of sharing a double bed with another man, even a friend, is not something which appeals. Funny though, back then it didn't bother me or Trevor in the slightest! We found a bolster that usually went underneath the pillows and placed this down the middle of the bed to mark the frontier between our territories. This was done without any embarrassment and worked well throughout the dozen or so weeks we shared that room.

Trevor turned out to have something of an iron will and he persuaded me that if we put our minds to it we could live really cheaply, save as much money as possible which we could then divide equally when we left. Thus it was that we started to put our weekly pay packets into one of the now empty suitcases we had tossed onto the top of the large wardrobe. In order to leave those pay packets largely untouched, we adopted an almost tramp-like existence. We let our hair grow long, hardly ever washed, picked our newspapers out of the bins, limited ourselves to one pint of scrumpy each a night from a little pub known as 'The Scrumpy House' which was conveniently situated in one of the back streets that was a cut-through to The Dorchester Road and thus on our way home each night. The main problem was food. We solved this in the following manner. There was a large café, situated on the corner opposite the Jubilee Clock, called 'The Rose Marie'. We timed it to always enter this cafe at about 8 p.m., a time when most of their serving meals business was nearly over. As a consequence, Bert Hunt, the manager, was happy to pile our plates high with food he knew he wasn't going to sell. Never before have I ever faced such a food mountain on one plate and, as those who know me will testify, I have represented England in big eating contests on many occasions! It took Bert and his pretty dark-haired assistant Pat, who was on the chips, at least a couple of minutes to pile up the fried chicken, sausages, peas and the rest onto our plates. This was done in such a way that the food would not suddenly start slipping off the top of the mountain commencing a landslide over the edges of the plates and start dropping onto the green tiled floor! Seriously, we ate like this night after night and this one lone huge meal a day was more than sufficient to keep us going.

Trevor was a hard taskmaster and was adamant that we must keep to our plan and he would frequently deny my requests for some relaxation as in 'Come on mate, let's have another pint tonight, it is Saturday!' The only entertainment we allowed ourselves was also for free. Every week on the Pier Bandstand there was professional wrestling which Trevor was really keen on although he seemed to have a problem accepting that the whole wrestling thing was make-believe. Be that as it may, along with quite a few locals who also, literally in this case, knew the ropes, we would take off our shoes and socks, wade out a few feet underneath the pier and shin up the rope which had been dangled down for us by a collaborator who had previously legitimately gained admission. The result was that we had a whole evening's entertainment for nought, unless you count having wet feet for half an hour! Trevor really loved to boo the baddy and cheer the goody once the grapplers got going. We would wait right to the end on these occasions as Trevor was a real fan and he would try and chat to some of the wrestlers as they left their dressing room. I remember he eventually became quite friendly with one named 'Judo' Al Hayes.

So, our Bohemian existence stretched right across that summer. It had all been worth it. On the day we left we lifted the suitcase down from the top of the wardrobe and tipped all the money onto the bed. There was a lot! We picked it up in handfuls and cascaded it over one another! We both took quite a lot of money off to College with us and it says much about the essential difference between us regarding finance that Trevor would have put his money to good use immediately. 'Give me a pound to make a pound' was one of his favourite sayings whereas my own pile had largely slipped through my fingers by the first half term of my College life. I'm better nowadays but back then, with me, it was a cast iron case of 'a fool and his money are easily parted'! Unfortunately!

....tipped all the money onto the bed.

It was two indescribably dirty, dishevelled and smelly individuals who rolled up together at the bathhouse on Weymouth Quay at the end of that Season. The bathhouse was primarily for the use of sailors and yachtsmen passing through Weymouth Harbour. Well, we washed, wallowed and scrubbed ourselves for a couple of hours! After that, with pockets full of pound notes, I headed for the nearest barber shop on the way to the train station. Feeling pretty cocky, as I was off to College in Birmingham and a new life the following week, there was nevertheless one thing I knew I absolutely couldn't do under any circumstances—turn up in front of my Mother with long untidy hair! This, without a doubt, would have well and truly given her 'The Screaming Ab Dabs'!

Chapter Ten

Birmingham

THE ONLY REASON I think I applied to Teachers' Training College in Birmingham was because, having been brought up with a southerner's standard prejudice that Birmingham was a truly awful place, then it followed that fewer people would want to go there and therefore there would be less competition to gain admission to College! Not exactly a positive reason then! The fact was that I had done a whole round of applications to Teachers' Training Colleges the year before and got absolutely nowhere. My qualifications were minimal and competition was fierce. This was just before the years of massive expansion in Higher Education so places in Colleges were limited. Additionally, there was a policy operating amongst the Colleges of holding places open for those young men who were still doing their National Service. All these factors mitigated against my obtaining a place. Hence the conclusion that I had best try somewhere that few others would want to go... like Birmingham!

This was all distorted thinking of course but it seemed to make some sense at the time. In my imagination Birmingham was a ghastly place of factories belching smoke, blast furnaces setting the night sky permanently aglow and a weird, cloth-capped population all speaking with an accent sounding like a collective speech impediment. This region of William Blake's 'dark satanic mills' could be just the place to turn my luck around! So indeed it turned out, although my preconceptions about dear old Brum were somewhat unfounded!

The finger post to the rest of my life

Of course I need not have been half so negative in thoughts of Birmingham. In time I would grow to love the place and going there at the age of twenty was, without a doubt, the finger post to the rest of my life. Another story!

When the letter, inviting me for an interview in Birmingham, dropped onto the mat of our little prefab in Henleaze Road in October 1959, its implications would have produced mixed feeling for my Mother. On the one hand she would have been pleased that I was getting on, at last, but she also would have been thinking that I may have to leave home and she would be left to live alone. This was a prospect that never appealed to Mother. True, my sister Jill lived nearby and she would always look out for Mother as best she could. In some ways, though, Jill and her ever increasing family were just another of Mother's worries. Jill and Mick had added two more daughters, Sally and Katy, to their family by this time. They were forever on the breadline and struggling along from week to week even though Mick was nearly always in work. To be fair, he was never afraid of hard work. The problem was that the kind of work he was able to obtain was poorly paid and dead end. It was no surprise, whatsoever, when a few year's later, Mick and Jill jumped at the chance to emigrate to Canada with their kids. This move was to have a huge impact on Mother's life from which, in many ways, she never fully recovered.

Another difficulty Jill and Mick faced was that the curse of the Duttons had struck their second daughter Sally and she had been born with the dreaded talipus. Her left foot was twisted right around the other way. No longer, though, were victims of this condition sentenced to life in an ugly, heavy surgical boot like our dear Auntie Sis and others of the Dutton Clan from the past had been. At this time, the remedy was surgical, to correct the angle of the foot. The infant Sally therefore had a number of surgical procedures, none of which were ever completely successful, leaving the poor girl with a physical legacy that has thrown a shadow across much of her life in many ways. In spite of it though, she grew up to be a talented, humorous and career successful person. Sally nowadays lives in Australia specialising in teaching less able and handicapped children who no doubt benefit from her own experience. Quite a girl!

During the time just prior to my going off to College and Jill and Mick emigrating to Canada, Mother was very mixed up in their affairs. There were crevices, too, starting to appear in the marriage itself. These were to widen into cracks and then into chasms not too long after they got to Canada. This was no great surprise considering the shaky foundations on which the marriage had been built.

Our Mother had a wonderful gift of making a special relationship with each of her grandchildren. All of my brother's children too, dearly loved their 'Nana-Jam', as they called her, and my two older children, Jane and

Allan, were close with her also. Only my younger two, David and Amy, never knew her.

So, it was off to Birmingham for an interview at The City of Birmingham

Here I am at C.B.T.C.

Training College (henceforth C.B.T.C.), certainly with my Mother's good wishes and blessing but probably a touch of deep-down apprehension on her part as well. Arriving by train at New Street Station in Birmingham was a steamy affair with billows of the stuff enveloping the walkway which traversed across the tops of all the platforms. A few years later, New Street Station was to be redeveloped, along with a great deal of the rest of central Birmingham. In fact, throughout the sixties and seventies and indeed up to the present time there have always been bits added and subtracted to the Birmingham skyline and landscape. In truth, I think they've ended up with something of a dog's dinner. I hate to say it, being much more of a Brummie than a Mancunian (although I have lived in Manchester now for thirty years), that Manchester has a more coherent and pleasing central area.

There were several more young men who had come up to Birmingham for interview at that time. Indeed, it turned out we were a very select little group since we were the first men ever to be interviewed for admission to C.B.T.C., which hitherto had been an all female establishment. We stayed the previous night at a hostel on the Bristol Road. I recall two other fellows who were, like myself, to be successful candidates. There was Tom Young, who was somewhat older, perhaps in his early thirties and already had a bald spot on the top of his head. He was a short man who had previously trained as a draftsman but had become discontented and wanted to get into teaching. He became an ace geographer when he got to College and the standard of his sketching and map work had to be seen to be believed. I know this as Geography was one of my subjects when I started at C.B.T.C. I used to sit by Tom in lectures and admire (and envy!) his work. Incidentally, I was switched from Geography to English as I couldn't really 'hack it' with all that Physical Geography stuff. Ask me the capital cities of countries, no problem! Seemed though that Geography was something more than this at College level. Did surprise me though!

Similarly, I was switched from Physical Education to History. It had been my ambition to become a P.E. Teacher but, alas, dislocating my thumb in the gym during the first week, coupled with some concerns regarding my medical history, persuaded them that P.E. was probably too risky for me—so History it became. I never regretted the changes I made in both my courses as they ultimately worked to my advantage without a doubt. The other person I recall from our little group who successfully gained admission was a young fellow called 'Mac' Moore. 'Mac' was a greasy haired Yorkshireman still suffering from acne. He had a very 'sinusy' nose and was continually sniffing. When he arrived at College the following September, he did so on a motorbike and one rarely saw him throughout his College career without his leathers on.

Back to the interview morning. We arranged to get a black cab from the hostel on Bristol Road up to the College in Edgbaston. I myself would have been happy enough to have taken one of Birmingham's cream and navy blue coloured Corporation buses. In the event though it made more sense to 'throw in my lot' with the others and share a taxi fare with them.

Well, that trip up over Lea Bank to Five Ways was a real eye-opener. This area had been classic nineteenth-century cobbled streets and back-to-back housing but now the bulldozers were out and it was like passing through a war zone. What we saw was typical of what was going on all over Birmingham in the 1960's as the City undertook major programmes of redevelopment, trying to shed the worst remnants of

The Birmingham Accident Hospital.

its Industrial Revolution past. Our taxi took us past The Birmingham Accident Hospital. This was just about the only hospital in the country that had been established to treat injuries sustained largely by people while they were at work. It really spoke to the numerous injuries occurring daily in Birmingham's factories, forges and furnaces over the previous hundred years or so. Birmingham, 'The Workshop of the World'. This old saying had the ring of truth!

The difference between the frantic and messy activities on Lea Bank were in such contrast to the large set-back houses and wide, leafy peaceful roads of Edgbaston where you emerged once you reached Five Ways. 'Yow now, there wuz a nastee mewda just ova theyer,' remarked our taxi driver in his

flat-vowelled, Brummie drone voice. 'Sum young wench 'ad 'er 'ed cut off!'
He was nodding towards a building on our left on the corner of Calthorpe Rd.
and, in fact, referring to an infamous crime that had taken place a few weeks
before in the Y.W.C.A. Hostel. A young girl named Stephanie Baird had
been strangled and decapitated. As a result of this crime all the downstairs'
windows in Heathfield and Mariemont, the two female hostels at C.B.T.C.,
had had secure bolts fitted to them. It transpired that the murderer, who was
caught pretty quickly, had been working for several weeks on some of the
demolition work going on all around that area. The demented fellow must
have targeted the Y.W.C.A.

Entering Westbourne Road, our taxi turned right by St. George's Church.
The College itself was a modern three-storey building of strictly functional
design. My first encounter with Miss Margaret Rigg, the College Principal,
was as she sat at the centre of a five-person interview panel looking at me
from their side of a long oval table. Miss Rigg was extremely short in stature
and only just seemed to rise above the height of the table itself. So one was
only really aware of a voice emitting from a solitary disembodied head
balancing on the edge of the table opposite. She spoke in a curious high
pitched Scottish voice which sounded almost as though she were only
pretending to be Scottish: 'Wheel, Misterr Dutton, weere extreeemlee
pleesed that yuv allreedy commenced yur teeching careeer.' Remember, at
the time of this interview, I was still doing my stuff at the Crescent School
and ducking and diving around Mr. Harmer-Smith and all his nonsense.

I left that interview with the warm glow of a feeling I was going to be
accepted. I have to say at this point that, as my subsequent teaching career
confirmed, I've always done rather well at interviews. Something about the
benefits of making good eye contacts with the people interviewing you,
someone once advised me!

Thus it was that the letter confirming my acceptance at the College turned
up within a few weeks of that interview and the following September, on a
sunny morning, I arrived with my suitcase at the bottom of the steps to the
front entrance of C.B.T.C.

Standing at the top of those steps to welcome me was a Welsh girl named
Carol Davies. Carol was my 'College Mother' who had been designated to
write to me before my arrival to give me information and advice. 'Hello,'
she said smiling brightly and extending her hand, 'nice to see you Harry, you
made it then.'

It seemed as though the top of 'The Bumpy Lane' had been reached at
last.

Perhaps!

Lightning Source UK Ltd.
Milton Keynes UK

173135UK00002B/29/P